Critical Essays in Modern Literature

Critical Essays in Modern Literature

The Novels of Anthony Powell

The Novels of
Anthony

Powell

Robert K. Morris

University of Pittsburgh Press

Library of Congress Catalog Card Number: 68-12728
Copyright © 1968, University of Pittsburgh Press
Manufactured in the United States of America

To Penelope,

whose patience has been more than classic

Contents

Abbreviations
and editions
of novels
quoted in text

AM   *Afternoon Men* (London, 1960)
V   *Venusberg* (London, 1962)
FV   *From a View to a Death* (London, 1960)
AP   *Agents and Patients* (London, 1962)
WB   *What's Become of Waring* (London, 1961)

A DANCE TO THE MUSIC OF TIME

QU   *A Question of Upbringing* (Boston, 1955)
BM   *A Buyer's Market* (Boston, 1955)
AW   *The Acceptance World* (Boston, 1955)
LM   *At Lady Molly's* (London, 1958)
CCR   *Casanova's Chinese Restaurant* (London, 1960)
KO   *The Kindly Ones* (London, 1962)
VB   *The Valley of Bones* (London, 1964)
SA   *The Soldier's Art* (London, 1966)

The Novels of Anthony Powell

Introduction

For nearly forty years now Anthony
Powell has been writing books, but it is only in the last
ten that he has made more than a stir on the literary
scene and become recognized as a formidable practi-
tioner of the modern novel. His reputation rests almost
exclusively on a long novel sequence called *A Dance to
the Music of Time,* individual sections of which have
been appearing since 1951. The series has thus far
traced the fortunes of its hero-narrator, Nicholas Jenkins, from his childhood during World War I to his
lieutenancy in World War II; subsequent parts may
well cover another quarter century and carry his life
forward to the sixties.

Though reflecting a concern with this great period of
change between the world wars, and a constant obsession with divisions of society, *The Music of Time* is in
no way a sociological chronicle. Powell's fascination

1

with class is intellectual—to such an extent, in fact, that Jenkins remains detached and dispassionate even in the most personal situations. But this "intellectual" approach does not stifle Powell's sensitivity. If his persona has distance, he also has a more encompassing view; if he thinks, it is because he wishes to reason; and if he keeps from explicitly displaying his own emotions, it is so he can more vividly record the feelings of others. The novel, consequently, becomes something of a phenomenon: a massive work forwarding no philosophy, forcing no esthetic, fostering no strict ideologies, attempting no moral. It is, rather, a synthesis of observations and evocations built around themes and characters—an elaborate design by a novelist "whose imagination apprehends all the dogmas of our time and the uses men make of them without itself being at the mercy of them."[1]

Steering clear of dogma is perhaps the simplest task Powell's imagination accomplishes. With over two hundred characters in *The Music of Time,* Powell must manipulate those on-stage while informing the reader about those off-stage as well. The mere mechanics of such an operation require (in addition to imagination) intelligence, ingenuity, and a highly developed dramatic sense, all of which Powell demonstrates with ease and integrates through a tight control of comedy and irony.

Such talent was not simply inherited. Powell's apprenticeship dates from before 1931 (the year of his first book, *Afternoon Men*) and continues until the outbreak of World War II. Through the thirties he wrote five novels, all different from each other, and, even in the face of contemporaries like Huxley and Waugh, highly original. They are display pieces by a writer already skilled in technique, whose tone ranges from outrageous

1. Arthur Mizener, *"A Dance to the Music of Time,"* Kenyon Review, XXII (1960), 79-92.

farce to the subtlest irony, and whose themes embrace the central fads and dilemmas of his generation. Despite his talent and versatility, Powell was squeezed into that niche reserved for competent (which tends to mean minor) novelists. When the war came, among the many things swept into oblivion were his early novels.

There they might have remained had not Powell's growing popularity after the war rescued them. Few people would actually rank them artistically with the longer sequence, but they are more than curiosities of literature, more than finger exercises for the subsequent virtuoso performance. In them Powell mirrors the upper class and Bohemian England of the late twenties and early thirties: that odd quasi-order which tried bridging two periods of chaos while quietly rotting from within. Powell's novels amplify the "whimper" of these classes, but never so loud that it becomes a "bang." For Powell was then, as he is now, primarily a "comedian," accepting life and human nature for what they are without trying to change them.

Prodded by the comedian's pen, fixed in the gaze of his tolerant eye, the decade of the thirties seems to struggle up for a breath of fresh air before sinking beneath the wake bubbling around it. Powell's comedy can often suffocate, even when it is loving and gentle; but, whether benign or cruel, it never ceases to focus on what is current and topical. Psychoanalysis, Freudianism, Fascism, Communism, Expressionism, spiritualism, films, sex, parties, bluestockings, etc. are painted not only as social phenomena but as symptoms of human personality.

These early novels already reveal Powell's talent for comedy and his concern for structure and texture, but they gain in interest for anticipating elements in *The Music of Time*. Themes and actions echo and re-echo between the novels of the thirties and the later sequence, picking up as they do similar threads, weaving across many of the same years, cutting through identical class lines.

Afternoon Men, for example, while a comic anatomy of the futility surrounding Bohemian lives in the late twenties, underscores the ceaseless rounds of socializing that become paramount to the structure of *A Buyer's Market*. In *Afternoon Men* Powell lays the groundwork for themes he is to treat later in depth: themes such as identity, friendship, sexual intrigue, and above all the omnipresent mold of frustration, aimlessness, and boredom into which the characters are cast. Waugh's "bright young people"—older and tarnished, some even rusty—are still at it: lisping their profound banalities, drifting from bar to bar, party to party, playing musical mistresses, and waiting for something. Not the end, however. That is the same as the beginning. Indeed, boredom is the keynote of this first novel, which succeeds only because Powell exhibits immense energy in being continually fascinating about people who are continually boring.

The characters in *Venusberg* (1932) are less boring, but then they are less real. The novel, a partial exploration of a totalitarian state in the Baltic, becomes halfway through a mythical quest for love and ends up accepting what it set out to reject: a limited nihilism. "*Nitchevo,*" says one of the characters to the hero. "Say to yourself—*nitchevo.*" Nothing: almost the conclusive commentary on a novel in which values and human relationships are either dissolved or left unresolved.

But *Venusberg* is perhaps most important for its commentary, however oblique, on the erosion of ideals and aspirations by the forces of public life, and on the dissolution of personal and social values. This concept of "power" is immediately taken up in the last three pre-war novels and is of course central to *The Music of Time*. In *From a View to a Death* (1933) the basic power struggle between the socially mobile middle class and the decadent squirearchy is treated paradoxically and ironically to test the tensions between energy and apathy, sanity and eccentricity. Power, as wielded by the two rogues in *Agents and Patients* (1936), probes the ethics of exploitation, the mechanisms of self-delusion, and the responsibility of realistic choice. Here sex, the cinema, and psychoanalysis are indicators of adjustment in the world; and Powell gets at the impelling, compelling power behind each. *What's Become of Waring* (1939) spells out the theme of power directly and in that way is closest in spirit to *The Music of Time*. Power is wrapped up with the search for an identity, which in turn is explored through a first-person narrator who somewhat anticipates, in method if not in depth, Nicholas Jenkins.

So cursory an examination of the early novels only hints at their richness and their link with *The Music of Time*. One final parallel should be noted, however. The overall architectonics of a Powell novel is best seen in the dimensionalizing of an epigraph which, at its simplest, supplies a title, and, at its most complex, a central metaphor. The associations of *What's Become of Waring* with Browning's poem "Waring," and *From a View to a Death* with a popular hunting song, "John Peel," extend the implications of the major themes; connecting *Venusberg* with certain myths creates multiple levels of meaning for interpreting character and action. The same sort of play operates in books like *The Acceptance World* and *A Buyer's Market,* where metaphors of finance become involved with the human comedy and commodity, and in a book like *The Kindly Ones,* where the classic euphemism for the Furies is flanked by a legion of contemporary ones. In all cases, however, the epigraph does not function as an ingenious acrostic. A Powell novel is not a mere working-out of its title. On the contrary, the epigraph becomes the fixed point of reference by which themes are stabilized, and by which they are fitted into the novel's structure.

Especially in the early novels, such structuring may appear too neatly engineered. Yet realizing what animates the finely geared mechanisms imparts grander proportions to the world of Powell's prewar fiction. The prime mover is an ironic god, less fierce than skeptical, who controls a universe into which has been introduced a host of characters, some impelled by hereditary drive, others set in motion through kinetic contact. Scheming, seducing, experiencing, creating, even dying, they react like living puppets with the skin peeled off, frenetic bundles of exposed nerves, their impulses carried by filaments of sensation that are worked by the master's hand. Yet when everything is at last quiescent, when the spasmodic charade ceases, all the performers seem to share a common futility, an ignorance of what their actions have been or where their gyrations have led them. This, basically, is the important ironic interplay between form and content: the indication of an ominous and omnipresent aimlessness set within a perfectly ordered and perfectly planned framework.

Powell's early works are dynamically static, directed to portraying boredom, hopelessness, and helplessness as part of the intellectual and human tradition. *The Music of Time* is dramatically active, renewing its power through steady accretion, seeking to discover some form in the least thing, meaning in the most fleeting memory, a pattern of existence that is acceptable in the face of modern complexities. If the prewar novels are involved with showing the loss of certain virtues, *The Music of Time* demonstrates a concern with the "tentative reconstruction of values" that has been going on for over two generations.[2] Just as any of the volumes in *The Music of Time* could have been entitled "the acceptance world," so each of Powell's early novels might have been called "the rejection world." For, whereas Nick Jenkins uses his many encounters as standards by which to measure an existence that is reasonable (if not always utopian), the protagonists of the early novels, guided by their own narrow standards, reject what has potential worth and return to what is meaningless.

This disparity exists just as keenly in the tone of the novels. Those written before the war are farcical, or grotesque, or mannered, but they are overcast by a gloomy fatalism that can only temporarily be relieved by glimmerings of comedy. Indeed, for all its conflicts and struggles *The Music of Time* seems more sane and steady, a less painful document of the troubled personal (and societal) metamorphosis of the thirties. Perhaps the explanation is that Powell is reinterpreting retrospectively values that were too immediate to be completely detailed thirty odd years ago. Or perhaps in his artistic advancement Powell has learned to synthesize rather than diffuse his themes, thereby balancing the tone and conveying the impression of evenness and symmetry.

Take, as one example, a recurring theme in all the novels of Powell: the shattering of illusion by reality. As experience is acquired, the protagonists suffer the slow realization that the potential promise is fraudulent. For Powell's protagonists of the thirties, such a process can unstabilize a personality, and in some cases may even destroy it. Atwater, Lushington, Blore-Smith, Captain

2. James Hall, *The Tragic Comedians* (Bloomington, Ind., 1965), p. 148.

Hudson do readjust to their new lives, but disillusionment has soured, even hardened, them against it. Experience, while breaking down illusions, should also lay a
foundation for further understanding. For those characters in *The Music of Time* who are able to learn from
experience, there is a promise of new standards and
judgments. Perhaps many of these are as objectionable
as the people who propose them, but they at least have a
vitality and purpose. One can either counter them (as
Stringham does in his way, or Erridge in his), exploit
them (as do Widmerpool and Quiggin, in their differing ways), or reinterpret them (as Jenkins himself does).

One might look also at Powell's treatment of marriage. In that arty world of *Afternoon Men,* marriage is
seen as something random and capricious; chance, which
dictates the choice of profession, dictates the choice of
spouse, as Barlow's speech makes clear. Later, in *Venusberg,* the central misalliance not only distorts the ideals
of Mavrin, his wife, Ortrud, and her lover, Lushington,
but implies that marriage is a condition apparently
made bearable only by infidelity. In *From a View to a
Death,* Powell's emphasis is placed on those marriages
that are made unbearable by fidelity, and on the disappointments that inevitably attend new alliances along
similar lines, while in *Agents and Patients* and *What's
Become of Waring* he nullifies entirely the slightest
sentimentality attached to marriage. In the latter work
especially, the act of getting married is never dependent
on love, but prompted by need, money, or merely habit.

All these considerations are reworked brilliantly in
Casanova's Chinese Restaurant. The themes are broad-
ened and given new dimension through their fuller
statement; isolated aspects of marriage are brought into
contact with each other; effect is linked to cause. Nick's
relatively happy and unobtrusive alliance with Isobel

Tolland provides a commentary on Widmerpool's pre-marital difficulties with Mrs. Haycock, while Stringham's divorce from Peggy Stepney throws into relief Moreland's relationship with Priscilla Tolland and defines Maclintick's own bitter marriage and ultimate suicide.

Contrasted with the diffuse treatments of marriage in the earlier works, *Casanova's Chinese Restaurant,* for its starkness of outline, its concentration of theme, becomes an impressive, stringent, even authoritative account. Yet more impressive than Powell's power of synthesis within individual novels of *The Music of Time* is his ability to relate and subordinate particular themes to the dominant motif weaving in and out through the sequence. Whether he is outlining the norms of behavior within the rigid system of the public school and university, as in *A Question of Upbringing,* profiling the configurations of love, as in *The Acceptance World,* limning the eccentricities of class, as in *At Lady Molly's,* or, as in *Casanova's Chinese Restaurant,* demarcating the limits of decay in marriage, Powell builds his analyses upon a dualism fundamental to human nature, yet peculiarly symptomatic of the twentieth century: a dualism that sets in opposition the man of will and the man of imagination, the power-hungry and the sensualist.

Emerging as an almost full-blown prototype in the person of Widmerpool, the man of will moves through *The Music of Time,* now as J. G. Quiggin, now as Mark Members, Ralph Barnby, Commander Foxe, Idwal Kedward; fathered by Stringham, the man of imagination becomes now Uncle Giles, now Edgar Deacon, Hugh Moreland, Rowland Gwatkin, or often Nick Jenkins himself. Their clash, direct or indirect, ideological or personal, comic or tragic, is at the heart of *The Music of Time,* sustaining the tension between characters, triggering the action, providing the overall suspense.

Caught up first in Powell's ethos, the men of imagination are often paralyzed, always fascinated by their own predicament in a vastly changing, complex world, and by the force of will—the men of power who work the changes.

These progressive, surprising, but general logical changes set *The Music of Time* in motion, provide the impetus that carries each novel in the sequence beyond its predecessor, in texture if not always in style. To discover new attitudes and attributes of the men of will and imagination, to make each novel the apparent apogee of what has gone before, while keeping the projected outcome questionable, demands an art predicated on accumulation and accretion, rather than resolution: an art, in other words, predicated on Powell's genius for characterization.

But to go on at length would demand here closer analyses than any brief introduction warrants. Those already familiar with the body of Powell's work will perhaps have already formulated in their own minds much of the substance of the introduction and of the following criticism. Those less familiar may find here and elsewhere in this study some random insights into an art that for nearly forty years has spoken again and again for itself.

PART I

The Early Novels

I

Afternoon
Men

The originality of Anthony Powell's *Afternoon Men* resides in its paradoxical nature. It is a novel about "bright young people" written by a bright young person, yet the surface seems dulled by an incipient lackluster and scored with the furrows of a jaded age; it is a novel of wild parties and easy seductions, but the festivities tamely fizzle out like leftover champagne, and sex is more laboriously worked at than the most routine vocation. It is a novel in which language and action progress rapidly, yet people say little of substance and are restrained by their own inertia; it is a novel that holds out the promise of hope and retreats into despair. It is a novel presenting boredom vitally and futility comically.

Little actually "happens" in *Afternoon Men*. From design, not accident, the sense of any "story line" is conspicuously absent, for Powell's calculated rejection of formal plot enforces the theme of emptiness reflected in societal and private lives alike. Action, if it can be called such, is confined to successive and often frustrating attempts to acquire and exchange lovers and mistresses, which at best may have limited appeal to the less morally oblique. The manner in which people dedicatedly, though somewhat grimly, transact affairs in this sexual stock market fluctuates with the circumstances, which clearly do not fluctuate much themselves. After one round of London parties (and several rounds of drinks), a gallery seat at a seamy boxing match (and more rounds of drinks), a promiscuous weekend junket to the country (with a generous sampling of drinks), and London parties once again, a person might consider a cozy translator's corner an alluring refuge indeed.

Such a translator of sorts is William Atwater ("a weedy-looking young man" lazying on toward thirty), who is present throughout the novel and through whom, directly or indirectly, the action is filtered. Having failed twice for the Foreign Office, Atwater holds down a job in an archeological subdivision of a national museum. His professional position, quasi-creative, quasi-genteel, makes him, like Nicholas Jenkins later on, a natural link between fashionable and Bohemian London. He walks a fine line between these worlds, deriving only fringe benefits from each of them, for he is undecided as to where his allegiances lie and is often left suspended in a limbo of his own devising. In one way, Atwater is the earliest portrait of a recurring Powellian type—the man whose ambitions are checked by a weak will and a vacillating temperament. Drifting from party to party, affair to affair, Atwater finds himself steadily relinquishing middle-class security, without proper compensation, and sinking deeper and deeper into a spiritual bankruptcy.

If his credit seems higher with others than with himself, it is because even the so-called successful people in the novel are failures—not, certainly, professionally or financially, but in terms of a personal dissatisfaction that gnaws at their self-respect and accomplishments. What makes this dissatisfaction more deadly for its sufferers is its relatively ill-defined nature. It may originally have evolved from general feelings of frustration and hebetude, which are often symptomatic of reconstruction periods and which apparently are felt more keenly by those *soi-disant* artistic segments of society. But one suspects that Atwater and his coterie pay only lip service to the deity known as Art, seizing every opportunity to evade her discipline and perform their alienating rites at the shrine of the goddess Neurotica.

Because it focuses on the sort of people who should be relatively immune from boredom and futility and finds them the most susceptible, *Afternoon Men* becomes a particularly lamentable account of mismanaged lives. Powell's satire is directed strictly against those—be they artist or aristocrat—who obviously have had all the opportunities and have done nothing with them, who are bored by their own talents and find even their successes futile. Their every action and gesture is somehow tainted with defeat, for between desire for change and the will to accomplish it lies a gulf, widening in one great, continual, microcosmic yawn. As deep as the predilection for novelty goes, the depths of ennui go further, but are more easily reached. If consistent in any one thing, the characters of *Afternoon Men* are so in scrupulously exercising their lack of will.

The atmosphere, from the very opening of the novel, is clouded over with spiritual and mental fatigue. Raymond Pringle, "a naturally bad painter" who sells his work occasionally and subsists mainly on an inheritance, does not really want to be drinking in Atwater's club, and probably Atwater does not want him there either; but habit has dispensed with the need for innovation, at least in respect to something as tentative as the relationships in *Afternoon Men:*

> They had met in Paris three years before . . . one night at the Coupole Bar. From the first they had felt a certain mutual antipathy, but, by contrast and comparison, fellow-countrymen had seemed more nearly tolerable that evening than might actually be the case in other surroundings. But for some reason the acquaintance had persisted, and quite often they went out together when Pringle was in London, long after the earlier reason for putting up with each other's vagaries had been forgotten. (*AM*, 2)

Ground so unfertile does not produce the best soil for comradery; but as neither of the men demands anything of the other, there is apparently little reason why this kind of friendship should not flourish. Indeed, those liaisons which are cultivated assiduously generally bear the poorest fruit, as Pringle discovers with his sometime mistress, Harriet Twining, and Atwater with Susan Nunnery. To perfect friendship or love requires exertion of the will, and few people in *Afternoon Men* are resolute enough to barter time and effort for anything so decisive and lasting.

Such flabbiness of will is embodied in Hector Barlow's dialogue with Atwater:

> "If I marry Sophy," said Barlow, "I shall never see anybody but my own friends. If I marry Julia, I shall never see anybody but her friends. A third course would be Miriam, who anyway might refuse to marry me when it came to the point. It would also mean living in the country."
> "In comfort?"
> "At least in luxury."
> "You must make up your mind one way or the other."
> "They are fine people, the Jews," said Barlow. "What I

like about them is they always act on clearly defined
principles. You know where you are with them."

"She's a nice girl, Miriam."

"Yes. I shall marry her," said Barlow. "I shall marry
her and become a Jewish painter. There are no structural
objections." (*AM*, 16)

Barlow, of course, has little intention of marrying anyone at this point. His resolves are as erratic as his art,
and as thin as his pocketbook; his fervent expressions of
sincerity and determination—brought on not so much
by soul-searching as by alcohol—are challenged only a
few months later when Pringle catches him (in Pringle's
country house) making love to Harriet.

Making Atwater the sounding board for so many
loosely strung wills is a device that an ironist could
hardly resist. Acutely aware that he treads the mill of
habit, Atwater should be the first to attempt escape. But
sensitive though he may be to his failings, Atwater
bridles when Fotheringham, a restive copywriter also
sucked into the vortex of despondency, laments the use-
lessness of their lives. " 'Try not to think about it,' "
suggests Atwater, as if this glib advice (echoed later by
Bobel in *Venusberg*) were an infallible panacea for the
psychic ills of himself, the Fotheringhams, and the other
afternoon men and women. As a cure, however, or even
as a mild anodyne, it is unsuccessful. Everyone *does*
think about it; for the most part, thoughts are among
the few things most strongly directed—on the one hand
toward personal frustration, and on the other toward
the belief, but more generally the doubt, that things
will improve. Such pessimism naturally generates an
aura of aimlessness and despair, and reviewers of *Afternoon Men* were prompted, fairly perhaps, to suggest
that since Powell's characters seem indifferent, Powell
must be indifferent, too.

Yet to take, always, the deed for the thought, is as precipitous as the converse; and to view *Afternoon Men* solely as a naturalistic, if humorous portrait of the minutiae of apathy is to slight a more significant picture—that of the human will constrained to immobility through the fear that action produces nothing of lasting value. In treating this theme, Powell becomes as classic a moralist as Samuel Johnson, and *Afternoon Men* attains the force and distinction of a modern day "vanity of human wishes." In much the same fashion as Johnson's poem, Fotheringham's monologue combines the lugubriousness of a jeremiad with the truculence of a malediction:

> "When love has come to mean the most boring form of lust, when power means the most useless pots of money, when fame means the vulgarest sort of publicity, when we feel ourselves exiled for ever from the pleasant pastures of debonair insouciance (pardon the phrase), which is, I suppose, the one and really only possible mitigation and excuse for the unbridled incoherence of this existence of ours, it is then, and only then, that we shall realise fully, that we shall realise in its entirety, that we shall in short come to know with any degree of accuracy . . . what friendship means to each one of us and all of us, and how it was that, and that only, that made it all worth while. . . ." (*AM*, 61-62)

Johnson's moral warriors—Patience, Obedience, Faith, Charity—were possibly, at one time, crack opposition to vanity and indifference; but for an age where such troops have become outmoded and outmaneuvered, the naïve appeal to ethics would be vain. In their stead, Fotheringham, having tested his wings, proposes "friendship." The cynical Atwater, of course, perceives the platitude and cuts short his companion's mawkish flight. The theme of friendship is, however, quite serious with Powell and dominates *The Music of Time,* where, by faithfully recording shifts in relationships and alignments of personalities, he displays an express concern with something he dismisses here. Part of Powell's method in *Afternoon Men* is, indeed, a playing down of relationships, since he is pursuing the idea of how his characters can escape from, rather than cohere with, society and each other. Shackled in servitude to tedium, they seek escape through sex, art, or, most radically, a new environment.

Obsession with change of milieu is conspicuous in the novel; the escape route opens (as it always does) westward—to America. The magic of its name draws on Fotheringham, who, paralyzed by inertia, never sets the date to leave and consequently does not, and Susan Nunnery, who sexually exploits the pliant Verelst and finally does leave. But the one who has already escaped before the novel opens, and who vainly becomes the symbol of escape throughout, is Undershaft.

Though he never once appears on the scene, Undershaft remains legendary with those still plagued by the life he has apparently fled. Apart from his thematic significance, Undershaft structurally provides that bit of suspense which few novels ever suffered from possessing. "What's become of Undershaft?" everyone asks now, just as in the future the question arises over T. T. Waring and Kenneth Widmerpool. In addition, Undershaft's very name becomes a leading motif. Cropping up here and there at odd moments, it often takes on a comic significance and produces somewhat the same impact as a running gag. Like the favorite funny man who has this stock tool to extract the painful laugh, Powell has his Undershaft.

The particular elements of comedy arise chiefly through repetition of a banal piece of news circulated with apathetic devotion. At the opening of the novel, Pringle and Atwater discuss him in their usual desultory fashion:

> "Have you heard anything of Undershaft? . . ."
> "He's in New York."
> "Playing the piano?"
> "Playing the piano . . ."
> "Has he written to you at all?"
> "He's living with an Annamite woman."
> "In New York?"
> "He says she's pretty good." (*AM*, 3,5)

Atwater's vague appraisal may be related to a personally disturbed libido, since his recent love affairs have not been working out well, while Barlow, who never suffers from lack of women, but who often dangles at loose ends for portrait commissions, inquires along different lines:

> "Is he making any money?"
> "Doing very well, he says." (*AM*, 7)

Powell gains still another perspective by bringing on the scene the petulant homosexual, Walter Brisket, who swishes in to offer his own tithe of tidings:

> "I hear Undershaft is in Boston, living with a woman of colour."
> "He's in New York. I had a letter from him."
> "I shall be so acid when I see him."
> "Why?"
> "He and his women." (*AM*, 9)

Later, at a party given by Naomi Race, a stellar patroness of the arts around whom revolves the demimonde of high culture, Brisket elicits a typical response from the superannuated suffragette and bluestocking:

> Brisket said: "Have you heard about Undershaft, Naomi?"
> "The Siamese?"

"Yes."

Mrs. Race said: "I think he's so wise." (*AM*, 73)

The conceit is ironically clinched during a frustrating dinner rendezvous between Susan Nunnery and Atwater:

> Susan said: "You're a friend of Undershaft's, aren't you?"
> "Do you know him?"
> "I used to. I hear he won't look at a white woman now."
> "He's in New York."
> "I must go there."
> "I'll take you." (*AM*, 91)

Atwater, of course, takes her nowhere, for their tête-à-tête is rapidly terminated by the intrusion of a half dozen or so people, among whom is Verelst. Indeed, with Undershaft's offstage return at the end of *Afternoon Men*, and Susan's hurried departure, the two have literally exchanged places, indicating, perhaps, that there may be a superior fatalism which conspires to maintain the status quo. Escape *may* mean hope; but those who remain behind are certain to find that life continues in the same vapid fashion. *Afternoon Men* forecasts a future that is bleak because it is without either a past or a present; it is a future built upon the subtotals of zero.

Afternoon Men is the *reductio ad absurdum* of boredom and futility, but so organized that form becomes as important as character and action. The novel is divided into three sections: "Montage," "Perihelion," and "Palindrome." These terms—drawn respectively from the jargon of the cinema, astronomy, and literature—define structural extensions of the theme. The titles are basically dry and abstract, connected by their common allusion to some mechanical operation or technique, and reflecting the progressive impingement of habit and routine on a world atrophying through lack of will.

"Montage" is a quite free literary adaptation of the

film technique that uses a rapid succession of short scenes to present a stream of interconnected ideas. In Powell's novel, the pace is by no means as frenetic as that produced through movie sequences, nor the scope as wide; yet Powell's brand of montage, developed through economical use of narrative and crisp, laconic dialogue, maintains the illusion of mobility and widens the latitude of action.

Thus Atwater is seen gossiping at his club, circulating at a Bohemian party, working in the museum with his eccentric colleague, having tea at Barlow's, drinks with Fotheringham, and dinner at Naomi Race's—all the action rendered with cinematographic fidelity, but all tending to go nowhere. Powell, perhaps, forces too strongly the irony implicit in the subtitle, for the montage technique relies on a principle basic to cinema art: that all the scenes and images which have whirled and flashed at random will eventually cohere at one point. This is hardly the case in *Afternoon Men,* unless it be the point at which one realizes the very pointlessness of such movement.

As work becomes deadlier, parties duller, and seduction triter, Atwater finds his small world describing an orbit that allows for even less mobility than before. Trying to get out of this circular rut, Atwater gravitates toward Susan Nunnery—his "sun"—and by the second section of the novel, "Perihelion," they are in close conjunction, although she refuses to sleep with him. Atwater then seeks a convenient sexual outlet in Lola, as frustrating in her own way as Susan is in hers and, from a cosmic (or social) point of view, neither particularly illuminating nor magnetic. Atwater's momentum carries him forward for the little else he gets done; since he expends most of his energy chasing Susan, it is not much. Like a planet in perihelion, Atwater is momentarily suspended by the push-pull of the greater force, until he is drawn off toward aphelion, beginning the dreary revolution again.

Whereas the fields of moral vision and physical selection have perceptibly narrowed from "Montage" to "Perihelion," it is only with the last section, "Palindrome," that one understands how thoroughly delimited they have become. The London of *Afternoon Men* may have seemed circumscribed, but it had a multiplicity of persons that imparted the illusion of activity. In "Palindrome" there are a mere handful of people, guests at Pringle's country house, and they spell "boredom" written in bolder letters than before.

Actually, there *is* nothing to do at Pringle's place—or rather nothing *more* to do. Some random reading and painting, an excursion to the local pub, brief games of tennis, and rather longer ones of sexual musical chairs constitute the daily regimen. The oddest thing that transpires is Pringle's half-hearted suicide attempt, and even this fails to get the proper response. That death is no more meaningful than steak-and-kidney pie is an indication of how constricted the world outlook has become. "Palindrome" offers no exit from futility for those boxed in their little squares, who believe they still possess freedom of choice yet clearly display through repetitious patterns that choice has been withdrawn. Like palindromes, their lives are merely extrinsically clever and mechanically arranged.

The machine, however, still functions; and by using imagery drawn from the universe of mechanics Powell manages to suggest his characters' metamorphoses from afternoon men to mechanical men, endlessly repeating the same programmed motions and emotions. Just how dependent on outside agents they are, or how "mechanically" receptive to motivation they can become, is revealed through graduating perceptions, sometimes those of the narrator, often those of the characters themselves.

A recurring (and, in this case, potent) image in the novel is the telephone,[1] which links the external and internal worlds of *Afternoon Men*—those of hope and despair—and jangles with the merciless insistence of a Pavlovian stimulus. Atwater, for example, on a typical morning's bout of daydreaming, during which he has been brooding over "existence and its difficulties," is recalled to actuality by the ringing of the telephone:

> Atwater felt shaken. The secret of life had seemed at that moment not far away. A few more minutes and absolute reality might have been grasped. Now things were as far off as ever before. Years of thought, years of labour, years of dissipation might never bring the conception so near again. He took up the receiver. (*AM*, 43)

Atwater's philosophical pipe dream and his delusive Berkeleyan idealism contrast sharply with the mundane discovery of what reality is—namely, Lola, with whom Atwater makes a date. Later on he receives a phone call from Susan Nunnery at the very restaurant where they were supposed to meet for dinner:

> "So sorry I shan't be able to see you tonight. I'm in the country."
> "I see."
> "I can't get away."
> "Can't you? . . ."
> She said: "I feel an awful little bitch about this."
> Atwater said: "No, that's all right."
> "I do really."
> "These things will happen."
> She laughed again.
> "Good-bye," she said.
> "Good-bye."
> She said: "Ring me up soon." (*AM*, 117)

1. An early new critical reading by G. U. Ellis, *Twilight on Parnassus* (London, 1939), p. 380.

The telephone now frustrates Atwater's real desires as before it had thwarted his imagined ones. The irony is complete, of course, when Atwater reverts vainly to thoughts of the telephone, the weapon others have so expertly turned against him:

> They had written each other no letters, but he thought of the inflections of her voice on the telephone. . . . He thought of all the times that he might have been with her or near her when he had chosen to do something different. Or when he had just done nothing. When he had just sat in his room and read a book when he might have been talking to her on the telephone. (*AM*, 214)

Atwater's appreciation of Susan Nunnery comes too late, though his failure to seduce her is a somewhat anomalous feature of *Afternoon Men*. The game of seduction employs strategy perfected through routine; the rules prescribed are a wink, a nod, a phone call, a languid gesture in the right direction. Skill depends on sedulous practice and application of principles. Lola, an habituée of Soho parties who makes a career of being loved and left, seems to have been as aptly coached as Atwater in the mechanical art of seduction:

> Slowly, but very deliberately, the brooding edifice of seduction, creaking and incongruous, came into being, a vast Heath Robinson mechanism, dually controlled by them and lumbering gloomily down vistas of triteness. With a sort of heavy-fisted dexterity the mutually adapted emotions of each of them became synchronized, until the unavoidable anti-climax was at hand. (*AM*, 83)

Here the hard core of cynicism, though not penetrated by comedy, is softened by it. Elsewhere, however, Powell juxtaposes the cruder, everyday realities against the incongruities that suddenly rise in the realms of experience, and enlarges the ironic portrait of his characters' nugatory existences.

Pringle's grand, but thoroughly inept, gesture is a case in point. Having resolved to drown himself because of Harriet's indiscretion with Barlow, Pringle prepares for his death with the same mechanical precision that has governed his life:

> He stood there for a moment and then took off his wrist-watch and put it in his pocket. He began to undress. As he stripped he folded up his clothes and made a neat pile of them. . . . At last he was naked . . . he stood there scratching himself. He did this for some time and then walked towards the sea. (*AM*, 180)

Pringle is later rescued by fishermen and charged with indecent exposure. But the ironies extend beyond this. By chance, Harriet and Atwater have strolled to the sea cliffs earlier that morning and witness Pringle's preliminaries. He does not know they are watching; they are unaware that he is contemplating suicide. After he disappears from sight, they retire to the woods (where she commits her usual indiscretion) again without misgivings at deceiving Pringle. Indeed, infidelity never engenders remorse—only fatigue, and ultimate despair:

> Harriet said: "Do you think that one of these days everything will come right?"
> "No."
> "Neither do I," she said. She laughed again.
> Atwater said: "What's going to happen about all this?"
> "I don't know," she said, "yet."
> "What do you think?"
> "I don't know." (*AM*, 182)

For concentration of thematic material and multiplication of ironies, this scene may possibly be the most forceful in the novel. Powell's concern over the erosion of morals and the decay of health culminates in Atwater's and Harriet's mechanically mutual seduction, and in Pringle's attempted suicide. The latter has the added significance of perhaps symbolizing the self-destruction of everyone; it principally complements the theme of illness running through *Afternoon Men*, which takes the forms of physical sickness and madness, both the results of melancholia (as Robert Burton had anatomized three centuries before): "As if they had heard that enchanted horn of Astolpho, that English duke in Ariosto, which never sounded but all his auditors were mad, and for fear ready to make away with themselves . . . they are a company of giddy-heads, afternoon men . . ." That Powell finds this a trenchant epigraph for his novel presumes some affinity on his part with Burton, and both, indeed, are masters of the art of minute dissection of ills.

The opening dialogue of the novel, in fact, involves some new medicine Pringle has gotten for his nerves. Later, when he returns home, his major concern (after the suicide note he has written) is his medicine bottle. Pringle is subject to twitching and fidgeting; Atwater suffers from headaches, spots before his eyes, and general malaise.

More hopeless (and more numbing) is the madness of J. Crutch. Like many of the "originals" cropping up now and again in Powell's novels, he is a full-blown creation, significant both comically and thematically. Crutch, who visits the museum with the wild scheme of purchasing some of the national collection, runs up against Atwater's own brand of madness, that of switching off the outside world at will:

> He did not listen. He knew that the best he could hope for was that he should avoid hearing it all more than once. He considered other things. He achieved the complete detachment of thought of one who listens to the words of a schoolmaster. He became lost in his own introspections. The old man, Dr. Crutch, continued to talk until his outline became blurred. (*AM*, 39)

Remote from reality, Atwater is likewise subject to a somewhat disturbed visual sensation upon seeing Susan Nunnery; several times he notices that she seems to be separate, "like someone in another dimension." Atwater's mental network, designed to feed illusion and reality alternately, depending on how quickly it can switch perceptions on and off, is short-circuited in evoking memories of Susan:

> And so she was gone, ridiculous, lovely creature, absurdly hopeless and impossible love who was and had always been so far away. Absurdly lovely, hopeless creature who was gone away so that he would never see her again and would only remember her as an absurdly hopeless love. . . . There had been meetings when he had felt that the whole thing had been a silly mistake and that she was not like what he thought she was like and he had not enjoyed being with her. But always when she had gone he had known that he was wrong and it was his imaginary picture of her that was real and her own reality the illusion. (*AM*, 214-15)

Susan's legacy to Atwater is her eccentric father, George Nunnery, a ruined financier inhibited by port and crossword puzzles from carrying out schemes to recoup his losses. Atwater visits him at his cluttered flat and finds the old man under the intoxication of both. Wandering in his mind, Nunnery questions Atwater about Susan and her friends, and inadvertently makes a crucial and ironic connection:

> "Have you been away?" he said.
> "I've been in the country. It was rather nice."
> "I don't care for the country," said Mr. Nunnery. "Were you staying with people?"
> "With Raymond Pringle."
> "The man with red hair who always used to be ringing Susan up? . . . How was he?"
> "He seemed fairly well when I left."
> "I expect he'll kill himself one of these days," said Mr.

Nunnery. "He looks as if he would."

"Yes, I expect he will."

"Have some more of this," said Mr. Nunnery, and added: "Of whimsical design? Seven letters?"

"Baroque?"

"That's it." (*AM*, 210)

Powell's wit here approaches the metaphysical. Pringle *is* baroque, or at least the most whimsically designed character in *Afternoon Men*: half-comic, half-pathetic, without a controlling will, without a consoling imagination. Pringle is plagued by a host of eccentricities, and his life by a series of small disasters that aggravate his case of nerves. His successes in painting and love—though considerable—are inferior compared to Barlow's. Unlike the Bohemians of the twenties, Pringle is horribly middle-class in outlook, and although he lives on a comfortable income he is mercenary to the point of monomania.

Powell effectively capitalizes on this crotchet toward the end of the novel. While Pringle is sleeping off his ordeal-by-water, one of the fishermen knocks at the door and asks for the clothes Pringle had borrowed after being pulled naked onto the ship. It is suggested to Pringle by his guests that he supplement the return of the clothes with a reward:

"Don't you want to give him some money?" [asked Mrs. Race.]

"Why?"

"I don't know."

Pringle said: "Well, if you all think so, I suppose I ought. How much shall I give him?"

Mrs. Race said: "I think ten shillings would be enough. The others think a pound."

"Ten shillings?" said Pringle. "A pound? . . . But I mean, a pound is enormous."

"Give him ten shillings, then."

"Ten shillings isn't enough," said Harriet. "You must see that. . . ."

Mrs. Race said: "Why not compromise and give the man fifteen shillings?"

Pringle said: "I might do that. . . ." He fumbled about in his note case. . . . "Will you give him this, Sophy?"

He gave her a ten-shilling note and the two half-crowns. Sophy took the money and went out again. When she came back, carrying the coffee-cup, Mrs. Race said:

"What did he say?"

Sophy said: "He just said, 'Tar'."

"Nothing more."

"No."

"That was obviously the right sum," said Pringle. (*AM*, 204)

Here, as always, Powell employs comedy with the intention of exploiting it ironically; and basically he is asking the same questions that he has asked throughout *Afternoon Men:* if life is worth nothing—or less than a pound—has it any more value or meaning than death? Is not the madness, the fear of routine that incites these "giddy-heads" to "make away with themselves," of the same sort that induces them to continue in the futile way they do? "'A few days in London will put him right,'" says Naomi Race, shortly after Pringle's near drowning, oblivious of the sardonic implications of her remark. For to be "put right," for him, Atwater, Barlow, or any of the others, is to sit around clubs discussing lavatories and derbies, dancing and whiskey, mistresses and the next party.

Powell, the comedian, asks and observes; but he declines to answer or editorialize. He achieves such total detachment that whether he is writing narrative or dialogue one can almost hear the snap and click of the camera shutter. Yet, in spite of his sheer objectivity, he often betrays compassion for the human condition. While never waxing sentimental, nor relinquishing his firm belief that life, at every turn, is subject to (and predicated upon) ironies, Powell provides, here and there, touches of pathos: Crutch and Nunnery fostering their delusions, Pringle scratching his absurd naked body on the beach, Atwater wandering alone through the London streets—these are pale flickers of humanity, if nearly imperceptible in the glare of constant afternoon.

2

Venusberg

Venusberg is less a fiction than a myth. Like *Afternoon Men,* it exposes, anatomizes, and flays human weaknesses, but the ethos in which it operates is, ostensibly, timeless, and the attendant denouement is tragic rather than pathetic. Whereas the significance of *Afternoon Men* derives from its recounting of the humdrum parties and liaisons of upper-class English Bohemia, that of *Venusberg* depends upon fabricating an absurd society in a fictitious Baltic country just recovering from the throes of revolution.

Powell manipulates his characters against a backdrop hung with the frills and trumperies of a stage set; but the urgency of their plight is totally envisioned in a kind of "higher pessimism" that keeps them teetering on the brink of realization like marionettes until the strings are jerked to snatch them from the stage. "And then one day Count Scherbatcheff died," writes Powell, dismissing a minor but important character; yet as we come to understand the novelist's method in *Venusberg*, it is obvious that the count could be disposed of in no other way, that in Powell's scheme of things these strange reversals are integral to structure and theme.

In creating this topsy-turvy state peopled by barons, countesses, fainéant embassy attachés, and chocolate soldiers waiting in the wings for their cues, Powell momentarily obscures what is serious; but when death and apathy reverse the stock "happy ending," one realizes that comedy, even of this bizarre nature, forces to the surface the underlying earnestness. *Venusberg* is so structured that the grotesquely unreal is adroitly (if violently) juxtaposed with the real; the absurd is thereby used to underscore what is meaningful:

> In the ballroom the mazurka came to an end and there was a great deal of clapping. . . . People began to come through the doors in a stream. The American Minister passed the alcove and, pausing for a moment to point his finger in the shape of a revolver at Ortrud, said: "Bang!" and walked with great deliberation down the stairs. (*V*, 159-60)

Mere minutes later Ortrud Mavrin and her escort, the British attaché Da Costa, are accidentally gunned down by revolutionary thugs bent upon assassinating the pro tem dictator, General Kuno. Afterwards, the general's aide, Captain Waldemar, informs the hero that at the scene " 'a drunk man was seen brandishing a revolver, but after his arrest it was found to be but a cardboard pistol that they distribute at Maxim's on the nights of gala.' " Above all, this sense of the unreality of life, the knowledge that something as awesome as death is deprived of dignity through the ridiculous postures of antic ministers and debauched nobility, becomes a dominant theme in *Venusberg*.

Through the eyes of Lushington this sense of unreality is enlarged. A hack for a metropolitan London daily, Lushington grinds out platitudinous articles dealing with "real life," though his crowning ambition is to become a dramatic critic on a reputable paper. Like most of Powell's early heroes, Lushington is an intellectual drifter, an *artiste-manqué*, who has so retrenched his emotions that he can enter into neither art nor life. Psychologically, if not professionally, the heir of William Atwater, Lushington seems damned. But an assignment as foreign correspondent to cover political ferment in the Baltic offers a reprieve from his institutionalized professionalism (the stone stairs of his office building remind him of a "prison or lunatic asylum") and from his quondam mistress, Lucy, who suffers from a "mild but insidious megalomania."

Although Lushington's initial glimpse of the Baltic seacoast revives memories of happier times with Lucy, he is troubled by changes in his own feelings, an increasing uneasiness as the strangeness of his new surroundings obscures the division between the real and the illusory. Having never comprehended the "real," Lushington naturally finds it difficult to assimilate at once the "unreal."

This is potently exemplified in his affair with Ortrud. Though the liaison is adulterous, and far from the socially acceptable norms of even élite Baltic society, Lushington's love is no less genuine. He no longer feels love to be mere spiritual yearning (as he had with Lucy) but a sexually liberating force, able to modify an intolerable situation and soften the harshness of reality. As he walks arm and arm with Ortrud on the terrace of a deserted baroque palace, "the gnawing of actuality seemed for the moment silenced. In this place which had been left without meaning, it seemed easier to feel meaning where there was perhaps none."

Powell ironically exploits Lushington's actual inability to connect what has meaning and what has not, by turning to account his ambitions of becoming a drama critic. Lushington becomes part of an absurd triangle (almost theatrically incredible) where he is at once Ortrud's lover and her husband's confidant. Even more disturbing, he has a genuine affection for Panteleimon Mavrin and loathes his fraudulent role as illicit paramour and friend. On one occasion Lushington's quixotic gallantry urges him to castigate Ortrud for publicly deriding her spouse. Indeed, Lushington seems perfectly willing to cuckold the professor, but not to insult him.

Absurdities snowball when Mavrin informs Lushington that he has analyzed—along Freudian lines—his wife's marital coolness, concluded that she is in love, and determined that the man she loves is Da Costa. Not wishing to confess where the guilt lies, Lushington can only protest for his friend and equivocate for himself, relieved that he need not duel with Mavrin, yet at the same time feeling cheated by Da Costa of proper recognition. Since it is, in fact, Da Costa that *Lucy* loves, Lushington has been bested twice—once by Da Costa as his real opponent, and a second time by him as an imagined one.

With Da Costa's death comes the first step in Lushington's mental deterioration. Helpless as he was before to discriminate the real from the unreal, he now formulates the axiom that everything in life is an absurdity, and any advance he has made on the road to rehabilitation is at once retarded; his bitterness and cynicism return. After discovering that Ortrud also has been shot, he collapses entirely, so dazed and shocked that he can think only about the fact that he has "missed an eyewitness account of the thing for the paper." Lushington has put his faith in other men and in another country, and this grim reversal confirms what he had always believed—that men can never be civilized. For if the steps of his office remind him of a "prison or lunatic asylum," the crumbling palace where he and Ortrud kept their assignation "was . . . a potential state institution for mental defectives." The illusion of happiness that life could have offered him now becomes the despairing reality. Inured to all feeling, and having lost his regenerative powers, Lushington leaves the horror of a double nightmare and allies himself once more with Lucy; both end up cheated of the people they truly love.

At its furthest remove from reality *Venusberg* is an allegorical portrait of one man's search for salvation through various testings of love. To reinforce this quest theme, Powell employs a framework based partially upon Wagnerian myth and hints at this device in the novel's epigraph, a quotation from Baedeker: "Here, according to popular tradition, is situated the grotto of Venus, into which she enticed the knight Tannhäuser; fine view from the top." Parallels between *Venusberg* and Wagner's libretti should not be taken literally, since it is Powell's intention to show how heroic notions are insubstantial, illusory things. Often, differences evolve before similarities, and final judgments can be made only through combined outlooks.

For example, there are close parallels with *Tannhäuser* itself. Like the legendary operatic hero, Lushington exchanges the vices of one woman for the virtues of another; but "vice" and "virtue" are not doled out along the lines of a medieval morality tract. The respite Lushington seeks is from a spiritually complete but physically jejune entanglement. If Tannhäuser recoils sated from the lure of Venus and finds a fleeting beatitude in the pure love of Elizabeth, then Lushington shrinks from perfecting his role as Lucy's "ideal man" and yields to the indiscreet but sexually candid overtures of Ortrud.

Sometimes more direct in approach, Powell introduces allusions that, although simple and static, convey by association a complex meaning. In the opera, Tannhäuser confesses his guilt to the Pope; he receives harsh remonstrances and is informed he will be accorded salvation only when his dead pilgrim's staff shall bear leaves. In the novel, Lushington's valet (named, significantly, Pope) accidentally hears Ortrud's confession of love over the telephone and is among the group of well-wishers seeing Lushington off for England after the double slaying:

> Pope was there too, *carrying a walking-stick* with a heavy-coloured glass knob and he wore an unusually wide-brimmed black hat. He had been running about quickly, giving orders to porters. . . . Now Pope stood in the background *leaning on his stick*. . . . The steam hooter sounded and a minor official in a peaked cap wound a hunting horn.
> "Cheerioh, Mr. Lushington!" Waldemar shouted and saluted. Cortney took off his hat and raised his arm in the fascist salute. In the background Pope *brandished his stick*. (*V*, 180; italics mine)

Lushington's final, in a way retributive, gesture occurs when he and Lucy—Tannhäuser's Elizabeth—set out to honor the memory of Da Costa by visiting a spot where the three of them had often gone. The prominent theme of the opera, and of the novel, is emphasized: "The place was reached with some difficulty because she had made up her mind that the way there should be an expedition, a pilgrimage, and they arrived later than they had intended."

Wagnerian echoes are not confined to *Tannhäuser*. Ortrud herself steps right out of *Lohengrin*. As her namesake had derogated Elsa's honor and prompted the combat in which Lohengrin triumphs over Telramund, so Ortrud Mavrin traduces her husband's honor and provides a potential cause for his duel with Lushington. Further, the image of Lushington as a Wagnerian knight is comically undermined by his coming and going on an ill-smelling cargo ship, quite unlike Lohengrin's ethereal swan.

Ships, of course, evoke associations with two of Wagner's most important romantic works—*Der Fliegende Holländer* and *Tristan und Isolde*. In the former, the Dutchman, damned, must sail without reprieve for seven years. He is then permitted a brief time ashore to seek the love of some woman. If she swears to remain faithful until death, and does, he is freed from the curse of eternal wandering. In the course of the opera Senta commits suicide as proof of her love and thereby procures the Dutchman's salvation; through Ortrud's death Lushington loses his salvation. The final image in *Venusberg* is that of a small dinghy being pushed off from shore by several anonymous men, mingling with and being obscured by the "sallow" Thames fog. Lushington still wanders among the damned.

Tristan, too, has bad luck with ships. It is on a voyage that he drinks the love potion which fatally binds him to Isolde. Powell has eschewed the device of an actual philtre, but the supernatural element is conspicuous in the novel's structure, for Lushington's first serious contact with Ortrud is in the ship's stateroom, where Baroness Puckler is spelling out futures with a pack of cards. The fate motif is further reflected in the design of the novel. Over the life and death of Tristan and Isolde hovers King Mark, ruler of Britain; in *Venusberg* General Kuno, the nominal head of the Baltic state, is a like omnipresent force, always felt, seldom on the scene, the ultimate cause of Ortrud's actual death and Lushington's spiritual one.

Though Wagner provides the most opportune touchstone for myth and motif, Powell extends his theme beyond romance to embrace the tradition of allegory, especially that of John Bunyan. Salvation for Christian in *Pilgrim's Progress* is achieved after a long, upwards struggle against fear, corruption, venality, and vanity. Bunyan's ending is naturally optimistic; Christian succeeds, the veil and mist parting from his eyes as he looks back from his eminence on Mt. Zion. But while Lushington encounters equally great difficulties before achieving his "fine view from the top," his success is limited. Hope and Faith help Christian on his way; love spurs Lushington on but frustrates him by the ambiguity of its nature. Christian's pilgrimage is carried on in comic joy, Lushington's in comic despair. His literal journeys from the "low town" of the Baltic capital to the "high town"—or rather his alternating journeys between the two—make him aware of the hopelessness of his position. But as the veil and mist gradually lift from his eyes as well, he realizes that love, no matter how inadequate, offers the only possibility for salvation.

Early on, Lushington observes that the city is constructed on two levels, a "Low Town, where most of the buildings were modern and the streets broad," and a "High Town on the other side of the river," which seems, at first, quite unreal to him. Lushington's initial ascent takes him to Da Costa's flat (in the "High Town"), where he meets Cortney and Waldemar. Later invited back to Ortrud's apartment, Lushington notes that the Mavrins live "on one of the higher floors." Again, at the "top," Lushington descries the marital fetters that bind Ortrud and Panteleimon. The "view from the top" becomes increasingly clear as Lushington encounters and assesses varying perspectives on love.

The tortured *mésalliance* of the Mavrins is no less painful than the hopeless idealism of Count Scherbatcheff. Excluded from society because he is an indigent Russian *emigré* in a rightist country, Scherbatcheff tends his perpetually moribund grandmother, provides for a host of thankless and sluggish relations, and is consumed by a searing, unrevealed love for Ortrud. Lushington visits the count in his squalid rooms—"on the top floor"—and learns of his secret passion. Scherbatcheff, in his delusion, presumes that Ortrud is not indifferent to him and that his own immediate family respects and values his self-sacrificing nature. It is fitting that he dies, suddenly, without rhyme or reason, a shattered man with shattered illusions.

The final stages in Lushington's ascent are reached through revelations. The most important of these transpires when he and Ortrud spend a mild winter's afternoon ambling through the palace grounds:

> From the top of the steps there was a good view of the town, where wisps of smoke hung round the shapeless citadel. . . . Among the beds without flowers and the chipped cupids, the gnawing of actuality seemed for the moment silenced. In this place which had been left without meaning it seemed easier to feel meaning where there was perhaps none. (*V*, 111)

In this decadent baroque setting, symbolizing the fragments of their pasts, Lushington believes for an instant that this "view" of love is the true one; but hope and "meaning" become lost when he discovers Ortrud has a small son, who is impeding her divorce from Panteleimon and flight with him. The final wrench is Ortrud's senseless death.

Still Lushington endures, certain that life cannot be entirely meaningless. Like Christian, who must wade through the turbulent river before reaching the City of Zion, Lushington undergoes his greatest challenge on the ocean when he sails for England. The terror of nothingness takes the guise of the charlatan Count Bobel, whom Lushington had met on his previous crossing. Bobel, a cosmetics hustler by vocation, who dabbles in pimping, prostitution, and in arranging foursomes, represents the hedonistic nature of man—the crass, sybaritic existence that Lushington has rejected. Alone with Bobel on the trip home, Lushington finds himself drawn into tentatively accepting a supple nihilism that would free him from striving for something higher. Bobel says to him:

> "In Russia we have an expression—*nitchevo*. It is difficult to render into another language. . . . It means *nothing,* or, more freely, *what does it matter.* It is a very popular expression, characteristic, in a way, of our people. I tell you this because I think this is a moment when such a philosophy of life might be of value to you. Say to yourself—*nitchevo.* (*V*, 186)

Does Lushington make the pronouncement? On the one hand, he does return to the "stone passages" of his newspaper office "into which the sun never penetrates"; but at the same time the "river" has been crossed, and he and Lucy can inaugurate a further attempt to reach the "top":

> Going eastwards there was a place beyond the Tower where they could sit and overlook the river. It had been Lucy's idea that they should go there. Lushington had once proposed to her on that veranda and after she had met Da Costa the three of them had been there together on several occasions. Perhaps as a sort of mourning for Da Costa she was wearing country clothes, tweeds and low heels. The place was reached with some difficulty

> because she had made up her mind that the way there
> should be an expedition, a pilgrimage, and they arrived
> later than they had intended. (*V*, 189)

The "view" of the modern pilgrim may not be that of
either Christian or Tannhäuser, but then love may not
have the same regenerative power for him as it did for
them. Even granting that Lushington has not attained
salvation, must one forever exclude him from it? After
all, in his "view from the top," Bunyan sees "there was
a way to Hell even from the Gates of Heaven"; must
Lushington, looking back, be deprived of seeking
Heaven even from the gates of Hell?

If Powell's fascination with Christian and Teutonic
allegory seems to have imbued *Venusberg* with an
overly stringent morality, then his utilization of the romantic myth operating within the comic opera has ad-
vanced the comedy of modern manners and foibles.
Heroes and heroines are puffed to prodigious proportions only to be punctured by the sharp edge of ridicule
or exploded on a pointed reversal. Powell has simultaneously pressed into service two distinct genres and at
the same time superimposed the comic on the tragic,
achieving a surrealistic verbal collage. It is W. S. Gilbert
rewriting Wagner's *Ring*, or Harpo Marx playing
Bunyan's pilgrim.

Quite logically, almost necessarily, a farcical novel
about a Baltic state invites comparisons with operetta
milieu. The gay grouping of beauteous flirts and fun-
loving revolutionaries, disguised princes and superannuated roués, has always been the simple stuff of
Strauss and Lehar. The easiness, however, with which
Powell inveigles us into anticipating the expected makes
the reversal even more caustic.

Lushington's earliest impression of Ortrud is that she
looks like a "leading lady in a German musical comedy,"

a recurring association, and the immoderately romantic Cortney associates her with two popular waltzes, *Tales from the Vienna Woods* and *The Blue Danube*.

Lushington himself plays an essentially *buffo* role, sending his newspaper local-color accounts of political skirmishes and diplomatic functions at the House of Knights. At a typical embassy ball, Waldemar confesses that

"[the] armour around the room . . . comes from the National Theatre. It is not genuine armour."
"Why not?"
"It is false. A mere trick. I would tell no other stranger but you. I am angry with my country. But the committee insisted that it should be so. They were very adamant."
"But this is the invariable practice in all countries. The use of stage properties on such occasions as these."
"You astonish me!"
"I assure you."
"I am much relieved." (*V*, 156)

Like actors in a play, the characters in *Venusberg* mask their true personalities with rehearsed emotions, repeating and exchanging stock responses and gestures. Because of these pretenses and barriers, language no longer enables people to connect; at best, it becomes an elliptical cover up for vital feelings. Just such a case is Lushington's and Ortrud's seduction of each other, which gains its tragicomic point through periphrasis:

"Which of the two Counts shares your cabin?" [Ortrud asked.]
"Neither of them. I have a cabin to myself. . . ."
"[Do] you find that [the sea] rolls much on your side?"
"Not so much as you might think. I am lucky to have a cabin to myself. Don't you agree?"
"Does it roll there more than it is rolling now? What do you think?"
"I don't know. I think it does."
"It rolls very badly on the side I am on, too."

> "You share a cabin with your friend, of course?"
> "Yes. . . ."
> "Would you like to come down to my cabin and see if
> the boat rolls as much on that side as the side that you
> are on?"
> "Yes," she said. "It would interest me to see." (*V*, 32)

Language, too, becomes suspect at social functions.
People are always being admonished to speak *this* particular language or not to speak *that* one. German,
French, Polish, Russian, American, and English ebb and
flow with lunatic caprice without, it seems, being absorbed; the art of communication loses all value. On
one occasion Lushington desperately tries to summarize
in French the plot of Galsworthy's *Loyalties* to a Polish-
German countess. And on another he carries on a maddening conversation about *The Ordeal of Richard
Feverel* with a Meredith aficionado who apparently reads
English but cannot speak it. Lushington is " 'astonished
at the degree of excellence with which everyone in the
country speaks English' "; yet he confides his feelings to
no one, not even those closest to him. His very trade as
a journalist, while facilitating his writing, has atrophied
his speech. The inability to verbalize the unreality of
his experience to Lucy is perhaps his last aphasic gasp.

When it becomes impossible to use language as gesture, Powell's characters have no choice but to substitute
gesture for language. The ruling symbol of gesture in
Venusberg is the dance, which represents physical tension and mental relaxation, spontaneous movement
whose impulse carries one forward without intellectual
volition. Later, when Powell comes to write *The Music
of Time,* "dance" assumes the position of central metaphor; but its appearance in such diverse contexts as the
crowded nightclub, Maxim's, the chilly cosmopolitan
gathering at Baroness Puckler's, the ball at the House of

Knights, or the gloomy attic rooms of Scherbatcheff, is less an articulated formula than a primitive but nonetheless effective symbol.

Because of the speed with which characters gyrate, they present themselves as fronts or backs or profiles, seldom as the flesh-and-blood article, and Powell's way of defining them is closer to Fielding's than Zola's. To suggest depth and dimension, Powell, like Fielding, sandwiches together several "flat" characters rather than developing fully a "round" one. The complementary natures of Western and Allworthy, Thwackum and Square, Molly and Sophia, even Jones and Blifil are opposite sides of a single coin that diminishes in value as one impression or the other grows fainter. Seldom are the pictures in Fielding's gallery realistic at every turn, but as a total collection they are priceless indeed. Powell, too, forfeits (in part) realism by counterfeiting character, but the powerful twin-barreled ironies originate from the same comic stock.

In the characterizations of Lushington and Da Costa, for example, Powell confronts ambitious "Whig" professionalism with insouciant "Tory" dilettantism, a theme reworked in *The Music of Time* with greater artistry and profounder significance. In *Venusberg,* however, he seems uncertain in which direction the theme is moving. Ostensibly neither Lushington nor Da Costa has any idea of measuring up to the mark his class has set, or, in fact, to any mark at all. The former has succeeded in "remaining securely out of touch with life," and the latter has betrayed his tradition of regency nabobs and "empire building" by "[hanging] about working at a thesis on comparative religion."

Yet Da Costa turns out to be something of an empire builder after all, and Lushington keeps the pot boiling through Grub Street hack work. Powell recognizes that both existences may be vain of purpose; but, then, weak natures cannot formulate hopes and ideals as readily as they can relapse into a fatalistic atavism. Even with their basic cultural and hereditary differences, Lushington and Da Costa embrace the identical failing of being unable to replace outworn values.

Lushington's innate toughness derived from the middle class—"the god-damn bourgeoise" of Lawrence—is his only asset for survival in a modern world. Da Costa is a sensitive plant, poorly transplanted. His death, structurally, is a quirk of fate; but symbolically it is a "class" death, and a foreshadowing of Powell's pressing concern with aristocratic decadence.

Character complexities of a similar nature revolve about Ortrud and Lucy. Lucy, like Susan Nunnery of *Afternoon Men,* is witty, intellectual, and neurotic, slick but insecure in her amoral excesses. On the surface Ortrud appears to be only the usual caricature of the femme fatale, until we find she possesses a grace and seriousness, a genteel "remoteness" that imparts more solidarity. The strengths of each are displayed more prominently as their characters merge. They become, in effect, together, the perfect woman. To Lushington, partisan, yet sufficiently detached to be objective, they might be one and the same. At his first sight of Ortrud, she reminds him of Lucy, "although this woman was not like her in appearance nor in manner." And, later, after Ortrud has told Lushington of her early career and marriage, he cannot dissociate her from his former mistress:

> Again she reminded him of Lucy, but because she was different and not because their careers had been a little the same. There was the rather sparkling hardness that gave meaning to what both said, but the force behind it here was all instinctive and unsupported by any of Lucy's semi-philosophic buttresses. (*V,* 32)

Social barriers between Lushington and Ortrud are broken down after their love-making. She is free and animal, sexually healthy, while Lucy is possessed by sex, views it medicinally, possibly as a cure for her megalomania. Still, it is Lucy who remains uppermost in Lushington's mind, even throughout his affair with Ortrud. Though she appears only at the beginning and end of the novel, Lucy continually makes her presence felt. To both Da Costa and Lushington, she perhaps remains, whether chivalrously or chauvinistically deified, the avatar of the sexual-cum-intellectual English female. Like Lushington, she endures; Ortrud, her other "half," for reasons not unlike Da Costa's, does not.

Yet for all Powell's interest in this quartet, one cannot help feeling that his most devastating ironies revolve about the composite counts—Bobel and Scherbatcheff. Bobel, the sensualist of vague origins, has toadied to modern day commercialism and sold his aristocratic birthright for a mess of beauty aids. But poor Scherbatcheff, the idealist, "the man of feeling," cannot dirty his hands with the mundane material necessities of the middle class and dies from an overdose of blue blood. Significantly enough, Scherbatcheff, too, is an advocate of nihilism. On the voyage to the Baltic capital, he tells Baroness Puckler: " 'I fear, Baroness, that you will find my fortune a sad one. The fortune of a man who has lost in the gamble for life. A man who in that game has often thrown the zero.' " Powell exhibits a nostalgia for men like Scherbatcheff, uprooted nobility who retreat into a vain, but harmless, idealism. Bobel's nihilism, on the other hand, is depressing, not because it is hopeless, but because it is insincere. The deaths of Ortrud, Da Costa, and Scherbatcheff are the inevitable consequences of naïve, upperclass effeteness contending with the more vigorous dynamics of middle-class modernity. The aristocracy is not armed for the contest; the bourgeoise are. Lushington, Lucy, Bobel have all built up durable shells that seldom can even be scratched.

The themes of *Venusberg* rotate about a paradoxical center of conflicting yet ameliorating forces; the serious is not easily extracted from the comic, and truths are often present, but only tangentially. Such a truth is revealed in Count Bobel's highly symbolic and prescient conjecture that " 'it is the sentimental who do most harm in this world of ours.' " Bobel's words are frightening because they conceal, under the mask of cynicism, a formidable energy. Bobel is indeed a product of his mentor, Nietzsche—an *Übermensch* who heralds the new order. He perseveres. He endures. He represents the crude prototype of modern supermen who will later adopt the names of Widmerpool and Quiggin. But for the moment he is the immediate predecessor of Powell's next "hero," Zouch, another superman who discovers that tradition can prove as fatal as novelty.

3

*From
a View
to a Death*

F_{rom} *a View to a Death* plays on the tensions set up by an urbane satirist writing a country novel—the city slicker duping cloddish bumpkins, seducing village virgins, both toadying to and tweaking the time-honored customs of a fox-hunting aphasic gentry. Up until the moment the hero, fatally thrown from a horse, lies crumpled on a frost-covered rural road, the novel displays all the earmarks of a small, but perfect, bittersweet comedy.

But with death perspectives change; surfaces are seen from the underside; ambiguities are clarified. The hitherto farcical tour through the jolly eccentricities and skeleton-infested closets of country families becomes a sardonic circuit leading to frustration and insanity. The tensions are greater than one at first imagines and the forces creating them sufficiently powerful to expand personal conflicts into universal ones. Powell's basic theme

—a theme that has grown more important in *The Music of Time*—is the clash between the realistic, coldly intellectual, ambitious Modernist, and the romantic, emotional, apathetic Traditionalist.

The conflict is characterized in this novel by the introduction of a cosmopolitan *arriviste* into the society of an ever-decaying but eternally indestructible English squirearchy. He is Arthur Zouch, a sharp, unscrupulous young painter of twenty-nine who does work on commission and has made a name for himself in London. His success is the result of kowtowing to commercialism and the vanity of patrons. He relies on a modicum of talent and a great deal of enterprise; he takes as much as he can and gives as little as possible in return, "treating life as a sort of quick-lunch counter where you helped yourself and all the snacks were free." More predatory than his predecessors, Atwater and Lushington, Zouch is also more energetic. Bolstered by the knowledge that he has manufactured a reputation with the minimum of materials, he evinces the pride of the modern, self-made man:

> His life had not been too easy at the start. But this was a strength to him because it had left him with a contempt both for persons who had themselves had no early struggles and also for those who found themselves compelled to continue struggling in later life. (*FV*, 6-7)

Zouch is the classic example of someone whose attempts have brought success but with it a perversion of personality. Like most parvenus he is not above sneering, nor above feeling socially insecure either. He may have a reputation, but he has no position. Mary Passenger has, which is one reason why he cultivates her affections, indeed, uses her. To be sure, Zouch himself cuts a dashing figure, with his trim beard and arty environment, and represents "a world with which she had no first-hand contacts." But Mary's world—that of the landed gentry, rambling homes, rolling hills—is equally attractive to Zouch.

Zouch has foresight. He is an able schemer who has the knack of manipulating without necessarily manhandling, but life in the country is not so simple that it raises no problems. From the first he feels out of his element; and all the Passengers, save Mary, sense in him a disruptive force challenging their settled ways. Their initially cool reception develops, for the most part, into individual antipathy and even, in the case of Vernon Passenger, thinly veiled hostility.

Like Atwater and Lushington, Zouch has problems with women, though he never allows them to interfere with his future, a fact that Joanna Brandon discovers after she is seduced and jilted within a single week. When Mary accepts Zouch's marriage proposal, Joanna is the first sacrifice to his dreams of social position. She is no match for Zouch, who knows all the rules of the game and, with any sort of sporting chance, would easily win the pedigreed heiress. But he is never given one. Through Powell's selection of ironies, the fittest are matched against the unfittest, and it is the unfittest who survive. This is precisely why Zouch's death is so shocking. In his ability to manipulate, cajole, flatter, and humbug a second-rate society, he is first-rate. Theoretically he should come out on top, since he ardently professes the credo and possesses the superiority complex of the pushy modernist:

> Zouch was a superman. A fair English equivalent of the Teutonic ideal of the *Übermensch*. No one knew this yet except himself. That was because he had not been one long enough for people to find out. They would learn all in good time; and to their cost. (*FV*, 6)

Like some of the ingenious contenders in *The Music of Time,* Zouch organizes his life about a simple concept: Knowledge is Power. Many of his hours in the country are spent in acquiring the former and dreaming of a future when he can wield the latter at his leisure. When it becomes apparent that his ingratiating attempts to wheedle his way into family confidences have resulted in suspicion and dislike, he reflects bitterly that "except for Mary the Passengers seemed to be a difficult, tiresome family with their eccentricities and prejudices about ambition, which he himself had always imagined to be a virtue." Zouch's "virtue" becomes his tragic flaw; and his "ambition" loses all its utility when everything, including his own life, is sacrificed to it. As he leaves Passenger Court at the end of the summer, his bravado and rashness in accepting Mary's invitation to return for the autumn hunt (although he cannot ride) is the ultimate extension (and corruption) of the *Übermensch* philosophy:

> In the heat of the moment his inexperience in this direction seemed a small thing compared to the importance of the goal at which he was aiming. . . . he remembered that he was a superman and he saw no reason why he should not learn to do the things which were required of him with perfect ease. The will to power should teach him how to ride. *(FV,* 145)

Learning to ride will not, however, reconcile Zouch to Vernon Passenger, symbol of the opposing weight of tradition, and a formidable antagonist, as Zouch recognizes immediately: "Mr. Passenger . . . was an *Übermensch.* A pretty grim figure in fact. Indeed part of Zouch's uneasiness . . . was due to an instantaneous fear that in Mr. Passenger he might have met his match." Zouch overrates his host somewhat. It is no more difficult for Passenger to be a superman in his domain than for the one-eyed man to be king among the blind. Surrounded by social climbers and declining families, Passenger is undergoing an aristocratic agony, jealously guarding the last vestiges of class in a realm riddled with mental and physical decay.

Signs of such decadence are visible everywhere—there is scarcely a well-balanced person in all the county—but they are especially prominent in the Fosdicks, a quartet of eccentrics tortured by family ties. The matriarch is volatile, irascible, loud, and gossipy, thoroughly indifferent to the needs of her family. By comparison her sons are notably mild; Torquil's vague intentions of breaking into law keep him at Oxford and Jasper's interest in breaking eighty-two keep *him* on the links. In one way or another, both their intellects have mildewed. Torquil, for example, seems beset by "senile decay . . . while still in the grip of arrested development. Prematurely young, second childhood had come to him at a time when his contemporaries had hardly finished with their adolescence."

But it is Major Fosdick who is the most eloquent example of the gentry's decline. Plagued by an excess of fantasies, he spends long afternoons cleaning his guns in the drawing room and dreaming of past glories. His ultimate decline is caused by a complex of things: an insupportable existence with his harridan of a wife, total disappointment in his children, and the crushing necessity of abandoning his secret life. Still, for all his eccentricities, Fosdick emerges as one of the novel's truly pathetic creatures: the remnant of a once glorious era, a symbol of rough-hewn gentility, chiseled out of the same stuff as empire and subject to the same forces of decay.

An equally affecting portrait of waning gentility is Joanna's recluse mother, an ex-actress who withdrew from society after her husband's death. Having lived a sedentary, almost mummified existence for over twenty years in a house as damp as a mausoleum, she is now debilitated by a dreamy inertia and a despairing hypochondria. Though pretty in her youth, Mrs. Brandon is undergoing an insidious deterioration and her vain remedy is a tasteless application of makeup, which makes her "look like a favorite doll that has been worn to nothing by excessive use." Ironically, it is over Beauty that she rhapsodizes when Zouch visits her, dwelling nostalgically on the past beauties of stately country mansions: "So you are staying at Passenger. What a lovely house it is. . . . What a pity they can't afford to keep it up better. But it is the same all over the country. All the old places falling down or being sold."

Mrs. Brandon's awareness of decay is matched by Zouch's realization that she too is decaying and by the reader's perception that decay is rampant in the province. Joanna is the only one to escape the corrosion of habit which, in varying ways, takes its toll of nearly everyone. As Mrs. Dadds, the Brandons' housekeeper, reflects disquietingly: " 'There's something unhealthy about this town. That's what it is. It pulls you down. It made poor Major Fosdick go as he did. It wasn't any wonder.' "

This ambient decadence is most concentrated in an itinerant trio of organ-grinders:

> The Orphans were at the corner of the street with their organ . . . taking it in turns to work the handle, the unoccupied pair making it their business to importune, when it occured to them to do so, anyone who passed by and at other times, when the street was empty, to twitch and grumble at each other. . . . The three of them had small round heads and beady half-closed eyes. Hair grew on their faces but not successfully. . . . the Orphans lived together in a cottage with a sister who shared their mental attitude and who did the cooking for them. (*FV*, 18-19)

The Orphans are mental, physical and sexual deviates supported by charity from the locals, who seem to overlook these defects that reflect their own. The Orphans occupy the lowest link on the great chain of madness that ascends from them to the Passengers, supposedly models of robust sanity but in many ways as feeble as the demented musicians.

Vernon Passenger is perhaps the most melancholy portrait of the decadent traditionalist. Though he belongs to the cultural and social élite, his life has been a travesty. Measles (contracted several days after he landed in South Africa) prevented him from becoming a hero in the Boer War; sketchy research for his edition of a seventeenth-century poet was responsible for its being withdrawn upon publication; and World War I found him backing "the wrong horse." Although to the outside world of the hunt and pub Vernon Passenger appears popular and successful, he

> was gnawed inside with megalomania. He wanted to get away from all that he had been brought up to because it bored him and yet he felt that it was only by the accident of his position that he had any power at all. He used to brood over this, longing to be something more, and yet knowing at the same time that when he had come to live in the country he had deliberately chosen to be what he was. What he wanted to be he did not know. He knew only what he did not want to be. By allowing this to work in his mind he became every day more and more like what he wished most to differ from. (*FV*, 26)

The advent of Zouch gives Passenger's vague desires some direction. He recognizes in the artist a worthy antagonist, "another superman," and some of his old fire returns. But the flames are fitful. Although Zouch is killed, his accident defeats Passenger's major purpose—to make him look ridiculous at the hunt. The horse bolts before they even arrive there.

It is on his visit to Major Fosdick that Passenger suffers his severest setback. A protracted (if polite) hostility over shooting rights in a border wedge known as North Copse has given rise to mild antagonisms; but Passenger becomes actually inflamed when an alliance between Betty, his daughter, and Torquil Fosdick seems imminent. Vowing to take a firm stand on this more important issue, he drives to the Major's and discovers him roaming about an empty house while dressed in female clothing. For all intents and purposes, the moment of glory has come. A true superman has seldom been presented with such an opportunity for displaying his powers. But the situation overwhelms Passenger. The Major gains the upper hand over his incredulous caller by calmly offering to sublease the disputed woodlands; Passenger withdraws obsequiously, another of his lifelong ambitions bitterly defeated:

> He was overcome with a sense of failure. He had not risen to the situation. As a superman he had let himself down. In this moment of emergency he had been thrown back on the old props of tradition and education and when he might have enjoyed a substantial revenge he had behaved with all the restraint in the world. (*FV*, 185)

In this scene Powell frames his favorite sort of paradox, relying on the clash and reconciliation of the novel's antithetical forces. Tradition—frustrating, dreary, stultifying—offers the only reliable retreat in moments of crisis, shields the eyes from the ugly, the grotesque, the vulgar, and provides an excuse from ever becoming, in the modern sense, committed; yet it is from this very tradition that escape is sought.

Major Fosdick's transvestism is perhaps the most notorious example of escape, though he himself views it as a period of "mental relaxation," a "temporary [retirement] from the arena of everyday life." In the sanctuary of an upper-story room he casts off the cares and garb of a waning masculinity:

> Major Fosdick undid the loose knots of the first parcel and took from out of it a large picture-hat that had no doubt been seen at Ascot twenty years before. The second parcel contained a black sequin evening dress of about the same date. Removing his coat and waist-coat, Major Fosdick slipped the evening dress over his head and, shaking it so that it fell down into position, he went to the looking-glass and put on the hat. . . . In this costume he read until it was time to change for dinner.
> (*FV*, 17)

Thus attired, the Major spends his afternoons perusing hunting magazines or writing poetry in exercise books while "humming and singing to himself," until Passenger's surprise visit puts an end to this alternate existence. After his discovery Major Fosdick goes mad. In a sense, his crack-up is as final as Mrs. Brandon's death; and, oddly enough, although these two are never brought together in the novel, it is with her that he has the most pronounced affinity. Both lead secret austic lives in the world of books and in the past; both are abnormally obsessed—Major Fosdick has converted a not uncommon introversion into eonism, Mrs. Brandon has perverted a normal desire for beauty into callomania.

The family at Passenger Court fairly wallows in private obsessions though none so dramatic as the Major's or Mrs. Brandon's. Each is geared to his particular escape mechanism, needing only the impetus of the intruding Zouch to accelerate withdrawal. Vernon Passenger's excessive interest in his superman role allows him to "mentally compare himself" with the titanic figure of Lear, who has also seen his kingdom sink into chaos and his daughters turn against him. More contemplatively serene, Mrs. Passenger never really knows what is happening to her household, cares little anyway, and consequently remains tranquil (almost bovine), occupying herself with thoughts of bath-salts and pageants, or threading her way through gladioli, monkey puzzles, and cauliflower. Betty, Mary's older sister, is sporadically preoccupied with acquiring a second husband and " 'falling for all the pansies in the neighborhood.' " As for Mary, Zouch's appearance and her own initiation into London's Bohemia have unsettled and made useless any traditional modes of escape:

> Lately she had not been at her best. Without having any clear idea as to what it was that she wanted, she had begun to feel dissatisfied all day long. In the past when she had been attacked by depression she had dreamed about a tall husband with a country house that was a manageable size and a modern flat not too far from Berkeley Square. But all that had begun to seem unreal, insipid, somehow, and the thought of this husband of her imagination, leaning back on his shooting stick at Hawthorn Hill with bowler tilted over his eyes and his field-glasses half raised as together they watched the horses coming over the last jump, in her present mood, merely made her feel exhausted. Somehow it did not seem any longer to be what she wanted. (*FV*, 100-01)

Zouch represents Mary's likeliest means of escape. By converting him to country ways she hopes to gain an artist without relinquishing her birthright. What Mary fails to grasp is that Zouch sanctions the conversion completely; he is perfectly willing to chuck art, provided he can nestle neatly into a ready-made bourgeois niche and assume the garb of middle-class respectability. And so, convinced that "Mrs. Passenger and the garden [symbolize] a dignified and more successful future," Zouch patronizes and manipulates her, growing progressively more certain that he has succeeded in his bid for Mary. When the time arrives for his first ride to hounds (in which he has willed to prove himself), he is nervous but confident; with three whiskeys under his belt, he waxes mellow. Soon he will be leading a new life. The sordid hustle of the city will fade into the background as the dignified leisure of the country assumes prominence; the rat race will give way to the fox hunt. But this dream will never materialize for Zouch; his pretensions bar him from even considering his downfall, and his view of the future encompasses all possibilities but his own death.

II

Zouch's death comes as something of a shock, though a glance back at Powell's design should indicate how inevitable it is. The tight, neat framework is founded on two lines from the popular hunting song, "John Peel," which describes the four stages of the hunt and supplies the novel's title and epigraph: "From a find to a check, from a check to a view, / From a view to a death in the morning." The novel proceeds, sometimes literally, through these stages, relying for its impact on the reader's realization that metaphor and characterization grow out of the structure and that all three coalesce at the moment of Zouch's death.

Of course, Zouch is no other than the fox himself, while the movement of the novel imaginatively captures the pace of the hunt. Zouch's initial appearance at Passenger Court is directly related to the "find," the moment when the fox is first discovered and the hunt begins. Not giving his pursuers the ready opportunity for determining his next move, Zouch maneuvers himself away from his tense antagonists and creates the sort of confusion that might result when hounds lose the scent and a "check" is called. Leaving the safety of his London lair after a brief interlude, he reappears at Passenger's for autumn hunting, exposing himself to the "view," which becomes the penultimate stage in his destruction. Like the hunt itself, more frantic and feverish for the actual sighting of the fox, the book gathers energy as it moves toward the denouement; both, of course, end in a kind of brutal death.

The beauty of the novel's relatively simple structure is reinforced by the perfect proportions of Zouch's vulpine character—crafty, pert, shifty, predatory. Moving with calculated temerity, ingratiating himself slyly, Zouch does survive much longer than one might have first imagined. But even in his most guarded moment he is susceptible to attack, for basically he is an invader—a Reynard come not merely to make off with Pertelote but to harry the household.

At his slyest, Zouch is unrivaled. Having become enamored of Joanna Brandon, he manipulates the most routine greeting or chance encounter into a clandestine rendezvous. Though Mary's house guest, he contrives visits to Joanna when the Passenger family is calling on relations and conducts these excursions under the pretext of searching out scenic subjects for his paintings. His efforts are finally rewarded by Joanna's acquiescence —she is foolishly romantic enough to believe he loves her—and her seduction is even accomplished under the Passenger roof.

Zouch's amours are but a single reflection of his wiliness; he tempers his craft with a caution which, whether instinctual nor sophisticated, dictates the moment to burrow or remain burrowed. He answers ambiguously a query from Passenger on the merits of John Singer Sargent because "he did not see why he should come out in the open after so slight an acquaintance." Later, chatting with Mrs. Passenger during their amble through the grounds, he affirms "cautiously" his interest in gardens, on another occasion feigns curiosity in

Mary's activities so that he might not "be cross-questioned too fully about his own," and even hedges with Mary's niece, believing "in acting with children as circumspectly as with adults."

Zouch's fear of verbal commitments matches his evasion of physical ones. He detests crowds, courting retreat as methodically as he does Joanna or Mary, slipping off now and then to resummon his forces:

> He . . . sneaked away to smoke a cigarette in the morning room. . . . Here away from the crowd he was beginning to recover his superman technique . . . Zouch stepped aside to avoid being seen. . . . Indoors these people would be worse than in the garden. . . . He therefore walked away through passages into a nondescript wing. . . . Here he was unlikely to be disturbed. (*FV*, 59-60, 67-68)

During the pageant rehearsal Zouch plays hide-and-seek with the Passenger clan and spirits Joanna away for a few moments of preliminary wooing:

> He remembered that there was an alcove under the sweep of the stairs which had the advantage of a certain privacy without any of the opprobrium that might attach, should anyone happen to discover them, to some more remote part of the house. (*FV*, 70)

However Betty and Torquil do discover them, and Zouch admits to his secret self "that as usual it would be better to be careful as . . . being good [would be] almost out of the question."

For better or worse, Zouch is never given any extended opportunity of being either. From the moment he arrives at Passenger Court he is beset by animosities as potentially fatal to him as hounds to the fox. Marshall (the butler) directs him to Mary "with just the hint of a threat in his voice," and persistently spies on him from around corners and behind doors. Betty—with whom Zouch shares a natural, mutual antagonism—is more direct in her approach, summarily appraising him as "lousy . . . an ambitious little brute. . . . He's just awful and there it is." Despite his meticulousness, flattery, and temporizing, Zouch inspires what amounts to an instinctive aversion on the part of all the Passenger trio—a kind of vulpophobia. He can have no doubts about the impression he has made when Betty's child spontaneously reveals the prevailing sentiment of the household:

> "Gran'dad says he'll be glad when you get out of the house. . . . He says he wouldn't trust you round the corner. . . . Granny doesn't like you either. . . ."
> "And why not?"
> "She says she doesn't know. She says there's just something about you that she doesn't like."
> "Is that all?"
> "She says it's just that. . . . Mummy doesn't like you either. She says she'll be glad when you're gone."
> "Is there anyone in the house who does like me, Bianca?"
> "Yes, Mary likes you. . . . Mary says you're rather sweet. She gets angry when Mummy says you're a tuft-hunter."
> "Does she?"
> "Yes. Mary gets very angry."
> "I'm glad to hear that."
> "What is a tuft-hunter?"
> "Someone who hunts tufts, I suppose."
> "What is a tuft?"
> "I don't know," said Zouch, rather bitterly.
> *(FV, 129-30)*

Vacillating precariously between his role as hunter and hunted, Zouch discovers that opportunism can be a two-way game. While reciprocating the instinctive mistrust of Mary's father—he has an "instantaneous fear" that her father is his "match" and knows he is a "dan-

gerous man as soon as he sets eyes on him"—Zouch
nevertheless accepts Passenger's proposals to mount him
on a restive, skittish horse. Actually, of course, there is
no monstrous plot against Zouch. By definition, the fox
hunter cannot commit vulpicide; apart from this, it is
neither good sport nor good form. Though the Passengers are apprehensive at the thought of acquiring Zouch
as their son-in-law, their most deliberate move is a resolve to let him dramatize his own ridiculousness in the
arts and graces of country life, and what fitter opportunity for such histrionics than the hunt.

Quite by chance, the Passengers are in for more
drama than they anticipate. Yet it is Zouch himself who
displays the greatest levity concerning his own mortality.
On one occasion he ruminates jocularly on the "place
. . . reserved for him" in the Passenger mausoleum; on
another, he fatuously indulges in the following exchange with Betty:

> "Mary tells me that your father is going to be kind
> enough to mount me."
> Betty said: "Oh, it isn't kindness with father. It's cru-
> elty. Absolutely pathological, I can assure you."
> Zouch laughed heartily, thinking that what Betty said
> was all too true. (*FV*, 173-74)

Considering how precise an augury this is, Zouch's
facetiousness strikes a macabre note. Death was pres-
aged, however, at the opening of the novel. Meeting
Mary in her own milieu for the first time, Zouch finds
conversation strained; for a moment the mutual embarrassment is oppressive: "There was a pause. To arrive
was to die a little. Half-past three in the afternoon was,
as always, a difficult time of day to deal with." Socially
insecure upon first "arriving" at Passenger Court, Zouch
naturally experiences the sinking feeling that attends
the initiation of new, bold designs. But as critical as this

early venture may seem, he reaches his climacteric when he returns; it is when he believes he has attained fulfillment of his social ambitions—when he has, in an ironic sense, "arrived"—that Zouch dies.

While the focus in *From a View to a Death* often shifts from the fox directly, Powell never lets one lose sight of the central metaphor. Allusions to the "hunt and chase" are planted early in the novel, growing more prominent as the climax approaches. At first these are only casual: glimpses of hunting paraphernalia, random discussions about dogs, references to past shooting and hunting expeditions. Not until Torquil's cocktail party does the hunt motif actually assume importance as the background for action.

What begins as a dreary gathering on the lawn in back of the local pub (significantly named the *Fox and Hounds*) becomes a drunken debacle. Though less bright-eyed than the other guests, Zouch relaxes his customary caution and inveigles Joanna into the inn and eventually into a deserted upstairs room, where his ardent attempts at lovemaking are checked by her tears. Zouch, his enthusiasm dampened, is saved from embarrassment by a row in the courtyard below. Paralleling Zouch's own designs on Joanna, one of the Orphans has been pursuing the rector's daughter, with a kind of playful, ignoble savagery. As if the party had not already been a fiasco, it presently disintegrates altogether. Tempers flare and the group breaks up. No one displays a shorter temper than Mary, who sardonically labels the gathering "beastly, beastly, beastly."

She is right, without comprehending the irony behind her epithet. The group, not simply the affair, *is* "beastly." And Zouch, though notorious in exhibiting brutish traits, is not singular. Joanna, for example, has "mouse-coloured" hair, an apt characterization considering her limited defenses against the preying fox. On the other side of the fence are Jasper, in love with Joanna "in a heavy, dumb-animal sort of way," and Torquil, whose disproportionately large head gives him a distinctly equine appearance. Whatever weird agency has metamorphosed these two also has had a hand in transmuting their father, who literally leaps into the novel (he is initially sighted jumping a ditch) and is subsequently designated as Canis Major: "Major Fosdick's face, blotchy in places, worked up and down convulsively as if he were chewing gum, his dewlaps giving him something of the appearance of a bloodhound."

Powell employs these (and other) animal images as character signatures. Disregard of any consistency is intentional, since Powell strives for a cumulative effect and is generally more eloquent stating conclusions than forming propositions. In this way he is like George Orwell, who invests the characters of *Animal Farm* with increasingly human traits until at the end "it was impossible to say which was which." Powell reverses the procedure, while adopting a similar method: he makes his humans more like animals until they become part of the "hunt and chase" to which they are inextricably committed.

It is the actual hunting meet that moves the main theme into the structural foreground at last. This chapter is a microcosm of the novel as a whole, a summary of what has gone before, a rehearsal of what is to come. Almost the entire cast of characters rides onto the scene, a motley crew united for a brief instant by tradition, yet marked even here by their eccentricities: Passenger, alternately curt and brooding, conscious of his position as Master of the Hunt; Major Fosdick, "mumbling happily to himself" about the past importance of meets in his day; Torquil and Jasper, uneasily perched on their mounts, looking respectively like Cervantes' knight and squire; Mary, tall, neat, proper in the saddle; Betty and Joanna, on the sidelines as usual, the former caustically commenting on the action, the latter dreamy and vague despite the bustle. Powell's deft, rapid sketches of the gentry adequately compensate for his neglect of any naturalistic details of the hunt itself. And easily the most successful description is Torquil's chasing hotly after the quarry:

> The fox had a good start, with the hounds some way behind and the rest of the hunt nowhere. Torquil—it was now clear that it was Torquil—led the field, because his mare with remarkable intuition had decided to run away with him at the precise moment of the find. The enormous bay charged the first fence, a low one, loosely built up, and went pounding on, taking it easy over some broken ground, the rest of them catching him up one by one. Yet it was evident that the mare intended to negotiate the next hedge, which was considerably higher and had no gaps in it, by the method which had proved so successful at the previous one. Torquil himself seemed prepared for something of the sort and when the mare changed her mind and jumped, he went into the air, swayed violently, and could be seen trotting across the next field, still mounted, but in a position that would have enabled him to pick up a handkerchief from the ground if there had been one there and he had been so minded. (*FV*, 168-69)

Borrowing the merest tinge of sadism from Smollett's more colorful account of Commodore Trunnion on *his* runaway, Powell writes one of his better pieces of extended farce, always mindful of the secondary implications. What is viewed objectively as a ludicrous and amusing experience for Torquil later is transformed into Zouch's fatal misfortune. This kind of prefiguration operates elsewhere as well. Powell drops the hunt in the middle of a long "check," keeping the reader ignorant of the fox's fate—a mystery heightened by the previous analogy with Zouch, who is himself away during the meet and whose own fate is still precarious. Indeed, in the hunt chapter and the brief interlude following it the action hangs fire, preparing to sweep quickly forward; afterwards, the movement is inexorable: Zouch returns from the city, Fosdick is discovered by Passenger and goes mad, Zouch is killed, Mrs. Brandon dies, and Joanna departs for London.

Except possibly for Joanna, the ones who escape the reverses of fortune seem singularly unaffected by the deaths and madness of the others. Nor do they possess a sensitivity masked by a superior stoicism. For them, character is not an expression of iron will but of wooden habit. They welcome, in short, a return to an existence where patterns vary little and where life takes on the routine aspect of anticlimax. For some, Vernon Passenger in particular, these little tragedies engender peace of mind. Now he knows that neither of his daughters will marry men he detests, that the feuds between himself and Zouch, himself and Fosdick are permanently ended, and that with all rivals removed he has clearly been restored to supremacy, however specious.

But Passenger's domain becomes even more lamentable in retrospect than it had seemed during the course of the novel. Customs and traditions, which at first appeared merely frivolous and diverting, are now recalled as futile attempts to recapture bygone brilliance. The much-publicized pageant held at Passenger Court, which initially strikes one as a product of amateurish incompetence, takes on the perspective of a grim masquerade— a travesty of the costumes, manners, and mores of the Restoration. And a further impact of Powell's irony is felt once one realizes that the misdirected energies of a whole town have been consumed in miming an era that was a prototype of decadence, internecine struggle, and political jealousy—a deserving subject (like Passenger's province) for the caustic summary of John Dryden, that century's most perceptive critic:

> All, all, of a piece throughout;
> Thy Chase had a Beast in View
> Thy Wars brought nothing about;
> Thy Lovers were all untrue.

4

Agents
and
Patients

*A*gents *and Patients* is Powell's flirtation
with two distinct literary models: the picaresque tale
and the philosophic fable. The rogue of the first has
tramped through English comedy for over three hundred years, maintaining his geniality despite the many
detours and dead ends, and enjoying a mobility denied
his more serious brethren who remain laced in the
straitjacket of class and tradition. The green youth of
the second has been traveling a good deal longer, always
with the hope that beyond the next turn lies a haven
called Happiness from which the harsher realities of life
are excluded.

In *Agents and Patients* these types appear as a pair of
picaroons and a naïve *philosophe* and are transported
from their accustomed genres to be set down in a
comedy of manners that is thinly farcical and solidly
cautionary. As "postwar characters" Powell's rogues may

possibly seem dated, but as confidence men they bear the ageless stamp of their profession:

> [Chipchase's] . . . emaciated physique and severe expression gave some indication of this historical background. He was an art critic by profession and an amateur of psychoanalysis. Maltravers, who was tall and in a genial way distinguished-looking, had connections with the film industry and might have been a better-class gangster figure of any period. (*AP*, 2)

Except that their methods have been streamlined and their manners polished, Chipchase and Maltravers are lineal descendants of Robert Greene's coney-catchers, noticeably feeling the pinch of the trade depression and the lack of a gullible backer for their newest schemes. Chipchase needs a "suitable patient to experiment on for a new system of psychological and psycho-analytical treatment [he] is developing": one, of course, who will not merely bear the burden of neuroses but of expenses as well. Maltravers requires capital to film a documentary—"founded to a considerable extent on the findings of psycho-analysis"—on the behavior of a small intellectual group without theatrical training.

Fortuitously, the coney wanders into their snares. He is Blore-Smith, a young innocent recently down from Oxford, whose only activities are reading desultorily for the Bar (in order "to have something definite to tell people when they questioned him about himself"), attending the cinema frequently, and piling up large monthly allowances in his hutch. He is neurotic and wealthy, with an unexceptional past, an unbearable present, and an unpromising future:

> Life at Oxford had been lonely and obscure, but his solitude and a lack of distinction did not become apparent to him until he had lived for some months in London. . . . Blore-Smith had even hoped on coming down

from Oxford that he would have opportunities for friendship with the opposite sex. But although in London this was not openly put a stop to by the authorities it seemed no less difficult to achieve. He kept up with some of his Oxford friends. . . . His comparative affluence seemed no help. In the first place he disliked the idea of spending a lot of money all at once, and in the second he could think of nothing that he wanted to spend it on which would not complicate life in a way which alarmed him. . . . Life showed every sign of being a disappointment. (*AP*, 10-12)

Above all else, Blore-Smith is seeking freedom from the humdrum rounds of his existence; but though his solvency allows alternative routes of escape, he is fettered by a weak will, unable to extricate himself, and unprepared for the consequences if he should. After witnessing a side show featuring a fakir trying to free himself from a "spiked board strapped to his back," Blore-Smith ruminates on his own helpless restraint:

He too felt himself chained. Chained by circumstances. Again he toyed in his mind with the idea of collecting hour-glasses or first editions or something of the sort. He knew that a little decision was all that was necessary. But steps of that kind needed a command of initiative. (*AP*, 12)

Chipchase and Maltravers are fettered as well, not by their wills (which in opportunists are always strong), nor even by the eccentricities of their projects, but by the lack of ready funds needed to carry out such projects. A near-accident, however, sends Blore-Smith almost literally into Maltravers' arms, and it is not long before he and Chipchase discover that the coney is well heeled. Within the week the two rogues have freed him from his "chains" and enmeshed him in the world of their schemes.

Blore-Smith's inexperience and expectations that life

should be something other than he had made it enable Chipchase and Maltravers to bend his will. The purely picaresque elements in the novel proceed from the farcical situations Blore-Smith encounters as he is taken on a romp through three world capitals. Though ostensibly liberated at last, he has merely substituted one sort of thralldom for another. As before he was fettered to the drab realities of life, he now becomes mesmerized by its more extravagant chimeras, since Chipchase and Maltravers are skilled purveyors of the two commodities that so completely nourish twentieth-century illusions: psychiatry and cinema.

Chipchase is the first to exploit this new source of funds. After a cursory diagnosis of Blore-Smith, he decides that a trip abroad is a prerequisite for bringing him "into touch with life" and leaving behind "the dream world in which he had been accustomed to live." In Paris Blore-Smith meets the dope addict, Gaston de la Tour d'Espagne, encounters a gaggle of eccentrics at the Duchesse de Borodino's, and is conveyed to a brothel where he is soon hungering after a plump French tart named Yoyo, who leads him to a rented room and rolls him. But Yoyo is merely one rogue among many, and her little prank seems almost artless when placed beside the swindle of Chipchase.

Obviously a world like this, obsessed with sex and sterling, may be something of a sordid one—as indeed the world of *Agents and Patients* is. But physical prostitution is insignificant compared to the prostitution of personality and talent. This theme is blatantly delivered in the opening lines of the novel:

> "I like sordid affairs," [said Chipchase.] "What I object to is the assumption that just because one's love affairs are sordid it doesn't matter whether or not they go wrong."

> Maltravers said: "Naturally, naturally. It's far worse. People who have unsordid love affairs have extraneous things to fall back on. Sordid love affairs have to be their own reward." (*AP*, 1)

For all the facile attitudinizing of Chipchase and the crisp, Wildean texture of Maltravers' epigram, the dialogue contains the sound, if cynical, forecast of Blore-Smith's sobering experiences. The seeds are sown in Mrs. Mendoza's florist shop (a hangout for Chipchase and Maltravers), portentously named *la cattleya,* the flower to which Odette de Crécy and M. Swann attached such significance. Like her Proustian counterpart, Mendie has led a fast Bohemian life. Driven by cupidity and aided by her sensuality, she now contemplates acquiring respectability through marriage with the bearish, bull-headed Commodore Venables. Blore-Smith imagines Mendie to be "the most beautiful woman he had ever seen," although his allegiances shift when he meets Maltravers' wife, Sarah. In its own way, the relationship between Sarah and Maltravers is as sordid as Mendie and the Commodore's, for their marriage is based on personal antagonism, professional jealousy, and sexual disinterest.

Aware of this marital tension, and more militant for being under the aegis of Chipchase, Blore-Smith lays siege to Sarah and is quickly repulsed and hustled off by Chipchase to Berlin to confer with Maltravers about the forthcoming film. Mendie, propelled by her own sordid motivations, turns up in Berlin, too, gets her claws into Blore-Smith, and leaving everyone in the lurch bolts with him from Germany. Blore-Smith sets up housekeeping in London with Mendie and soon perceives she is not the sexual philanthropist he had imagined. However, a car and cottage lessen the strain of living what she calls a "horrible constricted fussy little" life, though

Blore-Smith's neuroticism is not lessened an iota and his little life has never been *more* constricted. Mendie exploits him mercilessly: first by sapping his funds, then by letting Scrubb (a smutty, puerile medical student) move into the cottage, and finally by running off with Gaston de la Tour d'Espagne, whom Chipchase and Maltravers have calculatingly set out as a decoy. Mendie's defection, merely one aspect of the outlandish denouement, precipitates Blore-Smith's inevitable fall from his fool's paradise into an inferno where the scorching truth at last obliterates all false illusions.

Such illusions are part of the central design of the novel; they assemble with unusual speed and force because Blore-Smith displays (through his neurosis) a special vulnerability to them. As a farce, *Agents and Patients* naturally embraces the themes of appearance and reality; and, as an ironist working over these themes, Powell has sought substantial and comprehensive metaphors, pertinent to this decade, for illustrating them. One, "psychiatry," ultimately destroys Blore-Smith's hope of rectifying or strengthening his "emotional life"; the other, "the cinema," squelches irrevocably his artistic pretensions.

Like most of Powell's early novels, *Agents and Patients* is indebted to the films for much of its terminology, technique, and design; but in no other prewar work has Powell actually placed his characters into a motion picture milieu in order to animate the movement between the real and the imagined. At first, Maltravers' schemes to "photograph people existing," to illustrate their dreams, desires, and behavior, seem imaginative, but also vain and impractical. His brand of surrealism is, however, matched by Powell's. Trailing Chipchase through a maze of sets in the Berlin studio where Maltravers is at work on a commercial film, Blore-

Smith finds his powers of perception now eclipsed, now dazzled, but in either case confounded by the sudden juxtaposition of illusion and reality:

> Going through one of the doors they entered a pitchy-dark passage and, opening another door at the end, came out into a white-panelled room . . .
> Beyond the curtain Blore-Smith found himself in the depths of the jungle. Tropical foliage hung down from above him so that he had to pick his way carefully along the narrow path between giant cactuses and spiky clusters of equatorial blossom. Once he caught his foot in the wire supports of a rope of orchids and fell headlong, causing the surrounding undergrowth to shake violently. . . . They left this primeval forest by way of a sliding door in a hollow tree . . . [and] came out from behind a wing of scenery and into the blaze of light that shone from several powerful arc-lamps that were trained like searchlights on a group of people. (*AP*, 125)

This surrealistic interplay of darkness and light[1] fuses into a kind of imperfect chiaroscuro, blurring all definition. Not only visual images but identities as well remain tentative and ambivalent. As Paris distorted the psychological, so Berlin's movie world distorts the physical and presents to Blore-Smith a grotesque array of split personalities that necessitate constant adjustment of appearances to his own sense of reality. The director-dwarf Roth, Gaston de la Tour d'Espagne, the character actor Inglethorne, Adolf the waiter, the lesbian Fritzi, and the homosexual Willi are pertinent adjuncts to several central questions. Can we, Powell asks, ever satisfactorily penetrate behind the masks of others? Does any character in *Agents and Patients* really have a stable identity, one that can be fixed upon with certainty, one that even he himself recognizes? Or do not all of

1. The entire Berlin chapter (Chapter 4) capitalizes on light and dark imagery.

Powell's personae in some way wear masks similar to that of the bumbling art collector:

> [Schlumbermayer] handed a card to Blore-Smith and got into the taxi. As the taxi began to move, Blore-Smith ran forward and said:
>
> "But this card says *Mr. Joseph Simpson,* and there's no address."
>
> The taxi stopped. Schlumbermayer leant out. "Oh does it?" he said. "I must have given you the wrong one." He fumbled in his notecase and handed out another card, which was inscribed *Mr. E. E. Schlumbermayer, The Bibelot Club, S. W.*
>
> "The others sometimes come in useful," he said, and laughed angrily. (*AP,* 102)

Fragmented identities confuse Blore-Smith as much as multiple and jarring visual experiences, and his battered psyche almost disintegrates under a barrage of both. At Broadacres, Blore-Smith incredulously witnesses and participates in the rapid unfolding of events that transform his shattered illusions into physical sensations of "terror and nausea": Mendie's play for Gaston; Commodore Venable's verbal assault on Mendie; Gaston's physical threat to the Commodore; the landing of Pauline Borodino's airplane in Schlumbermayer's field; Reggie Frott's maneuvering of Schlumbermayer out of Gaston's estate; Gaston's and Mendie's mad dash across the field to the plane—pursued by the crazed Commodore—and their escape; Maltravers' wild camera direction to Chipchase; and his own flight (in an appropriated car) to his London sanctuary. When the game is up, he finds that he has done more than lose; he has been taken. Moreover, Chipchase and Maltravers (on their last visit to him) unwittingly define the central issue:

> "But what is really the matter?" [Maltravers] said. "When we met you your life was of a dullness so intolerable that you thought of suicide. You told me. I repeat

your very words. We take you in hand and in the space
of a few months you are in the thick of everything. Love
affairs. Business dealings of the most varied kind. Travel.
Strange company. Adventure. What else do you want?
What else do you imagine life has to offer? . . . And
what are your plans, may one inquire? . . ."

"I shall lead my own life again."

"I see."

"Not the life foisted on me by you two. Something very
different."

"I can imagine that."

"The real thing," said Blore-Smith, rather desperately.

"If," said Chipchase, "you imagine that the Real Thing
is ever going to be widely different from what you have
already experienced, I fear that you may be disappointed."
(*AP*, 213-15)

The literary echo does not force a parallel with the
famous story of Henry James, but it does suggest it.
Both "The Real Thing" and *Agents and Patients,* as
vastly different as they are in plot and technique,
broadly are stories about the breakdown of illusions,
and, more precisely, about "the process of undermining
our assumptions."[2] Powell, however, chooses to dig
through to comedy, James to pathos. Blore-Smith does
possess the advantages of youth; he is at least disillusioned early enough. Hopefully he can correct the vision
that distorts life into either of those vague abstractions:
a "disappointment" or "the real thing."

II

Powell's total artistic achievement in unifying the
moral implications of *Agents and Patients* with the
welter of farce should not be overlooked. The allusions
to cinema and psychiatry, highlighting the picaresque

2. Quentin Anderson's term found in his introduction to *Henry
James: Selected Short Stories* (New York, 1958), p. vii.

framework of the novel, complement the mythic symbolism that illustrates its allegory. The comic tale incorporates the fable and the ironic incorporates the moral;
human experience is thus placed under double criticism.
Powell's sights are leveled against the purchasers as well
as the purveyors of illusion, the naïve as well as the
sophisticated. Thus his heroes generally end up closer in
spirit to Gulliver than to Tom Jones, Candide, or even
Rasselas, for what starts out as their innocent infatuation with knowledge becomes an ultimate distaste for it
once it reveals how much grimmer and more intolerable
life really can be. Ostensibly then, the novel describes
the end of innocence and the expulsion from the lush
Eden of illusion to the dreary regions of reality. It is a
philosophic parable involving the Devil, Man at his
Fall, and the Garden.

Although Powell is indebted to the Bible and Milton
in developing his allegory, his own comic juggling of
archetypes provides *Agents and Patients* with its unique
character. Certainly the novel's opening is highly sugges-
tive of the early books of *Paradise Lost*. Chipchase and
Maltravers are plotting the fall of any anonymous innocent who might happen along to gratify their schemes.
Physically, both men are depicted as "historic" and
"gangster" types, and even their immediate milieu (a
London café) evokes associations with the underworld.
The room is "hot," draped in a "red curtain," and in
perpetual "twilight":

> When there was a fog about, the inside, only brightened
> by the reflections of the gas fire on the metal of the
> massive funereal urns in which the chicory stewed, was
> like a cave; and the linoleum floor a vein of grey-pink
> rock, some volcanic substratum. (*AP*, 2)

The spirit of Milton's Hell is again conjured up in
the sideshow sequence. Though the burning lake has

been metamorphosed into the pavements of a London
side street and the writhing band of fallen angels into a
single "handcuffed" fakir, the atmosphere is as noxious
as that of the inferno. The background is "surrealistic,"
the "disproportionate height of the surrounding build-
ings" induces a "claustrophobia," and the fog hangs
'about in wisps here and there like weeks-old poison
gas." Powell's anachronistic Acheron even comes complete with its own modest Sisyphus: "In the centre of
[an] open space a pile of stones lay beside a wigwam in
which a man sat all day long, awaiting the completion
of some unachievable labours on the cobbles."

Throughout the novel Powell excels in this sort of
ironic interplay of an actual human predicament and
an intellectual allusion. The description of the fakir,
goaded by sword thrusts, struggling and groaning like
an epileptic, is rendered in terms of a Renaissance portrait of Jacob wrestling with the Angel. The image is
ingenious and concise; the sense is all wrong. In the
Bible the Angel is the messenger of God, not of the
Devil; Jacob's combat is hard, but not cruel; and he
gains a blessing, not a curse. In Powell, *only* hellishness
and cruelty are emphasized. The sado-masochistic relationship of the fakir and his accomplice is an extension
of an identical relationship between them and the audi-
ence. Even their props are designated as "assorted
instruments of torture," an epithet that recurs after
Blore-Smith's ordeal in Paris. But the most fastidious in
his fiendishness is Chipchase. Leaving the scene, he non-
chalantly "steps over [a small child] who had fallen to
the ground" and eventually "[slinks] off, keeping close
to the walls of the houses to avoid the wind."

The child sprawled on the pavement and the skulking
art critic prefigure the Fall of the Innocent, Blore-
Smith: the middle-class English Adam, tagged, like his

adversaries, with a characteristically figurative name, and, by nature, ripe for deception. He first displays vulnerability at an art gallery, where his entrance interrupts a dialogue between the owner, Reggie Frott, and Chipchase:

> Reggie, when he saw Chipchase . . . grimaced diabolically. . . .
> He took a small bottle from his pocket and smelt the grey liquid inside.
> "Time to take my medicine," he said. "Have some?"
> "No."
> "Do. It's awfully good for you. Gets rid of all the poison inside."
> "I prefer to keep mine."
> "Just as you like, you old devil." (*AP*, 19-20)

Blore-Smith's offer to pay two hundred pounds for a painting of almost no value provokes "wide-eyed uncertainty, like a frightened child's." Frott, however, accepts the check; and Blore-Smith, with demonic laughter ringing in his ears, leaves the gallery, only to "fall" into the clutches of Maltravers and nearly under the wheels of his auto. As the Prince of Darkness is still a gentleman at this point, Blore-Smith willingly accompanies him to a pub. Taking up his protective perch by the fire, Maltravers tempts him with "life, women, a good time" and leads him up the path to the garden of illusion.

This particular part of the Garden is Mendie's florist shop, the first in a series of botanical allusions associated with Blore-Smith, and the place where he comes under the stricter scrutiny of Chipchase and Maltravers. After falling under their spell, he is taken to dinner by Maltravers, whose strategy in tempting Blore-Smith further parallels that of Milton's Satan: feeding dreams and flattering the ego. Later, at Blore-Smith's flat (in which hangs a sole print—Van Gogh's *Sunflowers*) Chipchase confidentially reveals some salient bits of the

absent Maltravers' biography. Though no Raphael nar-
rating to Adam, Chipchase shows a similar dispas-
sionateness in recounting Maltravers' refusal to become
"permanent under-secretary," his rebellion against his
own father, and the withdrawal of his father-in-law's
affections and financial support:

> "The old man . . . left most of his money to found a
> home for fallen women or something of the sort. That
> was because he disapproved of Maltravers."
> "Why did he disapprove?"
> "Well," said Chipchase, "you've seen him, haven't
> you?"
> "Maltravers?"
> "Yes."
> "But was it just his clothes?"
> "That sort of thing and the way he talked and the
> things he did. Maltravers gave up the civil service and
> got a job in pictures, which Sarah's father considered to
> be falling as low as it is possible to fall." (*AP,* 62-63)

Powell, like Milton, capitalizes on this structural
irony of having Adam informed of Satan's overthrow
preparatory to experiencing his own. It is not long before Chipchase drops his disguise of visiting angel and
tenders his own brand of temptation, quite different
from that of Maltravers' but equally Miltonic. Ultimately, both Adam and Blore-Smith fall because of an
admitted weakness of personality: uxoriousness in the
former's case, and in the latter's the susceptibility of a
wealthy, virginal, neurotic, dull Oxonian graduate for
adventure and psychotherapy.

To Blore-Smith, unlike Adam, knowledge (carnal or
otherwise) does not come immediately. An eternity of
incident and illusion is suspended between the moment
of the first protracted bite of the fruit and the final
realization of its bitterness. Yet Blore-Smith's initial reactions to these new experiences are basically similar to

Adam's. Both get drunk. Whereas Milton describes the agonies of Adam's mental hangover, Powell renders Blore-Smith's physical suffering:

> At first, when he turned over, Blore-Smith thought that he was going to die. The agony of movement, the strange dryness in his throat, and the fact that he was still wearing his underclothes all pointed to some sudden and fatal seizure. The blinds of the bedroom were not drawn and the sunlight was playing on his face. . . . Blore-Smith shut his eyes and felt the bed slowly revolving on its own axis beneath him; from left to right; and then up and down. . . . For some time he lay like this, hoping that the end would come quickly. Never in his life before had he felt in such a state. His parched throat drove him at last out of bed. He almost fell to the ground. He managed to reach the washstand where a bottle of Vichy stood, already opened, but still containing a little water. He drank this and broke out into a cold sweat. He sponged his face and lay down again on the bed. Later, looking at his watch, he saw that it was nearly lunchtime. (*AP*, 92)

Under such circumstances, lunch turns out to be a grim affair. Hardly "able to nod his head without prejudicing his physical state," and having his "line of vision . . . from time to time obscured by clumps of black spots that would appear suddenly," Blore-Smith reverts to a botanical fantasy:

> He sat back, watching the rest of the luncheon-party as through a mist, sometimes catching snatches of their conversation, but more often hearing the words as if they were part of the irregular buzzing of insects in a garden, the heat of the restaurant providing an additional illusion of high summer. (*AP*, 98)

Blore-Smith grows compulsive about having his fling with original sin. But lust is easier to contemplate than to satisfy, since obstacles naturally arise. In his attempt to seduce Sarah Maltravers, Blore-Smith confronts the two

most exasperating ones: her unwillingness and his inexperience at making her willing. The reference to Gide's
Si le Grain ne meurt in Blore-Smith's flat and Maltravers'
subsequent remark to his wife reinforce the irony of the
garden imagery, which multiplies with Blore-Smith's progressive temptations and sexual desires. Such symbolism
nearly overruns the Berlin episode. Greeted at the train
station by Fräulein Grundt, Blore-Smith is whisked off to
the *Niebelheim* studio lot and onto the terrifying jungle
set. As emblematic as his wandering through the foliage is
his emergence from it: "They left this primeval forest by
way of a sliding door in a hollow tree and in the distance,
as he stooped to avoid a python that hung, swaying, from
one of its lower branches, Blore-Smith heard the voice of
Maltravers." Compared to Powell's more skillful writing,
this juxtaposition of "python-Maltravers" seems somewhat crude, but it is none the less effective.

The fable gathers renewed effectiveness when everyone
is back in England. Here the pleasures revealed upon
tasting the forbidden fruit are at last experienced by
Blore-Smith as Mendie surrenders after only the briefest
of formalities. Loving nature, and having had her flower
shop seized by bailiffs, she suggests he take a cottage in
the country to house her simple, pastoral spirit. But the
anticipated idyll soon turns into a bucolic disaster.
Their metaphorical paradise becomes a wilderness in-
vaded by doubt, jealousy, and the persons of Chipchase,
Maltravers, Gaston de la Tour d'Espagne, and Scrubb.
Trying for Mendie's sake to placate them, Blore-Smith
agrees to accompany the lot to Schlumbermayer's estate
—the last stronghold of Eden:

> Broadacres . . . was a large red affair, built about 1900,
> and surrounded by closely cut grass, circular flower-beds,
> and high banks along which ran clipped yew hedges.
> There was a lawn in front of the house and on the

farther side of the drive a wide stretch of meadow where
the previous owner had played polo. Neighboring estates
were hidden by a high wall that surrounded the grounds.
(*AP,* 167)

Like Adam, Blore-Smith soon discovers that neither
seclusion, isolation, nor high walls can bar corrupting
elements inbred by nature. As Powell's comic-epic parable of the Fall moves swiftly toward the conclusion on
Broadacres' lawns and fields, Blore-Smith is at last un-
paradised, causing not the least tremor or quake of the
cosmos into which all his illusions are absorbed.

As for the "fiends," they get off scot-free. There is no
retributive act levied against them, no "universal hiss of
scorn," no serpentine metamorphosis. With characteristic bravura, they pay a final visit to Blore-Smith, extract
one more substantial check, and depart, tendering words
of good fellowship and a "small token of [their]
regard":

> They went through the door, leaving Blore-Smith stand-
> ing in the middle of the room holding [an] envelope in
> his hand. Blore-Smith heard the front door slam. He tore
> open the envelope. Inside was a snapshot of Maltravers
> and Chipchase sitting on either side of one of the urns in
> the garden at Broadacres. (*AP,* 215)

One would as soon consider giving a snake-skin purse to
Eve as such a souvenir to Blore-Smith. But after tossing
it in the wastebasket, he takes it out again and puts it
on the mantelpiece. It is, after all, the only tangible
memento of a lost illusion and new-found sense of reality. Even Blore-Smith recognizes that though life's problems cannot always be solved by experience, they never
can be solved without it. Tricked into tasting and test-
ing knowledge, and out of paradise, he still has this one
most important advantage over Adam: he has discovered what sort of land lies east of Eden before his exile
there.

5

What's Become of Waring

While unraveling one provocative riddle, *What's Become of Waring* suggests a score of others. The last of Powell's five prewar novels, it modulates (like the four earlier ones) from the sober to the eccentric, though the dark passages found in the preceding quartet have been considerably lightened and the blatantly farcical colorings often subdued by subtler shadings of comedy. The themes of the novel are rich and varied, which is not what is expected of a possibly suspect genre like the mystery-romance.

Curiously, *What's Become of Waring* is neither very mysterious nor very romantic—only enough so to dazzle superficially and create the illusion of a surface without a foundation. In fact, the novel has seldom compelled serious attention; and when it has, it has been pictured as some flapping appendage to the former volumes or a gasping, if conscientious, forerunner to *The Music of*

Time. For some reason it has proved easier to embrace the letter of Powell's book rather than the spirit. The novel has gained a reputation for being little more than a rather skillful story: a moderately paced marathon attempt on the part of a handful of persons to reconstruct the biography of a best-selling author who has remained incognito even up to his death.

In the unfolding action it becomes apparent that T. T. Waring, the author in question, is very much alive, perfectly well known to everyone concerned, and a fraud. Despite a nom de plume and additional aliases, Waring is at last unmasked. But Powell's obvious gimmick is merely a small part of a mechanism that investigates other personalities and psyches as well. The novel gains in thematic strength when one realizes that, as Waring's character comes into focus, the characters of those involved in the search also come under scrutiny, though the ultimate revelation of who *he* is still does not adequately solve the enigma of who everyone else is. *What's Become of Waring,* then, is patently a novel of discovery, but at the end one wonders what has been discovered. Is it simply that Waring is not Waring? That he is a common wastrel? an intriguer? a hypocrite? a genius? Or is it perhaps that Waring does not matter at all, or matters less than those who, in trying to uncover another's identity, discover how little they know about their own?

These considerations are never forced, but they are present, and gain a further dimension by their association with Browning's "Waring," which supplies the novel's title and epigraph:

> What's become of Waring
> Since he gave us all the slip,
> Chose land-travel or seafaring,
> Boots and chest or staff and scrip,

> Rather than pace up and down
> Any longer London-town?

Both works present worlds activated by complexities
and ambiguities and sent helter-skelter (in a kind of
Browningesque motion) through a suspension dense with
questions. Beyond abstracting sequences (and, at times,
tone and mood) from "Waring," Powell has drawn freely
upon Browning's ideas, using in some cases exact parallels
from the poem, but transforming them into something
new. The novel maps a never-never land that is meta-
phorically stable, but literally is in constant change.

The search for Waring begins in a London publishing
house on Grub Street, moves through the town houses of
spiritualists and the country estates of retired officers,
through the musty stacks of libraries and polished
drinking clubs of regimental barracks, and ends on the
grubby wharves of southern France. Powell's fiction has
ranged as widely before, but in no other early novel has
he so successfully cut back and forth across class lines—
not strictly for the sake of analyzing one class or the
other, but to portray, along with his customary eccentrics, characters of some depth.

His characters seem human because they also seem
probable. They are not (with a few exceptions) either
supermen or confidence men, paranoiacs or neurotics,
extroverts or introverts, but rather average plodders:
some successful and bright, others unsuccessful and dull,
many mediocre, but each secretly guarding in one way
or another an idealized picture of himself. It is, in fact,
the manner in which disillusion impinges upon these
romantic notions that provides the action of the novel,
and it is the austere or frivolous ways in which individuals adjust their identities that supply the central
theme.

As in Browning's "Waring," both action and theme

filter through the narrator, an unnamed young man who, like Nicholas Jenkins after him, is obligingly mobile. To be sure, the narrator here (anticipating the Jenkins of the early volumes of *The Music of Time*) exists in terms of the people whose lives he links, and he is necessarily shadowy. Rendered any more definite, he would become the center of attention and cease to function as the bridge between the experiences of others. Powell's concern with technique makes one believe that artistic motives lay behind this first-person innovation, for the most logical way to cast a novel about egos might reasonably be in the first-person; and when the story further involves a question of identities, what could be more logical again than to supply an anonymous narrator who so accurately reflects them!

The narrator is employed at a small publishing house owned by two brothers who manifest a fierce hostility toward each other's person and policies. As reader to the firm (and an aspiring critic himself), he is peculiarly susceptible to the caprices of the trade: one which can bury an author under his own remaindered books or, just as suddenly, turn best-sellers into legends.

Such a legend is T. T. Waring (the only feather in the firm's otherwise fusty cap), who has been writing travel books with a philosophical punch for nearly fifteen years and who has grown as notorious and revered as Doughty or T. E. Lawrence. But, as many writers burn for recognition for fear of remaining unknown to posterity, Waring assiduously cultivates a mysterious aloofness, almost as though he dreaded personal discovery:

> T. T. Waring himself never appeared. It was even suggested that Waring was not his real name. His manuscripts were sent to Peppercorn . . . with detailed instructions as to how they were to be produced and sug-

gestions for advance publicity. . . . orders were given that
his "modesty" was to be plugged all along the line. In
short, by the time his third book appeared, T. T. Waring
had shown himself to be a master of the science of building up a literary personality. (*WB*, 26-27)

t is when the newspapers announce his sudden and
unexplainable death that the publishing firm of Judkins
and Judkins decides a "life" must be brought out rapidly to capture the market, and it is here that the search
for Waring's identity and the entanglement of lives
begin.

Identity is questioned early in the novel when the
narrator describes Eustace Bromwich, an ex-captain
friend:

No one could ever tell when Eustace was giving an imita-
tion and when a confidence. He threw himself with such
heart and soul into his impersonations of splenetic gen-
erals, White Russians, Cockney privates, and Levantine
panders that for the moment he actually became them.
(*WB*, 4)

Bromwich's effectiveness as a character is twofold. Structurally, he provides the opportune link between Waring
and Hudson, the young captain chosen as Waring's biog-
rapher; and, as it later develops, Bromwich becomes
engaged to Roberta Payne, at one time also allied with
the two men, but sexually rather than socially. His
thematic function is initially more difficult to assess,
since he exhibits all the earmarks of being but one more
eccentric, preoccupied with outrageous fabrications and
practical jokes. But he is in control of his identity at
every moment, never considering these metamorphoses
either as outlets of escape or inlets to self-delusion; it is
the others, those having the mistaken notion they are
being themselves, who most often relax their grip.
Beyond this Bromwich acts also as a kind of symbolic

mediator between levelheaded objectivity (the nameless
narrator) and profligate excesses (the protean Waring)
providing the norm by which to judge other frequently
unstable personalities.

By indexing the personalities of the Judkins brothers
who have slipped just beyond the pale of normality
Powell most skillfully makes the connection. That a firm
named Judkins and Judkins should be the publishers of
an author prefixing "T. T." to his pen name is an initial irony, compounded when the brothers' identities
become as suspect as Waring's. A casual allusion along
these lines is noted in some early byplay between the
narrator and Bromwich:

> "Still advertising?" [Eustace asked.]
> "I'm a publisher now."
> "Who with?"
> "Judkins and Judkins."
> "Whom do you prefer? Judkins? Or Judkins?"
> "Judkins, emphatically." (WB, 2-3)

From the novelistic standpoint, this impartiality is not
ill-advised. Aided by Powell's comedy, Hugh and Bernard
Judkins are turned into intriguing persons with a Dicken-
sian flavor about them. But they are not "flat," as characters, though sometimes their realistic qualities are
overshadowed by a thematic pertinence. In this respect,
they reflect most strongly the metaphysical Tweedledum
and Tweedledee, and like Carroll's mirror-images they
seem to predicate existence on "contrariwise" attitudes:

> Hugh, who was about ten years younger than Bernard,
> had always had revolutionary ideas. . . . From the day that
> Hugh entered the office, Bernard, never over-addicted to
> optimism, became increasingly embittered. . . . [He] be-
> gan to loathe books, so that it seemed he had only
> entered the trade to take his revenge on them. His life
> . . . became one long crusade against the printed word.
> Every work that appeared under the Judkins & Judkins

colophon did so in the teeth of Bernard's bitter opposition. Hugh, who had always disapproved of his elder
brother's worldly ambitions, did not take this sort of
thing lying down. If Bernard could annoy him by refusing
to publish authors Hugh wanted, there were ways in
which Hugh could annoy Bernard. He did not hesitate to
employ such methods. (*WB*, 8-9)

Hugh's "methods" (which are not particularly devious)
are directed toward publishing books that boost sales; few
could consider him guilty of anything but good business
sense. Yet, despite his competitive involvement with his
brother and within the trade, he retains the lofty ideals
that once made him a respected public school master. He
finds a simple pleasure in romanticizing the youth of
others so that he may identify with it himself:

> T. T. Waring was exalted in his mind to the incarnation
> of Youth Triumphant, the sort of figure photographed
> on the cover of magazines advising Germany for your
> Holiday. It was a form of adolescent hero-worship that
> Hugh must have caught from his pupils when he was a
> pedagogue . . . [Shirley Handsworth, another of the
> firm's young authors] did not, of course, come nearly as
> high up the lists as T. T. Waring, whose preeminence
> was unassailable. But he had a special line in boyishness
> that Hugh liked. T. T. Waring stood for the glorious
> extra-mundane ideal of Youth: Shirley Handsworth, for
> its grubby schoolboy reality. (*WB*, 27-28, 39)

Hugh can fit youth, as an abstraction of the Real and
the Ideal, into his intellectual world. But when it becomes embodied in the provocative adventuress, Roberta
Payne, the temptation to go overboard is too great. De-
luding himself into thinking that "she is scarcely more
than a schoolgirl . . . [with] all the intelligence and
charm of a mature woman," he unwittingly pursues her
with shaky chivalry and zealous Puritanism.

Roberta is the first woman with whom Hugh has
dared let himself become involved, and her sophistica-

tion at twenty-five is no match for his naïveté at fifty.
When she declines Hugh's proposal of marriage he calls
her a harlot, a word which, while overstating her guile-
less (if liberal) immorality, comments on his own fastidious vision of sexuality. After her refusal, his perspective
narrows; with the subsequent revelation that his hero,
Waring, is a fraud, his youthful ideals and idealization
of Youth evaporate. Obsessed by the idea that all is
vanity, Hugh becomes weighted with insane standards
of morality—though one suspects these have always been
latent—and is eventually dragged down into a theologi-
cal quagmire. Refusing to publish books that are not
self-improving, and alienating the house's best authors
by criticizing their "personal characteristics," he steers
the partnership dangerously close to bankruptcy until a
final nervous collapse forces his retirement from publishing.

Hugh's removal from Judkins and Judkins leaves
Bernard to recoup the firm's reputation. Hugh returns
to his old master's post, presumably still uttering
inflexible moral dictums. Powell perhaps is promoting
further ironies still. Can a man who sees only black and
white teach others to perceive shadings in between? Can
one who has grown so disillusioned in the efficacy of
Youth be its mentor? Can a man so uncertain of his own
identity shape the identities of others? The art of the
comedian is, of course, to ask such questions without
providing direct answers.

Yet even those younger, more energetic and vigorous
idealists find that their moral fiber—originally tough
and elastic—grows progressively brittle as fancies are
dispelled by facts. One such person is Captain Hudson.
Like Hugh, he is bewitched by heroic phantoms and
idealizes Waring until reality intrudes into his world.
Despite an outward coolness and strength, he suffers as

great a disenchantment as Hugh. His actual involvement with the Waring myth only serves to bring on the
disaster more rapidly than under normal circumstances.

Leading a life on several levels (a life very much like
Rowland Gwatkin's in *The Valley of Bones,* one regu-
lated by the mechanics and ambitions of a military career and the other by a "profound romanticism"),
Hudson often contemplates the sort of escape Waring
typifies. When he swears he would "give something" to
meet the author, he is naturally oblivious of the ironic
outcome. What he "gives" is a part of his own identity,
perhaps the most important part since it holds his romantic vision of the world.

More than anyone else in the novel, Hudson becomes
fully immersed in the project to uncover the identity of
Waring. Sponsored by both Hugh and Bernard, he pursues his research tenaciously. To the narrator, who is
having difficulties with his own book on Stendhal, Hudson is a model of discipline and "industry" even though
he is dangerously close to being so entirely absorbed in
his work that he loses other valuable perspectives. In
compiling notes for the definitive biography, he runs the
risk of taking on the personality of his subject, "soaking
in the works" so thoroughly that Waring becomes paramount.

Only a few weeks along on the project, Hudson encounters certain problems that begin making his life as
difficult to sort out as Waring's. While diligently perusing stacks of travel memoirs on Ceylon—one of the
countries recently popularized by T. T.—he unearths
an old and obscure book from 1860, pieces of which
Waring has incorporated bodily (without acknowledg-
ment) into his own, thereby adding plagiarism to an
already lengthy list of eccentricities. Hudson's respect for
his hero is only momentarily reduced, but he is still

plagued by his ethical sense, which dictates that he mus
bring the matter before the public even if Waring'
reputation suffers.

The question of ethics is further complicated by
Roberta, with whom Hudson is collaborating on a collection of personal anecdotes for the biography. As work
draws these two into close association the inevitable occurs, and Hudson—strongly moral, if somewhat insensitive—breaks with his fiancée, Beryl Pimley:

> If he felt any sentiment in the matter, Hudson showed
> none. His real life, of course, was lived among the shim-
> mering domes and minarets of T. T. Waring's Orient,
> where all the men were brave and all the women, with
> the possible exception of Roberta, chaste. Hudson had
> the happy gift of detaching himself absolutely from his
> immediate past. (*WB,* 133-34)

The illusions fostering Hudson's new-found, vicarious
identity—illusions molded by his own mythicizing of
both Roberta and Waring—are at last overtaken by the
powers of reality. Hudson's fiasco with Roberta is the
first step toward self-illumination. His "romantic view"
is destroyed when he discovers that the girl he envisioned
as his dutiful wife, cheerfully abiding cheap rooms in
backwater garrison towns, is in fact taking a summer
cruise with Hugh Judkins.

Then, while staying with Bromwich at Toulon, Hudson comes across a work on Arabia (written by a Swiss)
that once belonged to Waring. Like the Ceylon memoir,
it too has been snipped here and there, transplanted
piece by piece, and passed off as an original. Suspecting
that Waring, who lived for many years in Toulon,
cribbed most of his books from other French accounts
gathering dust in the local library, Hudson does some
research and soon satisfies himself that his suspicions are
correct. When the shining armor is stripped away it

turns out that beneath it is not even a man, only a straw man. And when it later develops that the literary fraud has been committed by someone as prodigal and feckless as Beryl Pimley's black-sheep brother, Alec, even the insubstantial stuffing is whisked away on the wind.

Despite being paralyzed by Pimley's ingenious imposture and Roberta's promiscuity, Hudson does not stagnate like Hugh. The same fresh optimism and exuberance that originally inspired his venture stirs him from the doldrums. His resolve to marry Beryl and to transfer to the King's African Rifles is perhaps a comedown of sorts, but it is a realistic concession to romantic ideals. And in adopting this new outlook on life Hudson demonstrates how unwarranted and precipitous Hugh's blanket disgust with Youth has been.

What's Become of Waring is not, however, a paean to "Youth Triumphant," nor does it promulgate the view that only youth can reshape itself after the forces which deform ideals or identity have been removed. The mere appearance of Alec Pimley—a man who has played fast and loose with both for over fifteen years—disproves such a generalization. As much as Hudson serves as a foil to Hugh's fatal pessimism, Alec parries Hudson's cautious optimism.

Alec is Powell's ironic touchstone. Lacking any sort of scruples, breaking family ties, surrendering self-esteem and a respected name, he becomes an adept Jack-of-all-trades. He greatly disobliges those who have marked him down as "a hopeless fellow" and a "wrong 'un," actually succeeding where they have failed. As Alec Pimley, he wangles sums from his indulgent grandfather and even has the temerity to plagiarize the old captain's privately printed Ceylon memoirs, thereby launching a brilliant literary career as T. T. Waring. Under the name Robinson, he and Roberta pass a summer together; and as Alec Mason he makes a convenient marriage with the aging, but well-preserved, heiress, Mrs. Cromwell. Having played so many eccentric roles in his short span, Alec takes life for the sardonic jest it is.

After Hudson has discovered Alec's masquerade, he realizes how futile it would be to expose him. In finishing the biography and publishing the fraud, Hudson could be destroying the very myth that inspired his own dreams. Understandably, he decides to drop the whole affair and shows little interest when the Pimleys' craft slips its moorings and heads for the open sea, carrying Alec and his wife to Greece and the promise of endless isles and identities. But legends die hard, and often not without major catastrophes. Pimley and Mrs. Cromwell are caught in a violent summer storm, and their yacht (symbolically, if ineffectually, christened *Amphitrite*) runs aground somewhere off the coast of southern France. Though it is likely they both founder with the ship, the point is never satisfactorily settled. With men like Alec Pimley, nothing is ever certain. Perhaps he is dead; perhaps not. Perhaps this "death" is but another hoax, perpetrated to discard the no longer useful identity of Mason, as an earlier ruse disposed of Waring. Perhaps Pimley *is* a tortured soul forced to live by artifice and sham in the dark divisions of his mind, already a mere ghost to those who have seen the *Amphitrite* pass beyond the mole in the Toulon harbor. Yet, perhaps, like the nomadic Waring of Browning's "dramatic romance," Powell's hero represents some stellar incarnation, a small, bright symbol of the restless personality that is never content to "be" but must eternally "become":

> Oh, never star
> Was lost here but it rose afar!
> Look East, where whole new thousands are!
> In Vishnu-land what Avatar?

As the narrator dissolves in sleep and the tale closes, this last line from Browning echoes in his fading consciousness. It is a curious question, visionary in the poem, both retrospective and prophetic in the novel. It casts backwards to those who have tried (with ill luck) to preserve an ideal identity, and forward to one character—the anonymous narrator—still searching, it seems, for any identity whatsoever.

For this young man the search is a difficult one. Like Nicholas Jenkins, he is caught up in events, yet is more than some mechanical tool or technical device for slavishly recording them. He is faced not only with the crucial question of his own identity, but with a bewildering range of conflicting experiences concerning the confused identities of others. Even his physical identity is called into question by the pathetic and half senile Pimley patriarch:

> "What is your . . . name?"
> I told him. I added that I was a friend of Hudson, who had brought me down with him the day before. . . .
> "I thought you were my grand . . . son Al . . . ec."
> "Am I like him?"
> "What's that?"
> "Do I look like your grandson Alec?"
> "No."
> He brought out this with considerable emphasis. Conversation came to a temporary standstill. Then he spoke again:
> "My grand . . . son Al . . . ec"
> "Yes?"
> ". . . is a scoundrel." (*WB,* 61-62)

In spite of this comedy of discontinuity, Powell is serious about this fundamental problem. His narrator is a young man who admires energy, whether expended by sincere pluggers like Hudson, or reckless, talented prodigals like Pimley. It is he who gives unqualified support to Pimley's genius for fraud, informing Hudson that Alec is more admirable as a fake than Waring would have been as the genuine article. Lack of energy is his own particular weakness, periodically lamented, and reflected in the apathy he exhibits toward completing his own critical study: "Stendhal: or Some Thoughts on Violence." Even Stendhal's novels have failed to galvanize the narrator into activity, or to transform social boredom and the feeling of vacuity into anything remotely approaching art. Ironically, Stendhal's two best works are objective, dispassionate studies of strong-willed, self-made men, both introspective and energetic, both caught up in power struggles. While not as profoundly motivated as Fabrizio or Julien Sorel, Waring understandably provokes the admiration of someone whose life is ineffectual.

Through the narrator, then, the theme of identity becomes linked to that of power. *What's Become of Waring* goes further, however, in crisscrossing the actual plexus of power with a maze of diverse identities. Insecurity and inferiority dominate those who must demonstrate how ably they can control others; but Stendhal's exceptional ego-brandishing heroes (who have inherited titanic wills) have now been supplanted by the socially ill-adjusted average man, intoxicated with acquired authority over his minute sphere of influence.

Hugh Judkins, for one, clings doggedly to the control of affairs in the publishing world, possibly as compensation for personal shortcomings. He is not unaware of the prolonged sexual continence that has persisted into his middle age and to some extent he seeks the solace of others' inadequacies in love to bolster his own wounded self-image. He manifests his power in another curious way, attending séances at which he distinguishes himself as a quiet oracle of skepticism. Being torn between a strict, Puritan rationalism and a youthful romanticism,

Hugh dabbles in these spiritual exercises as a concession to the latter. Yet it is the rationalistic principle that deserts him in the end. At a séance he goes temporarily mad, spouts salvation gospel with evangelical fervor, and eventually collapses. His return to the academic life might even be a salvation of sorts. There, at least, he can wield power over young boys, once again having become the respected martinet.

Hugh obviously fails as a "Stendhalian" where Roberta Payne almost succeeds. Tight-lipped and calculating, she is singularly effective in contriving relationships that inspire both intimacy and apprehension:

> Roberta's spy-system was remarkable. It was impossible to guess how she had discovered that Hugh knew Lipfield. By mentioning this she established an instantaneous and double hold on Hugh, because she could flatter him and at the same time quell him by her knowledge of what in the office amounted almost to a guilty secret. (*WB*, 91)

While balancing Hugh in one palm (she persuades him to publish her "memoirs" and to reproduce some of her journalistic trifles in book form), Roberta counterpoises Hudson in the other. Part of her success is that she manages not to fall in love with the men she exploits. She seduces Hudson and lets him take the consequences, just as she summers with Hugh in Scandinavia and lets him do the same. But her power over men is at the same time limited because she tires of them so soon. When she and Bromwich (who claims to have been married seven times) become engaged, one suspects that Roberta has finally met her match—or at least come up against someone as sexually sophisticated as herself.

Whether she has or not remains conjecture. Like many threads of the novel, this particular one crosses and becomes tangled with the countless others, of which Waring's life is the most prominent. In Waring, the

entire range of Powell is seen: to the public he is a
legend; to women a constant enigma; to Hugh the
idealized portrait of Youth; to Hudson the abstraction
of the romanticism after which he hungers; and to the
narrator an emblem of energy, the ultimate symbol of a
quantity which so many wish to possess and which so
few can wield:

> Everybody wanted power. Bernard wanted power. Lipfield
> wanted power. . . . It was power Hugh wanted too. . . .
> Roberta wanted power. T. T. Waring wanted power. Did
> Eustace want power? It was an interesting question. . . .
> T. T. Waring. He wanted power more than any of them.
> Curious how that poem must have struck him. *In Vishnu-
> land what Avatar?* . . . T. T. Waring. . . . *(WB, 235-36)*

T. T. Waring! To the drowsy narrator, even this bright
strand in the complex fabric of life becomes a grey
thought, mingling with the consequential and inconse-
quential—an identity, an illusion, which, like some
elusive will-o'-the-wisp, flits down corridors of memory
leading to sleep and forgetfulness.

PART II

A Dance to the Music of Time

6

Time and Nicholas Jenkins

Sixteen years ago Anthony Powell launched a literary windjammer that displays all signs of tacking safely to home port. At his own leisurely pace he is writing the longest novel in English, and one of the best. The latest installment of *A Dance to the Music of Time* brings the number of volumes in the series to eight, making it only two-thirds complete, but already the thickest, meatiest slice of British upper-class life since Galsworthy served up *The Forsyte Saga*.

According to Powell himself, the idea for *The Music of Time* originated in 1937 or 1938, but owing to the war the first measured step of the dance—*A Question of Upbringing*—was not published until 1951; and, while revealing a mellowness and maturity over the early works, it gave few indications of the complexity and scope that subsequent volumes confirmed. In an interview several years back, Powell broadly outlined his intentions for *The Music of Time,* touching somewhat on its *raison d'être,* if not its main argument. The series will cover

> English social life in different aspects from about the First World War to the present time. . . . [It is] concerned with the inter-relations of individuals, their lives and love affairs, and is intended to illustrate and bring up to date consideration of the way in which the middle and upper classes live in England—a subject that continues to be written about by many novelists and playwrights as if no changes had taken place during the last fifty years or so, or at least as if these changes were only superficial ones.[1]

Powell's full title—*A Dance to the Music of Time*—is clearly both literal and metaphorical. The opening of the first novel depicts a group of workmen warming themselves over a coke stove on a wintry English evening; but the flicker of light from the fire, much like the play of some antique magic lantern, raises other projections, and the present fades out of focus, merges with memory, and metamorphoses into the dominant image of the sequence:

> The physical attitudes of the men themselves as they turned from the fire suddenly suggested Poussin's scene in which the seasons, hand in hand and facing outward, tread in rhythm to the notes of the lyre that the winged and naked greybeard plays. The image of Time brought thoughts of mortality: of human beings, facing outward like the Seasons, moving hand in hand in intricate measure: stepping slowly, methodically, sometimes a trifle awkwardly, in evolutions that take recognisable shape: or breaking into seemingly meaningless gyrations, while partners disappear only to reappear again, once more giving pattern to the spectacle: unable to control the melody, unable, perhaps, to control the steps of the dance. (*QU,* 2)

1. "Taken from Life (An Interview with Anthony Powell)," *Twentieth Century,* July, 1961.

The metaphor is necessarily elaborate; it attempts to capture the rhythm of humanity itself. Moving in Time, never static, Powell's characters align and realign themselves, define and redefine relationships. Such alignments and definitions can be measured at once, but not at the moment fully understood, just as one might grasp the individual figures and gestures in the Poussin painting without immediately recognizing the tension and drama at work within the closed world he creates. This use of Poussin shows, on the one hand, Powell's sensitivity to art, on the other his receptivity to life. For while "taking off" from something representational, he is less interested in turning life into art, than art into life. Conceding to artifice—there are just so many dances, so many house parties, so many club chats a chap can attend—he moves from it to construct a totally realistic society.

The classical cast of Poussin's painting, as well as its form, shapes the design of Powell's dance. Here is neither the fury of the bacchanalia, the flamboyance of the Viennese waltz, nor the looseness of the Charleston, in which dancers lose track of the accompaniment, but a formalized ballet (from moment to moment containing the comic or grotesque ingredients of the above) in which partners and choreographer seem forever aware of the music. *The Music of Time* emerges from the synthesis of dancer and dance, yet as much depends on the quality of the orchestration as on the mimetic character of the action itself. Balanced, formal, kinetic, intricate, music and dance are linked as subjects in a double fugue.

Fugual construction permits various themes—episodes as they are called in music—to alternately fall and rise from inferior to superior positions as they contrapuntally contrast with or complement each other. Such displays of counterpoint on the plot level are orchestrated by Nicholas Jenkins, the narrator, at the end of *The Acceptance World,* as he partially recapitulates the chain of events that have inadvertently developed into his liaison with Jean Templer, his mistress:

> I had enacted such scenes with Jean: Templer with Mona: now Mona was enacting them with Quiggin: Barnby and Umfraville with Anne Stepney: Stringham with her sister Peggy: Peggy now in the arms of her cousin: Uncle Giles, very probably, with Mrs. Erdleigh: Mrs. Erdleigh with Jimmy Stripling: Jimmy Stripling, if it came to that, with Jean: and Duport, too. (*AW,* 212-13)

On the surface, Nick's listing suggests an endless sequence, but Powell does not ploddingly link subject to subject, statement to statement; he varies the steps of the dance. Thus, Peter Templer's marriage to Mona begins as a brilliant allegro and declines into a sad adagio that is restated in Charles Stringham's unhappy alliance with Peggy Stepney; Mrs. Erdleigh becomes the chief subject in a scherzo involving Nick's Uncle Giles and the racing motorist Jimmy Stripling; and Nick himself trips a sweet, sensual andante with Bob Duport's wife.

Even these changes in time and pace do not always indicate the complexity of Powell's method, for the movement here is not strictly linear. The richness of the novel comes not from the reworking of an old motif in a different light, but by a sudden transposition of the theme, almost a vertical lift in construction. Aldous Huxley, similarly occupied by transference of formal techniques from one art to another in *Point Counterpoint,* has Philip Quarles enter this in his notebook:

> The musicalization of fiction [depends not on subordination] of sense to sound . . . but on a large scale in the

construction . . . the changes of moods, the abrupt
transitions. . . . You alternate the themes. More interesting, the modulations and variations are also more difficult. A novelist modulates by reduplicating situations and
characters. He shows several people falling in love, or
dying, or praying in different ways—dissimilars solving
the same problem. Or, vice versa, similar people con-
fronted with dissimilar problems. In this way you can
modulate through all the aspects of your themes, you can
write variations in any number of different moods.[2]

Musical modulation controls the thematic vertical
movement; dance hastens the action horizontally. But
these spatial concepts, placing the novel in several
spheres at once, fall finally under the sway of time, which
turns a once suspended memory into a revelation as it
dictates the duration of the dance.

Time is the controlling medium in Powell's novels,
but it is viewed neither philosophically, psychologically,
nor scientifically. One finds little of that Bergsonian
mysticism which informs *Remembrance of Things Past,*
the Freudian stream-of-consciousness refined in *Ulysses*
and *The Sound and the Fury,* the Einsteinian relativity
absorbed in *The Alexandria Quartet.* In all these cases
time becomes internalized, subjected to personal ordering, as though the individual believed—perhaps rightly
—that he could at last control the hitherto uncontrollable.
With Proust time is intuitional: past actions are sustained
in the present and the present is interpretable only in
terms of the past; with Joyce and Faulkner time is splin-
tered into tiny bits, allowing an eternity of fragmented
thoughts to flash in seconds through the subconscious;
and with Durrell (though not always successfully) time is
four-dimensional, beyond even the common, everyday
temporal conscious or subconscious, and relative to a

2. *Point Counterpoint* (New York, 1947), p. 293.

plurality of minds through which it courses simultaneously.

For Powell, however, external time (clock time) is the flux. Time is actual; its very sheerness brings about events as it relentlessly pursues the dancers who, loving, marrying, dying, are reluctant to admit that they are changing at all. Powell returns to the classical conception of time: the musical old greybeard who conducts the rounds of the seasons, or the cold goddess Mutability, altering people and events from day to day. Consequently, time functions critically, not mystically. Passing because it must, it is not mysterious, only at moments indefinable. Powell is concerned with time, not obsessed by it; for while he sees it as blasting the hopes of some, wasting the promises of others, he knows that it is also the sole arbiter for shaping in the future the formless formulae of the past. It is this outlook that enables him to focus on the essential aim of the novel sequence: to play changing sensibilities against the continuum of human history.

This concept is at the center of *The Music of Time*. Stated with thematic force, it resounds as a note of resignation, often melancholy or sad, sometimes even tragic, but mostly pitched to the comic stoicism of the narrator, which keeps the sequence from growing tedious, oppressive, or unwieldy. It is Nick's attitude throughout *The Music of Time* that prescribes the comic perspective on admittedly joyless and unpleasant topics: change and decay. Here, for example, are the final paragraphs from *A Buyer's Market* and *Swann's Way,* each discussing the controlling agency of time:

> For reasons not always at the time explicable there are specific occasions when events begin suddenly to take on a significance previously unsuspected; so that, before we really know where we are, life seems to have begun in

earnest at last, and we ourselves, scarcely aware that any change has taken place, are careering uncontrollably down the slippery avenues of eternity.

The places that we have known belong now only to the little world of space on which we map them for our own convenience. None of them was ever more than a thin slice, held between the contiguous impressions that composed our life at that time; remembrance of a particular form is but regret for a particular moment; and houses, roads, avenues are as fugitive, alas, as the years.

Proust obviously is hypnotized by the mystique of time. Points and places, having in themselves slipped away, fled into the past, are recaptured at the expense of making us slaves to our sensibilities that we grieve for because they have changed. Time turns Proust into a sober myth-maker; one doesn't smile at the conclusion of *Swann's Way*. It is otherwise with *A Buyer's Market*. Unlike Proust, who is saying that the places the mind has known have been exiled to timeless space, waiting for memory to imbue them with new life, Powell holds that all past actions have had meaning *in themselves, in the past,* all present actions meaning in the present. That the pattern of action is not clear from moment to moment does not mean that it will not be clear in the future.

This concern of relating cause and effect, of descrying the figure in the carpet, of prodding or pressing the past into shape is that of the narrator-hero, Nicholas Jenkins. Son of a retired army officer, Jenkins moves casually through public school and the university into publishing, later into script writing and most recently the army, writing several novels along the way and enjoying unlimited openings into the sophisticated echelons of England's upper classes. The handy second for a tête-à-tête, the essential third for a discreet triangle, the perfect fourth for a spur-of-the-moment weekend party, he has the knack for being tractable, eager, alert—and relaxed. Through all changes—the failure of friends, the decline of family, the shaking of class, the fall of nations—he leisurely narrates his life and the lives of those he intersects: a narration notably marked by a coolness which masks the intenser feelings running like powerful undercurrents beneath the surface.

There is at times something glacial in Nick's reserve, in the cultivated aloofness perhaps necessary for proper narrative omnipotence. Even when "involved," Nick keeps his distance, hangs in the background, more concerned with what is happening around him than to him, aware that excessive attention to his own particular steps might mar the general design of the dance. Nick, like other major characters in *The Music of Time*, develops finely and subtly until we know as much about him as about anyone: but his personality is often a reflection of other personalities, and what we gather about him is often picked up rather than spelled out. While some of his acquaintances succeed, and some fail, Nick manages to endure, free from the excessive introspection that might easily plague men of sensibility, propped up by his comic perspective.

Such a perspective does not tamper with his view of history. Nick is a faithful narrator and no facetious historian. Having witnessed hard knocks and reversals, he accepts experience with no thought of forecasting its long-range significance. He is surprisingly original in an age when heroes are generally either neurotic, angry, or foolish; he wishes neither to mourn a lost past nor dynamite the present. Nick reacts with sympathy, amusement, or mild astonishment to the things happening around him, for he refuses to be daunted by change and is, in the last analysis, only fascinated by it.

Proper, fashionable, sincere, self-reliant, he is the above-average, upper-class all-right-guy wanting desperately to "fit in" and keep from becoming defeated, excessively eccentric, too notoriously successful, or too scandalously simple. These, so far, are the alternatives in *The Music of Time* for those who contribute to Nick's education. Characters whose convictions prove mistaken fall prey to delusion, while those whose perceptions have failed at the outset are beset by illusions equally destructive. Adherents to outmoded beliefs and untenable positions, they travel toward destruction of one sort or another, taking society with them. Nick, bolstered by his attitude, primed by experience, sees the dissolution and charts a course between extremes, measuring the smallest signs or gestures against contemporary standards and holding fast to humane and sensible values.

The Music of Time develops from the premise that its characters contribute both to Nick's personal and artistic growth, yet never suggests that they are mere foils for the narrator or his creator. As a consequence, the series, manageable at the outset, grows more complex as characters—in conjunction with the narrator but independent of him—proliferate, interpenetrate, and fuse. Nick, not having had the opportunity of following each line of development, may suddenly (and bravely) confront situations that fall shorter or soar higher than his expectations allow. Powell is not so straight-faced, however, that he overlooks the reader's amusement at watching Nick keep up with events.

" 'My dear Nick, you know everybody. Not a social item escapes you,' " says one of Nick's friends in *The Soldier's Art,* thereby blurting out what everyone has been thinking all along. Nothing much does escape Nick, though characters who enjoy less vision than he,

who even seem less trustworthy, often better interpret
what he muddles. Nick's shortcomings, however, and his
ingenuousness, make him equally credible as narrator of
the series and as a person. He may grow intense about
experience, yet he will seldom construct from it rigid
rules for assuring the right or graceful gesture in the
future. His errors are never as egregious, his faux pas
never as noticeable, his bumbling never as total as any
one else's. Surprised but never paralyzed, utilized but
never exploited, he can remain committed to his time
and class without sacrificing principles or personality,
without surrendering his probity. Nick, in short, never
blots the scutcheon; unmistakably Powell's most con-
vincing persona, he is, too, one of the most original and
realistic figures in contemporary fiction.

7

A Question
of
Upbringing

The primary act in Nick's genesis—and that of *The Music of Time*—begins when he is completing the higher forms of public school. Powell launches into the narrative proper by creating an atmosphere similar to that evoked by the Poussin analogy several pages back. *A Question of Upbringing* complements the entire sequence; it is concerned with shadows and foreshadowings: of some shadows that will fade in the light of reality, of others that are reality itself. Here, in the stern but safe atmosphere of school, tentative steps are taken; here, character and career are prefigured; here, personality begins to evolve; and here, Powell sets forth some implicit questions. What, he seems to ask, is involved in making you the person you become? What things in youth foreshadow adulthood? What measurable quantity, a constant, can assure others that you will be later what they imagine now? What, in the last analysis, is "upbringing"?

The novel opens on a dreary English day. Fog rolls up the valley through a thin, chilling drizzle, and an amphibious form appears in the distance, materializing from the mist: Kenneth Widmerpool, huffing up the road, willing himself to run off excess weight, trotting out of the private public school into the public private lives of the English upper class:

> It was on the bleak December tarmac of that Saturday afternoon in, I suppose, the year 1921 that Widmerpool, fairly heavily built, thick lips and metal-rimmed spectacles giving his face as usual an aggrieved expression, first took coherent form in my mind. As the damp, insistent cold struck up from the road, two thin jets of steam drifted out of his nostrils, by nature much distended, and all at once he seemed to possess a painful solidarity that talk about him had never conveyed. Something comfortless and inelegant in his appearance suddenly impressed itself on the observer, as stiffly, almost majestically, Widmerpool moved on his heels out of the mist. (*QU*, 4)

Here Powell symbolically couples the natural and human phenomena: mist and Widmerpool, who even this early looms as a force, chilling and omnipresent like the English weather itself. Cold, undemonstrative, self-assured, Widmerpool, the loner, with his "good sensible shoes" and "wrong kind of overcoat," hobbles determinedly about the countryside, while the charming Charles Stringham, almost sacrosanctly removed from the eternal forces of weather, warms himself within before a cozy fire:

> He was tall and dark, and looked a little like one of those stiff, sad young men in ruffs, whose long legs take up so much room in sixteenth-century portraits: or perhaps a younger—and far slighter—version of Veronese's Alexander receiving the children of Darius after the Battle

of Issus: with the same high forehead and suggestion of hair thinning a bit at the temples. His features certainly seemed to belong to that epoch of painting: the faces in Elizabethan miniatures, lively, obstinate, generous, not very happy, and quite relentless. (*QU*, 8-9)

More than merely opposing physical types, or signifying the usual heterogeneity in schoolboys, Powell's sketches suggest—even at this early, amorphous stage of the novel—basic distinctions that are later elaborately treated. In a very minor way, the outsider who has his "being in obscurity," and the insider who, like the great Alexander, is the darling of the Establishment, represent the universal struggle between the English classes that has been reflected in nearly every novel since *Robinson Crusoe*. But Widmerpool and Stringham reflect more than class consciousness: they are part of Powell's fictional world where class has been replaced by character. And it is in this world one must seek the antithesis between them as previewed by Nick in his winter's vision: a contrast regenerated by the clash of class, but generated by the conflict of personality and temperament.

The most singular character in *The Music of Time* finds his element in water.[1] Hulking, hydrous, Widmerpool—the name itself is saturated with puns—leads an aqueous, at times fish-like existence. "He's so wet you could shoot snipe off him," remarks Peter Templer, and into Nick's last vision of Widmerpool at school is absorbed the image of "a fish recently hauled from the water, making powerful though failing efforts at respiration. . . . his mouth opening and shutting sharply, more than ever like some uncommon specimen of marine life."

---

1. An observation originating with W. D. Quesenbery, Jr., in "Anthony Powell: The Anatomy of Decay," *Critique*, VII (1964), 5-26.

Some years later Widmerpool infiltrates an Eaton Square dinner party and Nick notes that he still exhibits "that curiously piscine cast of countenance, projecting the impression that he swam, rather than walked, through the rooms he haunted." Added to this the host's daughter informs Nick that Widmerpool's father had been, while alive, a dealer in liquid manure.

This flow of allusions is channeled, Nick later realizes, into symbols, as Widmerpool begins taking on universal significance, becoming "one of those symbolic figures of whom most people possess at least one example, if not more, round whom the past and the future have a way of assembling." Later the once poor fish—"bred in those depths by the slab, amphibious perhaps"—stirs with kraken certainty, becomes as forceful as a sea-beast or as the maelstrom itself. But at this stage of the game he is still a figure of fun to be taken for granted, tolerated, dodged. By Nick's standards Widmerpool ranks low, poles apart from Stringham, with whom the contrast is violent but not yet fatal.

At odds with Widmerpool, Stringham is equally at odds with himself. Elementally he is air and fire: puckish, impetuous, heady, passionate, precipitous, "completely reckless . . . even when sober." But the physical in Stringham will not jell with his mental attitude. Living in a rarefied atmosphere, burning with a flame tormenting and ardent if not hard and gemlike, he is consumed by his own imbalance of humors. Now choleric, now melancholic, he is close to being manic-depressive. In every sense too highly strung, Stringham can only snap.

While Stringham's decline is brought about by internal conflict, Widmerpool's mental and social growth is built upon an internal harmony, a lack of ambivalence in his makeup. In him the elemental complements the humorous, making him less complex, more certain and single-minded. Once having made incursions he is uncontrollable. Stringham's bit of imagination is stifled by Widmerpool, inundated by him. Long after the flame in Stringham has died down, Widmerpool surges to glory. Nick even comments on this irony. Paradoxically it is Widmerpool, all water, impelled by pressures from within and without, who rises like the phoenix "from the ashes of his own humiliation"; and it is Stringham, his intoxication for life turned to alcoholism, who is drowned through his own weakness, as much as another's strength. At school, when Stringham sighs with mock exasperation that Widmerpool will be the death of him, it is this very death of fire by water that he unwittingly anticipates.

Humors and elements are not meant as substitutes for character analyses, however. As fire may symbolize imagination and sensuality, so water can suggest power, strength, a driving phenomenon like the will. One, indeed, may discover here the antithetical poles of the novel, and, perhaps, as Arthur Mizener has written, the major contrast in twentieth-century natures: Stringham, the man of imagination, Widmerpool, the man of will.[2] Yet this classification—of which Mizener himself is wary —embodies too rigid a dichotomy, a blackness and whiteness that doesn't admit the grayness of gradation. Doers and dreamers, redbloods and mollycoddles date from Esau and Jacob. In every epoch, in every age, men of imagination have arisen, refused to knuckle under to

2. Powell originates this thesis in *The Music of Time* and enforces it throughout. Mizener's essay in the *Kenyon Review*, XXII (1960), 79-92 (later reprinted as a chapter in *The Sense of Life in the Modern Novel*, Boston, 1964), is a creative interpretation and synthesis of Powell's statement. Important now as preliminary and pathfinding, Mizener's study was perhaps even more important in 1960 in bringing Powell before the American public.

those of stronger will, and succeeded—often, in fact, where the others have failed. The question here, then, is why do Powell's men of will seem fated to succeed, his men of imagination seem doomed to fail?

Surely the failure of the latter is not lodged in the imagination—a conclusion unlikely to originate with a successful novelist—but obviously in the men themselves. The opposition of Widmerpool and Stringham should be viewed as symptomatic of the century, if indeed not peculiar to it, but always with the understanding that Stringham might have excelled in some other era, in some other way. Because of his basic temperament, however, at this time he must disintegrate, for all Powell's men of power are in harmony with their *Zeitgeist,* while his men of imagination are not. Rather, in a dissonant way, they are transplantations from another age. Conflict, as Powell sees it, originates with these special types. And the novel may represent the struggle of the romanticist embodied in Stringham, who courts "strangeness" and "remoteness," who by analogy suffers "the strain of living simultaneously in two different historical periods."

A definition of this sort is not meant to subvert Mizener's excellent categories but to complement them, and in some way to answer the dilemma posed by the limitation of having only two alternatives. One must account for characters who, while neither particularly imaginative nor particularly strong-willed, are drawn first one way, then another: shaded characters lacking the absolute values of Stringham and Widmerpool.

Such a type is Peter Templer, the third of Nick's school chums, who comes later to occupy a critical position in the novel. Irascible, amorous, sanguine, Templer is, like Stringham, a sensualist; but he has in common with Widmerpool a mechanical tick ("a perpetual and

uite mechanical sparkle" of the eyes) that makes him
alculating and skillful when occasion warrants. The
ost important distinction, however, is noted by Nick
t that sensitive age when his own life has no "particular
rift. . . . For Templer, there was no truth except in
angible things: though he was not ambitious. String-
am, as I now see him, was romantic, and would per-
aps have liked to play a somewhat different role from
hat which varying moods, and love of eccentricity,
ntailed upon him." The pattern may be ill-formed in
he narrator's mind but little doubt there seems in
owell's that between the romanticist and the mechanist
noves the realist. Despite Nick's statement that, as a
outh, he had most in common with Stringham, it is
Templer's attitudes and affairs that ultimately have the
nore profound influence.

To place Nick and Templer at identical centers is,
however, to simplify Powell's characterizations. Though
Nick is a realist, his role as narrator means that he must
identify with any character and thus the problem arises
of how he can measure extremes without gauging the
norm. If the norm is to be gained at all, it is from the
influences that act upon his youth and either aid or
frustrate the process of maturing.

The question in the first volume of *The Music of
Time* revolves—as the title suggests—about environment, though environment only confirms what character
(heredity) has predicted. To explore the question,
Powell has imposed a symmetry on the novel, bearing
down on the two environmental factors that most critically affect upbringing: school and family. The balance
is careful and impressive. The first and fourth chapters
concern the former, the second and third the latter, and
each section provides variations that support the dominant motif. For as every act and gesture reflects upon

upbringing, upbringing itself becomes the mirror catch
ing the image of the contrasting types who dominat
Nick's world and decade.

The balances in *A Question of Upbringing* are struck
between families (Nick at the Stringhams', at th
Templers', at the Leroys' in France) and school (Nick a
Eton, then Cambridge). In each case similarities pla
against differences. While school may faithfully repre
sent certain youthful idiosyncracies, dreams, ambitions
it can give a false picture of the complex feelings an
attitudes formulated through family ties. The uninhib
ited schoolboy of the rambling countryside is seldom th
same as the precise son of the drawing room. As Nick
observes, "It is not easy—perhaps not even desirable—to
judge other people by a consistent standard." Nick's en
counters and experiences comprise, in short, a school
family syndrome which prepares him for society.

Visits to Stringham and Templer shatter Nick's pre-
conceived notions of their home life, and he can dispas-
sionately forecast that neither is designed for future
domesticity. Stringham is deracinated. Shuttled between
his mother (a beautiful aristocratic spendthrift who dabbles in remarriages) and his father (a wealthy colonist who
lives in Kenya), Charles finds his inheritance and affection being depleted. Gloom overcasts the superficial opulence of a house where matrimony is farcical, patrimony
crumbling. The catalyst for Stringham's melancholia is
apparent at the outset. In his own home he appears almost as much a stranger as Nick, spurned by a flighty
mother, trapped between the "overpowering" personalities of his stepfather, Buster Foxe, and the friend of the
family, Tuffy Weedon. Both Buster and Tuffy are, like
Widmerpool, cold and calculating. Miss Weedon's palm,
as Nick takes it in greeting, strikes him as "cool and
brittle," and Foxe diffuses "waves of personality, strong

chilling gusts of icy air that threatened to freeze into
rigidity all who came through the door."

Under such refrigeration Stringham's natural warmth
is neutralized, and his genial, potent spirit squelched.
Once having impressed Nick as resembling the Veronese
portrait of Alexander the Great—the worldly, gracious
conqueror who comes to right the disjointed world—
Stringham now conveys the image of Hamlet: weak,
confused, harried by conflict, a pawn for the powerful:

> His father had, of course, been shipped off to Kenya
> rather than murdered; but Buster and his mother were
> well adapted to play the parts of Claudius and Gertrude.
> I did not manage to get far beyond this, except to
> wonder if Miss Weedon was a kind of female Polonius,
> working on Hamlet's side. I could well imagine String-
> ham stabbing her through the arras. At present there was
> no Ophelia. Stringham himself had a decided resem-
> blance to the Prince of Denmark; or, as Templer would
> have said: "It was the kind of part the old boy would
> fancy himself in." (*QU*, 73)

On the other hand, Templer is fashioned for a quite
different part. He verges on total entrenchment in the
trivia of business. Born into the wealthy and optimistic
middle class, as solid and durable as the cement manufactured by his father, Templer is slated to be a bourgeois Brahmin. Stringham and his kind may be going
downhill quickly, but they have a verve about them.
The Templers have lifelessly dawdled into financial success and intellectual stagnation. Mercantile magic has
produced bourgeois mediocrity.

Consequently Templer's home life seems as dispiriting
as Stringham's. Characteristic of Nick's modes of experience, the prospect of visiting Templer is more exciting
in its anticipation than in its realization. Even as Nick
first sights the Templer house, impressively perched near
a precipice overlooking the sea, mystery is dissipated in

banality. "The Enchanted Castle—where any adventure might be expected" is governed by a gruff, laconic, dull, *paterfamilias* and the adventures turn out to be some wan pranks that reflect the boredom and lethargy about the place.

Yet all is not deadly. Peter Templer is only slightly tainted by the apathy and callousness that later infect him and his marriage, and he is often a jolly and instructive companion. Equally fascinating is Peter's younger sister, Jean. Nick falls under her spell. Half convinced that she is ill-equipped to survive in the impersonal world of ticker tape and blue chips, he sees her as a "saint" or "martyr." But he is not so smitten that he cannot recognize a blight settling over her as well. A paradox of insincerity and ingenuousness, she simultaneously repels and attracts him:

> The expression of her face, although sad and a trifle ironical, was not altogether in keeping with this air of belonging to another and better world. I felt suddenly uneasy, and also interested: a desire to be with her, and at the same time, an almost paralysing disquiet at her presence. (*QU*, 74)

As Nick intuitively suspects, Jean thrives quite well in the world of affairs and not long afterwards commits adultery to become his mistress.

Visiting the Templers instills in Nick an appreciation of those latent forces which go beyond the sanction or control of upbringing. Certainly part of this is an awareness of sex; but more, it is an awareness of the sheer physicalness of life itself, which he had never much considered before. The suppressed promise of Jean is translated into the person of a house guest of the Templers, Gwen McReith, when she spontaneously commandeers Nick to illustrate some fine points of the foxtrot:

I [became] aware, with colossal impact, that Lady Mc-
Reith's footing in life was established in a world of physical action of which at present I knew little or nothing.
. . . The revelation was something far more universal in
implication than a mere sense of physical attraction towards [her]. It was realisation, in a moment of time, not
only of her own possibilities, far from inconsiderable
ones, but also of other possibilities that life might hold;
and my chief emotion was surprise. (*QU,* 91-92)

Nick's education proceeds from a series of such slight
surprises which demonstrate the limits of raw knowledge. Willing to consider Jean an amiable image of
ideal love and Gwen McReith a manifestation of the
physical (sex in particular), Nick at first fails to fit
Sunny Farebrother into a category. While emerging as a
variation on the power themes, he complements it
oddly. Farebrother recognizes that "power [is] won by
self-abasement" and is successful in a sense. But he
strikes Nick, too, as a "saintly figure, ill-used by a coarse-
grained world . . . lonely and inaccessible," a counterpart of Thackeray's melancholy Colonel Newcome.
Sunny, in short, is another uprooted soul, "frayed" and
"battered"—like his clothes and luggage respectively—
through transplanting: an Edwardian relic, a power
man of an older order who must make way for power
men of the new order. But, as it turns out, this impression is true only temporarily. When Farebrother comes on
the scene seven volumes later in *The Soldier's Art* he is
on an equal footing with Widmerpool. Nick is then
only a little surprised, but only because he has come to
understand the workings of power better.

Variations on the themes of love and power do not
end at the Templers'. Another perspective is introduced
at the Leroys', the French family with whom Nick
spends his summer abroad before going on to the university. Once again, "family" is the milieu, but family as

an open society, not as a closed (one might say insular) unit. Life at La Grenadière is not exactly like life in the world at large, but it is the closest to a societal situation that Nick has come. To be sure, any enchantment it may preserve—Mme. Leroy, for example, is likened to Circe—is almost entirely dissolved before Nick's stay is over. Like the magic casements at the Templers', those at La Grenadière turn out to be cracked windowpanes. And the further breaking down of illusion becomes the prologue to a "ritual of initiation" into society.

The transitional stages are equally logical and well marked owing to the Leroys' guests, who, Nick soon discovers, are analogies for his English acquaintances and support his thinking. That M. Dubuisson is, as Sunny Farebrother's counterpart, fired equally by egoism and effeteness, that Mme. Dubuisson, enigmatic, unrestrained, passionate is associated with Lady Mc-Reith, that Suzette Leroy is linked to Jean Templer, comment on the consistency of human nature which Nick is able to discern but not decipher or control as yet. Clearly this is the great difference between him and Widmerpool; and just as clearly it is Widmerpool's effectiveness and single-mindedness that Nick continues to undervalue.

Widmerpool, *en famille,* is nearly as unpopular as Widmerpool at school, and as earnest. His purpose in visiting France is to gain instruction; and his rigorous regimen for learning French makes no provisions for enjoying himself. Obsessed by an almost Carlylean intensity for work, he can find interest in nothing not "labelled as in some way important or improving." Widmerpool's drive comes from his widowed, domineering mother, an inheritance that upbringing warps into three fierce inclinations: a slavishness to rules, an intrigue for "the game" (not as diversion but as the field of gainful activity), and a passion for power. Such are the bases for Widmerpool's cheerless decisiveness, his being set in motion, and his ready answers.

Nick's timorousness, though grounded in youthful insecurity, is lodged, too, in the need to question relationships and to delay acceptable answers. As opposed to Widmerpool's aptitude for simplification and bluntness which hit at the heart of complex matters—"Games are played to be won"—Nick's imagination complicates even the simplest of alternatives. Whether to share between the absent Jean and the handy Suzette a restless infatuation, whether to seduce the apparently willing Suzette in the summer house, become crises of considerable magnitude for one who often regrets not having turned chance to some account. Widmerpool, on the contrary, is never plagued by hesitation. Even in this first novel of the sequence, it is plain that Widmerpool, "the ineffective person, [the] freak who had no claim to consider himself as the equal of someone like Stringham," is the one to whom both Stringham and Nick will later be indebted. The supports raised by upbringing in the bosom of the family are razed in society. With the barriers down, the man of imagination locks horns with the man of power: puritanical in morals, Machiavellian in ethics, astringent in will.

The threshold of this society is the university, where concepts of power mature under the tutelage of Sillery, a don whose elevation to the ivory tower has not depressed his admiration for worldly success. Silver-haired, smooth-tongued, Sillery fawns over the already powerful and takes under wing the brilliant but unestablished seeking advancement through his many connections. Alternately flattering, berating, cajoling, insulting his select charges who suffer brief domination to spur their own ambitions, Sillery holds court in his study-cum-salon during weekly teas, traditional gatherings "to which anyone might drop in."

Sillery strengthens his influence by establishing a reservoir of diverse acquaintances among his students who might later prove useful. As an erstwhile student of political science and economics, he is aware "that in a society showing signs of transition it was essential to keep an eye on the changing focus of power." Consequently he is a highly developed power figure, emerging fully in his own right, and in opposition to Le Bas, the perennial public school master whose show of power (confined to enforcing smoking rules) is pathetic and vain, and whose vague romanticism labels him as a man of imagination. Temporally, as well as ideologically, Sillery and Le Bas are at odds: the one, Tiresias-like (as Nick calls him), foreseeing power as the spirit of the modern age, braced to meet the future; the other, wrapped in nostalgia for the past, unaware of the changing world, a transitional figure growing effete.

It is this "kind of deadness" that hangs about Le Bas during his visit to Nick's university apartment: a deadness in the master himself and in earlier values which Le Bas' very presence has thrust into disturbing relief. In the world of Sillery—for whom Le Bas expresses indifference—public school has only marginal influence on adulthood and proves an unreliable indicator for life. Stringham is excited at the prospect of leaving the university but Nick is far from certain about London being "fun" or about the future being rosy:

> Somehow, I felt doubts about this. Life no longer seemed to present quite the same uncomplicated façade as at a time when dodging Le Bas and shirking football had been the cardinal requirements to make the day tolerable. . . . The sphere towards which Stringham seemed to be heading, little as I knew of it, was scarcely . . . tempting to

me. Perhaps Widmerpool had been right in advocating a
more serious attitude of mind towards the problem of the
future. (*QU*, 207)

Nick suspects that the survivors will be those like
Widmerpool who, seldom surrendering to a sensuous
impulse or truckling to the superficial, become apostates
to pleasure, fetishists of the long-faced, prophets of the
important. Such are the two notable undergraduates
Nick meets at the university: Mark Members, a budding
poet whose esthetic easily reconciles materialism and art,
and J. G. Quiggin, a dissenting gadfly with Marxian
leanings who has set his sights on becoming a critic.
Favorites of Sillery, they develop almost spontaneously
an instinctive distaste and admiration for each other:
feelings that later turn openly hostile as each attempts
to commandeer the secretaryship offered by St. John
Clarke, the wealthy, weak-willed novelist.

Members impresses Nick, but it is Quiggin who immediately interests him. A more compelling counterpart
of Widmerpool, Quiggin is as openly aggressive and
strongly egoistical yet less ponderous. Both are abso-
lutists enthralled by naked power, and though their
means of attaining it differ, their ends are the same:
Widmerpool, a cautious manipulator, a patient, plod-
ding puller-of-strings, exemplifies the inexorability of
the will; Quiggin, "a fierce little animal" possessed by
an "angry solitude of spirit," a truculent in-fighter, symbolizes its turbulence. And as Nick moves from school to
family, family to school, he is eased into acceptance of
the spirit of contention (fleshed out as the novel pro-
gresses) and of the harshness of the world that later opens
up in *A Buyer's Market*.

Contention begins at preparatory school under the
guise of practical joking, but it is still, relatively, all in
good fun and quite harmless. The "duels" between Le

Bas and his charges are an accepted part of the duality in naturally rebellious and imaginative adolescents, and therefore ephemeral and slightly innocuous. Things are different at the Stringhams', however, where family pressures produce indelible, more serious scars. Stringham's clash with, and momentary triumph over Commander Foxe is on a par with his earlier humbugging of Le Bas, except now Nick tentatively understands the import of the second incident:

> I was conscious that some sort of duel had been taking place, and that Stringham had somehow gained an advantage by, as it were, ordering Buster from the room. Buster himself began to smile, perhaps recognising momentary defeat, to be disregarded from assurance of ultimate victory. (*QU*, 56)

Anticipation of "victory" stimulates the uncongenial competition between Stripling and Farebrother at the Templers'. Farebrother's collar-turner, which ably shreds rather than reverses several of Stripling's prize collars, is a failure from the commercial standpoint but a thorough success from the social one, since it becomes instrumental in effecting Stripling's temporary defeat. And while preparing revenge, Jimmy's attempt to slip a chamber pot into one of Sunny's hat boxes is foiled by the surprise appearance of Farebrother himself. Stripling has no alternative but to make off down the hall, bearing the pot before him like some "sacrificial urn" and undergoing the facial contortions of one "in actual physical pain." Though not himself pained by the incident, Nick is understandably made "uncommonly tired" by it.

Unquestionably, duels are fatiguing at any level. Örn and Lundquist's fracas on the tennis courts is immediately spurred by a dubious serve but is fundamentally lodged in secret rivalry over a woman. In a different way, *amour propre* motivates Sillery. His sparrings, shufflings, and wheedlings are triggered by the compulsion to emerge at the top of his academic stronghold. More strikingly, Members and Quiggin, who remove themselves from Sillery's influence, exhibit the excitement present in the duel of wills for those obsessed by a goal, while the final break between Templer and Stringham develops out of the mutual recognition that each lacks any direction whatsoever.

Aimlessness is destructive, but other paths have already terminated in dead ends. Such is the case of Giles Jenkins, a character as singular as Widmerpool though easily more humane. In the main thematic line of *A Question of Upbringing,* Nick's uncle directly links family and school, juxtaposing one with the other, but in *The Music of Time* he looms even larger as a figure beaten and nearly battered into punch-drunk eccentricity by stronger wills. Giles is the prototype of the eternal loser: the man who invariably chooses the sword that shatters or the pistol that misfires, whose "more than usually outrageous actions are approached, at least conversationally, as if they constituted a series of practical jokes."

Giles's fruitless contentions against family and society are concentrated in his hobbyhorse, the Trust: a vague sort of entity that brings in a moderate income and becomes implicitly transformed for the reader into an often ironic, often terrifying symbol of Giles's weakness and failure. Deprived of a saving modicum of self-illumination, Giles has muddled through the years, his failure long ago written off to lack of "influence," an abstraction as obsessive as "the Trust":

> This business of "influence" was one that played a great part in Uncle Giles's philosophy of life. It was an article of faith with him that all material advancement in the world was the result of influence, a mysterious attribute

with which he invested, to a greater or lesser degree, every human being on earth except himself. That the rich and nobly born automatically enjoyed an easy time of it through influence was, of course, axiomatic; and—as society moved from an older order—anybody who might have claims to be considered, at least outwardly, of the poor and lowly was also included by him among those dowered with this almost magic appanage. . . . As a result of this creed he was unconquerably opposed to all established institutions on the grounds that they were entirely—and therefore incapably—administered by persons whose sole claim to consideration was that they could command influence. (*QU*, 66-67)

Giles is here, of course, tilting against windmills; the nature of the "duel" has become almost mythical. For such "influence" that he broods upon—the weak man's mode of making his way in the world—only keynotes disaster in *The Music of Time*. Faults lie not in one's stars but in one's self; character, after all, is fate. To be sure, being deprived of "influence" does not, as in the cases of Quiggin, Members, and Widmerpool, assure success; Giles proves this by example. But on the other side of the coin, those like Stringham and Templer, favored by the "magic appanage," never forced into examining their own talents, end up de-vitalized by Influence's occult powers.

Nick confronts this very paradox at the conclusion of *A Question of Upbringing*. With the future before him, with the realization that upbringing can do no more, and with the added understanding that no "influence" will take over where upbringing has left off, Nick knows he must at last fall back on himself. Parting from Charles Stringham at Grosvenor Square, he to visit Uncle Giles, Charles to attend a dinner, Nick sees the farewell as the significant, perhaps crucial experience of youth:

This was the last I should see of Stringham for a long time. The path had suddenly forked. With regret, I accepted the inevitability of circumstance. Human relationships flourish and decay, quickly and silently, so that those concerned scarcely know how brittle, or how inflexible, the ties that bind them have become. . . . A new epoch was opening: in a sense this night was the final remnant of life at school. (*QU*, 229)

8

A
Buyer's
Market

The "new epoch" is treated in *A Buyer's Market*. Here the dilemmas fashioned by upbringing are inadvertently resolved for Nick as forces of school and family conspire to nudge him into deeper involvements with people and a vocation. But while he seeks the "right choice" as an aid to achieving an identity, he does not wish to become, like so many of his acquaintances, "formulated." The end of innocence brings the awareness that life must take on some sort of pattern, but it is meaning within the pattern that he really seeks. *A Buyer's Market* pictures Nick precisely at moments when he is precariously weighing such meaning and when he is drifting from identity to identity.

As far back as school, Nick anticipated this sense of aimlessness that he now feels. There, he puzzled over the existence and conduct of footloose, irresponsible Uncle Giles, "relegated [to that] limbo where nothing is expected of a person." A shade who drifts in and out of Nick's life, and disturbs his dreams, Giles at that time is "a being who [has] in him perhaps some of the same essence that went towards forming oneself as a separate unity." But while "separate" in the sense of "individual," he is dissociated as well.

If at an earlier point in Nick's development Giles provides the example of "separateness," Edgar Deacon supplies it in *A Buyer's Market*. Like Giles, Deacon is an eccentric whose "radical" traits motivate Nick's cautionary responses to his own predicament. But he is in some ways a more impressive and disturbing figure than Giles. Though his past career as a painter has become embalmed in the dust of his venture as a commercial antique collector, he has gained a bit of immortality for a work called *The Boyhood of Cyrus,* a kitsch affair which later takes on symbolic proportions for Nick. It is the recollection of Deacon's fame, coupled with the fear of missing the "spirit" that may later account for wholeness, which force Nick (as *A Buyer's Market* opens) into serious reflection. From the brief flashback of the sale of Deacon's effects at the beginning of the novel until Deacon's dreary funeral at the end of it, Nick is prodded into analyzing how life can be substantiated.

Nick is determined to create from his post-university life a unified being able to function both publicly and privately; however, he often reveals an awkwardness in fusing these two selves. Logic demands a "uniformity of pattern . . . rightly preserved in human behaviour," but experience reveals that life is inconsistent. When most insecure, Nick (given to Schopenhauerian musing) denies any pattern in human experience, and would have it conform to his subjective view as he sets "individuals and ideas in hermetically sealed receptacles." Only toward the end of *A Buyer's Market,* before a

dinner engagement at the Widmerpools', does Nick note
the significance of the novel's sequences, or define experiences as tentatively leading to cohesiveness, shaping an
identity:

> Nothing in life can ever be entirely divorced from myriad
> other incidents; and it is remarkable, though no doubt
> logical, that action, built up from innumerable causes,
> each in itself allusive and unnoticed more often than not,
> is almost always provided with an apparently ideal mo-
> ment for its final expression. So true is this that what has
> gone before is often, to all intents and purposes, swal-
> lowed up by the aptness of the climax; opportunity ap-
> pearing, at least on the surface, to be the sole cause of
> fulfilment. (*BM,* 254)

The search for fulfillment demands that Nick test
those values offered by opportunity. Aided by chance,
which lends suspense to the search, and motivated by a
precision and self-consciousness that give it direction,
Nick discovers how choices, sometimes tentatively desirable, sometimes thoroughly suspect, seem to multiply
with disturbing regularity and attend his every gesture.
Theoretically his position seems enviable. A youthful
bachelor in the market for an occupation, acceptance,
and love can hardly do better than move freely up and
down the societal ladder, waiting to buy in on the right
rung. But theory does not always forecast fact. While
the goods for sale are plentiful, and not particularly
shoddy, their value is still somewhat indeterminate—
like those Deacon paintings Nick recalls having seen
sold for a few pounds in some obscure auction rooms.
He knows how reputations can undergo deflation. Thus,
though the possibility of shifting fortune may dictate an
urgent choice, prudence as well as agility is indicated. If
the metaphorical complexities of Powell's title are to be
understood, one must view objectively Nick's relative
position on the market. In the world of bright young

men who tout their services, Nick discerns talent in abundance and finds himself a surplus item. The revelation that choices are more limited than he had imagined brings on a personal depression soon to be substantiated by the historic depression of the thirties. For, implicit though it be, the spirit of the Great Depression is suspended over *A Buyer's Market*.

With most persons in the novel optimism ranges high. There is a great security and energy in speculating, merging, and managing. Indeed, the informing agency of the book is the "professionally strong will[ed]," quasi-mythical Magnus Donners, who plans phenomenal expansions in the Balkans. Nick, however, cannot share in this infectious optimism. Although he may envy Duport for possessing a beautiful wife and townhouse, admire the suave Tompsitts or Truscotts and even the awkward Widmerpools for their promising futures, feel an inward pang at Members' and Quiggin's growing reputations, he is not at all inspired to emulate them. Fianchettoed by successes which grieve his sensibilities, Nick fears less that he has nothing whatever of value to sell than that there really isn't much he wishes to buy.

Such fears are strengthened by the several "opportunities" which appear to fulfill his needs but which, upon closer inspection, actually satisfy only momentarily. Leaving the university for the world, he finds that society comprises a set of three interlocked circles—laid out triangularly—each seemingly interested in him, but interested, too, in circumscribing his personality, delimiting his range of activity. Discomfited at the prospects, he discovers that he cannot yet commit himself.

Nick's movements within these circles provide the novel's structure. He runs the gamut of social experience from the fashionable milieu of Eaton Square dinners and dances, where no one comes too loose and no one leaves too tight; to the free-for-all at Hill Street (thrown by the exotic Milly Andriadis), where liquor and morals run equally freely; to Edgar Deacon's Bohemian birthday party in Tottenham Court Road, where art and power mix like some volatile cocktail. At best, these migrations are tangled affairs, and the homing instinct in Nick grows more disordered, his flight more undirected, as he realizes that, while he cannot ostensibly ally himself with any one clique, he may sensibly belong to them all. What is demanded of him is mere acquiescence in a single role, an assured and comfortable sort of gesture, but in *A Buyer's Market* he can never compel himself to make it.

The dinner party at the Gavin Walpole-Wilsons' and the subsequent society dance at the Huntercombes' are each hemispheres of respectability forming the first of the circles into which he steps. Family and public school connections have made upper-class functions most accessible, but Nick finds that these events interest him less for relations than relationships. Though he may be concerned about refining his rapport with the Establishment, he is more dedicated to effecting a liaison with Sir Gavin's niece, Barbara Goring, the reason for his being drawn into the Walpole-Wilson orbit and the cause of his defecting from it. Also, Nick's role as chivalric, refined lover is too chilling for his sensual nature. Place cards and dance lists are poor substitutes for assignation sheets.

Even more frustrating than wasting time and spirit in the fruitless pursuit of Barbara is the feeling that others seem unruffled by the urges so keenly plaguing him. Caught up in the business of politics, finance, literature, such young men cannot bother to moon about love. Widmerpool, for example, who like most of the set is bewitched by Barbara, can with admirable conviction forswear his infatuation and reject her. Nick must be impressed by a will that frees itself from an intolerable situation and moves on to other affairs. Whereas he views participation in society as an escape from involvement, an excuse for deferring choice, Widmerpool takes it as an expedient for advancement. Fearful of falling into the ineffectualness of his genially dilatory associates, Nick must at the same time confront the genius of the egoistic "pusher."

The condition is nowhere more brilliantly illustrated than in the scenes at the Walpole-Wilsons' and Hunter-combes'. Faithful in his rehearsal of the trivia, amenities, and bickering that pass for fare over the tables of the rich, Powell permits the ironies of Nick's position to unfold by associations of people and places. To move nimbly through discussions of Wagner, the Haig statue, Balkan enterprises, uniforms for Girl Guides, as though each topic were of identical importance, into the monotony of a ball, where "dance tune [follows] dance tune, and partner [follows] partner," might in itself reflect a certain vacuity. Nick rubs elbows with those who actually dedicate themselves to making these rounds, who extract pleasure from the routine, who exist for the whine of orchestras, the rustle of gowns, the swish of tails: the so-called "dancing men." His sole hope is to escape this ambience in which such mechanical professionals are wound up to whirl, whirl, whirl, and finally run down completely.

Contrasted with the atmosphere at Milly Andriadis', the Huntercombes' dance is a pale affair indeed. Nick's attendance at Milly's unconventional soiree, if not intimating a rejection of the upper rungs of society, at least implies independence from them. Chance encounters, first with Deacon and Gypsy Jones, then with String-ham, plunge Nick into a dangerous distraction. The excesses of the "dancing men" are always safely within the framework acceptable to upbringing, while those of Milly are not. And no matter how little Nick cares for Widmerpool, the latter emerges from the Hunter-combes' as a staying, sobering influence. Hardly the same can be said for Stringham, who significantly—if not symbolically—pops up from the past at a coffee stall and leads him toward potential abandon. Nick leaves behind at the Huntercombes' the mechanical world of Widmerpool and wind-up men to engage the romantic one of Stringham and sensuality at Milly Andriadis'.

Milly's party is the longest of several in the book, and it allows for a critical exchange of attitudes in and around the narrator. Nonconformity pervades the Andriadis home like heavy perfume. More so than the gatherings at the Huntercombes' or at Deacon's, Nick sees that Milly's crowd offers a farrago of "opulence" and Bohemianism, symbolized by

> champagne, beards, and tiaras . . . exotic embellishments . . . within a framework on the whole commonplace enough [in which] the shifting groups of the party created, as a spectacle, illusion of moving within the actual confines of a picture or tapestry, into the depths of which the personality of each new arrival had to be automatically amalgamated. (*BM*, 101)

Nick balks against "amalgamation," and the very heterogeneity of the party translates his inner conflict into the crucial conflict of the novel, crystallized in Edgar Deacon's studied assertion about the painter Barnby and the radical nymph Gypsy Jones that "Gothic manners don't mix with Greek morals." The symbolic extensions of the epigram, radiating like spokes from Nick's consciousness, become at once the many points on the circumference of *A Buyer's Market,* and its center.

Powell's symbolism is drawn from architecture di-

rectly, from philosophy indirectly, in order to substanti-
ate and amplify the clash between will and imagination.
As modes of the Gothic and Greek, power and sensuality are innately contradictory, and in these two forms so
historically and esthetically opposed Powell finds an
"objective correlative" for Nick's dilemma. Were it a
question of either-or, Nick would undoubtedly abandon
himself to Grecian sensuousness and simplicity. But this
is hardly the case. Although a cold commercialism un-
derlies the very foundations of modern and medieval
Gothic—the abstract realities of the Middle Ages
(Church and State, Religion and Politics) replaced by
those of the twentieth century (the Market, Marriage,
Money)—Gothicism, too, possesses a Ruskinesque vitality, that "degree of sterness and rudeness" one finds reflected in men like Barnby, Widmerpool, Donners, and
Quiggin. Convoluted, artificial, rough, thrusting as
Gothic manners are, they clearly dominate the freedom
and looseness of Greek morals: the one involving willful
participation, the other imaginative passivity. Half-Greek,
half-Gothic in attitude, Nick seeks the best of both
worlds, strives for a higher reality and ideal pattern, only
to endanger his decisions by lapsing into a brilliant eclec-
ticism—a kind of fluid, confused Hellenism—which attempts to meet complexities through adaptation of old
forms, development of new ones.

The dominant symbol for Nick's journey through Oc-
cidental materialism and Eastern exoticism, linked with
the metaphorical construct of the novel, is Edgar Deacon's *The Boyhood of Cyrus*. At the same time extrinsically marketable as an artifact and intrinsically effete
for its expression of diluted "Victorian Hellenism," its
subject a mirror of the union of latent power and
sensual setting (Cyrus hangs above a barometer in the
Walpole-Wilsons' front hall), the painting becomes a

touchstone for Nick's observations on love and vocation.

One such observation grows out of a walk with the two cousins, Barbara and Eleanor, and an incident on the steps of the Albert Memorial. The juxtaposition of the bas relief of "Manufacturers" (Western assurance?) and the statue of Asia (Eastern longing?) sticks in Nick's memory. Subsequent frustrations over the unsatisfactory affair with Barbara find confirmation in the mild eccentricities of Sir Gavin's self-recriminations: "For lust of knowing what we should not know . . . we take the Golden Road to Samarkand." Regularly intoned by "a man singularly lacking in intellectual curiosity," the quotation harbors its own ironies, Sir Gavin and Nick sharing something of the same caution.

Nick's insights, however, are keener. Though a "highly romantic view of life" colors his outlook at this time, he realizes that indefinable yearnings like those of Sir Gavin can prove dangerously retarding. A rational, rather than emotional, approach to the problem of the divided mind inhibits an easy abandon. And while the problem is not immediately resolved, Nick's course seems preferable to that of Peter Templer, who spurns the "unduly respectable environment[s]" of the Gothics for the laps of mistresses frequenting an exotic world of "mahogany furniture and Moorish brasswork." Nick momentarily flirts with this escape at the Huntercombes'. Feeling out of place, he is attracted by Rosie Manasch, who, resembling "a beauty of the Byronic era," looks out of place. A compact, voluptuous Jewess, she evokes the world of "some oriental potentate" and inspires visions of "occupying herself behind the scenes in all the appetising labyrinth of harem intrigue." In the foreground, similarly, but more oddly compounded, is Milly Andriadis. Part English, part Greek (both "ancient and modern" as Nick observes), Milly is literally made up of opposing strains, and her party provides the occasion for innumerable types (many are alloys like herself) to pass in review.

The purer Gothic valences, representatives of power, offer the least difficulty. Displaying a "colourless, respectable, dominating exterior," Sir Magnus, Widmerpool, and Sillery are men of irreproachable manners and Northern chill. The "Greeks" offer more of interest. Libertines like Stringham, homosexuals like Deacon and Max Pilgrim, Cyprians like Milly and Gypsy Jones may be subject to the severest class criticism, but their abandon seems less debilitating than their susceptibility to the incursion of Gothicism. If they attempt the Gothic role and fail (as they often do), it is not through misdirection of will but division of character.

The advantages of the free—or disturbed—life outweigh the disadvantages if one can accept the resultant split personality. But as compelling as love, or love affairs, may be, Nick recognizes that slaves bound to the senses are no freer than those bound to their wills. Although cold fish like Sillery and Widmerpool reek of frustrated perfection, Stringham and Milly, physically and mentally wearing themselves out in debauchery, smack of staleness. In the end, Nick sees the Andriadis party (like the Walpole-Wilson party before it) as something of a failure for both Gothic and Greek. His predawn revelation after the all-night revel finds him still on tenterhooks, but not unhappy that certain bridges have been burned. "The night had been an empty one," he assures himself, thereby signifying his rejection of Milly's way of life as he had rejected the Walpole-Wilsons' before.

Nick anticipates brighter days when he is invited to the country by Eleanor Walpole-Wilson. Removed from the pulsing urban existence, he enjoys "the sensation of starting life again . . . with a clean sheet," but he soon learns that tensions and eccentricities predominate no less in country isolation than in city involvement. The modes of life he has previously experienced unfold with identical, depressing regularity.

Odd, defeated, overcome by hankering after a vanished era, the aged Sir Gavin lives surrounded by artifacts of Eastern luxury symbolizing his past plunders in the Foreign Service. Sir Gavin is a forgotten man, taken seriously by no one, masking the vestiges of scandal behind a show of form. His decadence—and the decadence of his class—is uninspiring and unremarkable. And the climate at his country seat, Hinton Hoo, is routine, dull, and vapid.

The same conditions do not hold at Sir Magnus' country seat, Stourwater, to which Nick makes an excursion in the company of the Walpole-Wilsons and their other weekend guests. Superficially the castle emphasizes the basic physical contrast with the neat, classical Queen Anne style of Hinton Hoo, but its Gothicism makes Nick uneasy:

> Here was the Middle Age, from the pages of Tennyson, or Scott, at its most elegant: all sordid and painful elements subtly removed. . . . [However] something was decidedly amiss. . . . The impression was of sensations that might precede one of those episodes in a fairy story, when, at a given moment, the appropriate spell is pronounced to cause domes and minarets, fountains and pleasure-gardens to disappear into thin air. (*BM*, 185-86)

Like Spenser's blissful bower, or Tennyson's magic lands of lotuses or spinning ladies, Stourwater offers a luxury removed from the very power that has generated it. Nick contemplates drifting into the opiate ease of another passivity, "the beauty of the castle, the sunlight striking the grass and water of the moat . . . [making] sordid difficulties appear infinitely far away." His first real rub with power nearly woos him into slavery. Naïvely, he sees absolute power as offering an escape from decisions because it places one so far above them.

Despite the attractions of Stourwater, Nick does not become enslaved by authority. That role is still reserved for Widmerpool, whose appearance at Sir Magnus'—first as a voice in the gloom of the castle's underground tunnels, then as a face peering from behind a cell window —highlights Nick's tour of the dungeons and partially restores his comic perspective. As always, Widmerpool dispels any aura of romance. His "imprisonment" becomes only an optical illusion reflecting the reality of his condition:

> Now that my eyes had become accustomed to the oddness of his physical position, some of the earlier illusion of forcible confinement dissolved; and, at this later stage, he seemed merely one of those invariably power-conscious beings—a role for which his temperament certainly well suited him—who preside over *guichets* from which tickets are dispensed for trains or theatres. (*BM,* 206)

Pure power of the Magnus variety may be exotic and magic, but one must first operate like Widmerpool to achieve it, an ordeal Nick is not willing to undergo. To be sure there is something admirable in Widmerpool's cold, steely, resilient surface—but something frightening as well. He is arch-Gothic, so outlandish in design that he presents a ludicrous exterior to a Hellenist like Nick, but as a force he gains renewed life with every reversal. In one way, Widmerpool's social setbacks parallel Nick's own, although their directions are different, Widmerpool moving directly toward the spheres of power while Nick moves toward those of imagination.

Nick is helped along the path by Ralph Barnby: talented, libertine, engagingly Satanic, the Renaissance fusion of the socio-politico-professional man. Endowed with the sophistication and accomplishment of the artist-lover, Barnby enjoys simultaneously the patronage and mistress of Sir Magnus. His position as Bohemian-operator, while not perfect, is enviable and unassailable, for he seems to be everything that Deacon might have been, much that Nick wants to be. Composed and forceful, he indulges in few eccentricities and accommodates his broad taste for the basic matters of art and sex. That he lacks the perfection of genius detracts only imperceptibly from an esthetic which keeps him in touch with the times, "his pictures [personifying] a substantial proportion of that wayward and melancholy, perhaps even rather spurious, content of the self-consciously disillusioned art of that epoch."

Barnby has contracted a shaky, if expedient, reconciliation with power and imagination. His pulse attuned to the rhythm of the times, and gaining speed and strength with successive accomplishments, Barnby is the new breed able to reconcile Greco-Gothic within himself. Nor is it surprising to find present at Deacon's last birthday party Quiggin and Members, like Barnby emerging as types of the *Kraftbohemien,* energized by similar feelings of liberty and dissent:

> Quiggin, a kind of abiding protoype of discontent against life, possessing at the same time certain characteristics peculiar to the period: Members, no less dissatisfied than Quiggin, but of more academic derivation, perhaps even sharing some of Mr. Deacon's intellectual origins. (*BM,* 246)

Such "intellectual origins" herald physical ends. Deacon's drunken, fatal tumble down a flight of stairs is a symbolic one, sounding the muted, pathetic note of a dying era, signifying the ascent of a new Bohemian élite.

Where Nick belongs remains still problematical. "Toying with the idea of attempting to begin work on a novel" places him by inclination with men like Barnby, Quiggin, and Members, but certain prohibitions prevent his sympathizing wholeheartedly with them. While Barnby's "unusual variety of form [may provide] a link between . . . the world of Power . . . and that imaginative life," Jenkins perceives that "the artist who traffics in power does so, if not necessarily disastrously, at least at considerable risk." Less from cowardice than simple confusion, he defects from Barnby's world. But, as the novel ends, to spy him dining with the Widmerpools— exchanging, that is, the buoyancy of Bohemia's articulateness and ebullience for the gravity of ponderous, fatuous platitudes—by no means suggests that he has deserted Barnby as mentor. Still seeking "a satisfactory balance in [his] manner of conducting life," Nick is uncertain what the proportions should be, and he finds confidence in fractional acceptances. Widmerpool's decision to shun in the future that type of woman (i.e., Gypsy Jones) "who takes [his] mind off [his] work" confirms, for example, the opposite view advocated by Barnby:

> "It's unaccountable to me the way intimate relations between the sexes are always spoken of, and written about, as if of necessity enjoyable or humorous. In practice they might much more truly be described as encompassing the whole range of human feeling from the height of bliss to the depths of misery." (*BM*, 252)

In other words, while he need be no Lothario or Don Juan, the man of imagination must not neglect his sensual nature.

This last important theme in *A Buyer's Market*—the search for love—plays about the levels of choice Nick experiences as he moves on to "the acceptance world." The probing of surface emotions agitates profounder sensations, and love that has begun as merely intellec-

tual stimulation yields to more basic urges. Barbara Goring, Nick's first adult passion, is pursued as much for
convenience as desire. Various social encounters and
obligations force proximity; and, after all, Barbara
seems a likely choice to be drawn from the correct social
circles. But flirty, teasing, ragging, whimsical Barbara
balks at displays of sentiment. In a way she is as cold a
fish as Widmerpool and wields a similar power. Nick
acts the chivalric lover, mastering the refined posture
while aching for the unrefined one. Indulging Barbara
in extravagant social capers is his notion, significantly
dismissed, along with Barbara herself, at the Huntercombes' dance when she dumps sugar over Widmerpool.
In itself the gesture is minor, but it serves to strip away
the romantic patina. Barbara is revealed as a tiresome,
uncomfortable person, a just mate, perhaps, for the
playboy she marries.

What most appalls Nick about his breakup with Barbara is the discovery that Widmerpool has been enamored of her as well. Widmerpool later turns up as a rival
for the affections of Gypsy Jones, an affair more ironic,
for, while Gypsy would like to sleep with Nick, he is
never forward enough to press the opportunity; and,
while Widmerpool thinks her an easy mark, she will
have none of him, except to let him pick up the tab for
an abortion. The duping of Widmerpool is more comic
than sordid, however; and the affair seems a triumph of
the senses over the will. Gypsy, in fact, revels in the
sensual where Barbara has dabbled with power. To
Nick these two women possess "a good deal in common," reflecting as they do, from minute to minute, his
state of mind, and forming congruent relationships:
Barbara's defenses and aloofness toward Nick mirror his
toward Gypsy.

Finding it difficult to forget the world of proper (if

epid) love and plunge noncommittally into raw sex, Nick fails to capitalize on Gypsy. At last closeted with her, semi-nude, languishing, he cerebrates away the first serious opportunity to lose his virginity:

> Were Barbara and Gypsy really the same girl, I asked myself. . . . Here, at last, at the back of Mr. Deacon's shop, some conclusion had been reached, though even that inference, too, might be found open to question. At the same time, I could not help being struck, not only by a kind of wonder that I now found myself, as it were, with Barbara in conditions once pictured as beyond words vain of achievement, but also at that same moment by a sense almost of solemnity at this latest illustration of the pattern that life forms. (*BM*, 258)

Gypsy and Barbara embody distinct extremes, but both women are unsatisfactory to Nick because, in the last analysis, they are wearying. Accounting them such, however, does not alter the realization that a choice between a wife (which Barbara may have been) or a mistress (which Gypsy could only have been) seems imminent. Taking up with one or the other demands the social and moral commitment Nick has been unwilling to make. As usual, Nick is tossed about by the dilemma. Yet while dilemmas are disturbing they are not uninteresting. His fortuitous meeting with Jean Templer—who combines the best of both Barbara and Gypsy—sets the stage for a love affair, complicated certainly, but circumventing the niggling pressures of conventional choice. With some of his Greek luck still intact, Nick is at last ready to hazard his chances in the formidable "acceptance world."

9

The
Acceptance
World

The Acceptance World begins and ends with the arrival of a postcard. The first, which Nick receives a few years after the conclusion of *A Buyer's Market,* invites him to tea at Uncle Giles's; the second, received several years after that, announces Jean Templer's return from France. Between them pass an array of lives and actions more surprising than any Nick has hitherto encountered. Yet the complexities of *The Acceptance World* define more certainly than before his peculiar position.

The postcards announce two representative meetings (as symbolic as they are real)—one, a prelude, the other a coda—spanned by such occurrences as the initiation into the intense joys and disappointments of love, the dissolution and reformation of social allegiances, the substitution of new values for old, and the acquisition of an identity gained through an evaluation of individıals, not groups. What happens in *The Acceptance World* is no less than the coming of age of Nicholas Jenkins.

Though an increased emphasis on incident might indicate otherwise, the novel is more thematically compact than its predecessors, for its entire force depends almost exclusively on the kinds and degrees of "acceptance" it analyzes. Like the majority of Powell's titles, "the Acceptance World" fosters literal and symbolic connotations; but it is explicitly equated with Widmerpool's new occupation as a bill-broker who, "on the strength of [his] reputation," persuades banking houses to "accept" future debts for goods being shipped abroad. Nick relates Widmerpool's work with his own world:

> When, in describing Widmerpool's new employment, Templer had spoken of "the Acceptance World," I had been struck by the phrase. Even as a technical definition, it seemed to suggest what we are all doing; not only in business, but in love, art, religion, philosophy, politics, in fact all human activities. The Acceptance World was the world in which the essential element—happiness, for example—is drawn, as it were, from an engagement to meet a bill. Sometimes the goods are delivered, even a small profit made; sometimes the goods are not delivered, and disaster follows; sometimes the goods are delivered, but the value of the currency is changed. Besides, in another sense, the whole world is the Acceptance World as one approaches thirty; at least some illusions discarded. The mere fact of still existing as a human being proved that. (*AW*, 170)

While the economics of existence may not always be corollaries for emotions, the link between the commodities of both spheres is inescapable. To perceive the analogy is success (however limited) in itself, since adjusting to fate and the future becomes individual, not class responsibility; and *The Acceptance World* pictures the hero making such an adjustment.

The idea of the future broods over the novel from the first, connecting the seemingly unrelated worlds of Mrs. Erdleigh's spirits and Widmerpool's portentous business deals. But these worlds scarcely diverge; the ruling agents of both are concerned with predicting fate and ostensibly "willing" their prognostication into being. Assured success depends not on interpreting the past but in manipulating the future. By this standard, Mrs. Erdleigh and Widmerpool are figures of power, though their power presages different things: hers love, his wealth. Caught between is the man of imagination, who must accept them as concrete forces, as well as imperfect abstractions, and deal with them as best he can. Undeniably, familiarization with a sense of life necessitates in the hero a resignation to fate, at the same time producing within him the desire to dominate it. Or so say the "grey and greasy" deck of cards with which Mrs. Erdleigh tells Nick's fortune:

> "You live between two worlds," she said. "Perhaps even more than two worlds. You cannot always surmount your feelings. . . . You are thought cold, but you possess deep affections, sometimes for people worthless in themselves. Often you are at odds with those who might help you. You like women, and they like you, but you often find the company of men more amusing. You expect too much, and yet you are also too resigned. You must try to understand life." (*AW*, 14-15)

As Nick soon discovers, belonging, yet always questioning maintains the dynamics of character. And, as he nears thirty, love and wealth emerge as the most dynamically viable symbols of his role, the gauges of his willingness to accept and his ability to be accepted.

Yet while *The Acceptance World* is about love and wealth, while indeed the concrete and symbolic "acceptance" of these values comprises what may be the controlling theme of the novel, they are never for a moment romanticized. Powell, in his comic acceptance of a materialistic society, imposes upon it the greater considerations of love; nevertheless, he maintains a hard, dry, ironic view of relationships motivated by these prime movers of youth. *The Acceptance World,* driving toward Nick's acceptance of the human condition, is bent on constructing new values after youthful idealism has evolved into a harsher realism. His knowledge of the imperfectability of his fellows gradually tempers illusion, and in his search for the extraordinary he at last accepts that "all human beings, driven as they are at different speeds by the same Furies, are at close range equally extraordinary."

It is this balanced observation that moves Nick toward the future. *The Acceptance World* marks the end of his wandering in a limbo of nihilism and impotence. By the end of the novel the *bête noire* of acceptance no longer menaces his confidence and gnaws at his conscience. It has been tamed by Nick's dominion over himself. He has learned to relax, to accept people on their own terms, to understand that, after all, they function first as individuals, and only afterwards as mechanisms impelling the seesaw shifts of society.

In more ways than this the novel crowns the first trilogy of *The Music of Time.* The problem implicitly posited by *A Question of Upbringing* (where do you belong after being formed and fashioned by school and family?) and freely answered in *A Buyer's Market* (here, there, everywhere, nowhere, depending upon who you are!) is worked out in *The Acceptance World.* Love (sensuality) and wealth (power) now become the absolutes that differentiate the men of imagination and the men of will.

Thematically, then, *The Acceptance World* is an analysis of the potential power of love and wealth, explored through the central metaphor of "acceptance"; structurally, it proceeds from the philosophic (but fortunately witty) construct of "thesis-antithesis-synthesis," or, more mundanely, from personal alignments and realignments which form various triangles within the social framework. If an adherence to pre-established patterns is symbolized by the progression of a straight line in *A Question of Upbringing,* and an elliptical, noncommital attitude by the circles in *A Buyer's Market,* then the stress of total involvement in *The Acceptance World* is seen as a triangle at whose apexes the lines of tension and opposition converge.

In *The Acceptance World,* a Pythagorean logic within each of the triangles swells the harmony of the novel as a whole. The intricate, intimate scenes motivated through love and power, directed by the intelligence of fate, and acted against a backdrop of minor, pseudorevolutionary ripples, generate the novel's dialectical display. Disenchanted by the effectiveness of class props, one seeks support in people, for it is they, after all, who comprise the flux of society and its future. Thus, the novel's art and argument. Thesis: the breakup of class and overall societal disintegration. Antithesis: the search for patterns that can possibly aid in reconstruction. Synthesis: the acceptance of or commitment to a relationship based on love.

The "thesis" of decay—touched upon earlier in the series—is stated with full effect at the opening of the novel as Nick makes for the rendezvous with Giles at the latter's private hotel.

> The [Ufford] in Bayswater, where he stayed during comparatively rare visits to London, occupied two corner houses in a latent, almost impenetrable region west of the Queen's Road. . . . The . . . suspicion that the two houses were an abode of the dead was increased by the

fact that no one was ever to be seen about, even at the reception desk. The floors of the formerly separate build-ings, constructed at different levels, were now joined by unexpected steps and narrow, steeply slanting passages. The hall was always wrapped in silence; letters in the green baize board criss-crossed with tape remained yel-lowing, for ever unclaimed, unread, unchanged. (*AW*, 1-2)

Ironically parodied from the Romantics, the refrain echoes through the passages like a moan from Scott's minstrel or Byron's Harold. Easily the Ufford might be a symbol for Giles himself. The picture of a poor bache-lor of sixty, absorbed in the business of extracting greater shares from "the Trust," or occupied in the equally frustrating task of finding a wife, forced to in-habit for mortal eternity an Inferno of transient hotels, inspires a certain dread in Nick, who can not reasonably rule out like expectations.

Though separated from Giles by three decades and showing "some indefinable difference in class or bearing [and/or] moral standards," Jenkins often identifies him-self with his uncle. Embarked as he is on "an erratic ex-cursion through life," and doomed, it would appear, to an infinity of reversals, Giles, refractory but optimistic, puzzles over the shape of things to come. Nick, too, looks on the future with mixed hope and fear, anticipating anything, seeing "no reason to curb the wildest absurdity of fancy as to what might happen the very next moment." But he also senses the hebetude attending change; he knows that one fights off the past like a fever, however easier the temptation to succumb may be. The new year —the future—is momentarily held in the grip of the past during the transition from 1931 to 1932, the year in which most of the action of *The Acceptance World* occurs:

It was that prolonged, flat cheerless week that follows Christmas. My own existence seemed infinitely stagnant,

> relieved only by work on another book. Those inter-
> minable latter days of the dying year create an interval,
> as it were, of moral suspension: one form of life already
> passed away before another has had time to assert some
> new, endemic characteristic. Imminent change of direc-
> tion is for some reason often foreshadowed by such
> colourless patches of time. (*AW*, 30-31)

Love will work the change, though as yet Nick is
ignorant of the fact. Now, neither very assertive nor
assured, sexually or professionally, he sees signs of disintegration everywhere he turns.

There is, for example, his connection with the ailing
novelist St. John Clarke, who is working on an introduction to The *Art of Horace Isbister,* a book of
reproductions that Nick's firm is bringing out. More depressing than Clarke's being an allegedly poor choice for
writing the article, or than his procrastination in doing
so, or than even the confusion provoking the procrastination, is the suspicion that any encomium on Isbister is
actually an obituary of an era both the painter and the
novelist shared. It is as though the dying were eulogiz-
ing the dead. Fallen from popular heights into an abyss
of neglect, St. John Clarke has been denied in old age
the simple amenities accorded men of stature. His literary remains are squabbled over before he is dead.
Around him—right and left—churn the young, radical
forces of the new order, bent upon steering him from
identity to identity.

The need to gain ascendancy over the declining novelist through the secretaryship he offers becomes the
causus belli between Members and Quiggin. Both have,
in a sense, arrived: Members as a poet, Quiggin as a
critic. Tactful, charming, business-like, socially adroit,
Members would seem the logical man for the job, for
Quiggin is socially awkward, his coarse tweeds and gen-

erally crude bearing clashing with the waistcoats and gowns in St. John Clarke's world of high fashion.

That Quiggin deposes Members and woos the novelist from the Establishment is a slap in the face for tottering tradition. However Nick admires Quiggin's genius and vitality, he sees the critic himself as an agent of decay:

> Looking back afterwards, the dismissal of Members might almost be regarded as a landmark in the general disintegration of society in its traditional form. . . . Of course I did not recognize its broader aspects then. The duel between Members and Quiggin seemed merely an entertaining conflict to watch, rather than the significant crumbling of social foundations. (*AW*, 121-22)

On even this specialized level of the literati, disintegration reflects a kind of decadence. With Clarke's "acceptance" of Quiggin comes the rooting of infection, the "acceptance" and toleration by the upper class for its self-imposed destroyer.

Quiggin's movements are a new jig to the old tune. Widmerpool, in his onward and upward progress through society, has been charting a parallel course. While sharing with the critic the "determination . . . to live by the will alone," Widmerpool, aloof from human attachments (and consequently impervious to human weaknesses), has been systematically more effective at infiltrating the higher ranks. He has undergone a thorough metamorphosis. Once mocked and patronized, he is now respected and even admired. Like some ominous, lumbering, insensate machine, Widmerpool moves uninterruptedly and unfeelingly toward success. The callow boor of the Huntercombes' dance—"the kind of man people pour sugar on"—has become the competent voice of "the Acceptance World," the kind of man whose strength of "mind" can will into existence nonexistent taxicabs and into oblivion that vanishing vestige of society called "heart." The comedy of manners has momentarily become its tragedy.

At first only implicated in the novel's "thesis," Widmerpool turns antagonist in those scenes most notably concerned with physical and societal disintegration. Le Bas' heart attack at the reunion dinner (a seizure coincidental with Widmerpool's ceaseless, senseless speech on business practices and theories) and Stringham's subsequent drunk (slept off after Widmerpool and Nick have wrestled him into bed and quiescence) reflect the prepotency of the man of will. That Widmerpool endures while the world crashes and tumbles about him provokes a sobering revaluation:

> How strange a thing it was that I myself should have been engaged in a physical conflict designed to restrict Stringham's movements: a conflict in which the moving spirit had been Widmerpool. That suggested a whole social upheaval: a positively cosmic change in life's system. Widmerpool, once so derided by all of us, had become in some mysterious manner a person of authority. Now, in a sense, it was he who derided us; or at least his disapproval had become something far more powerful than the merely defensive weapon it had once seemed. (*AW*, 209-10)

By the end of *The Acceptance World* it is plain that repelling the attack launched by Widmerpool is impossible. However, the conviction that society is falling apart at the center makes Nick even more eager to interpret the realignments taking place on the peripheries. An increased self-consciousness in his vocation of novelist heightens his perceptions. Fully realizing the "complexity of writing a novel about English life" and its "intricacies" which "make English habits unyielding to simplification," he is forced to reconstruct sensible, workable patterns from the shattered pieces.

From this emerges the dialectic proper. The antithetical movement of *The Acceptance World*—the search for cohering patterns—involves less the blind opposition of abstractions than the order and degree of contrast. Neither human beings nor human relationships can remain, like class structures, categorical and impersonal. Even at their worst the triangles formed from relationships serve as the building blocks of reconstruction. To be sure, the inconstancy of wives and husbands, lovers and mistresses, and their constant shuffling and switching into more amenable combinations indicate considerable instability. Yet such permutations become not only permissible, but necessary once class lines dissolve. Private happiness, Powell suggests, is not consciously sought at the expense of society's dissolution but evolves because of it. People are plagued less by bungling or insecurity than by sheer restlessness, and to find satisfaction they conduct their lives on a pleasure-pain principle. Thus, a hedonistic utilitarianism undermines the public weal.

Just how the antithetical movement proceeds is reflected in Nick's involvement, here objective, there subjective, now with, now in each of the triangles. Formulated on gaining acceptance through the acquisition of love or power or, in some cases, both, the triangles display various intensities of thematic shading and range within these respective categories from the simplest to the most complex levels of motivation. And however isolated or unrelated, disparate or divergent the triangles may seem, each originates from a common hub, each is dependent upon the other for its shape and existence.

Only a strict, sure sense of form and materials can make such patterning work; lacking this, a novel, for all its solidity, must remain muzzy at the edges. In *The*

Acceptance World, the peripheries are more vividly defined than even the center itself. Illustrative of Powell's design is the shaping of incidents at the end of Chapter 4. At the core is the theme of "love": two lovers, two mistresses; at the edges a pair of triangles: Nick and Jean and her absent, wayward husband (a triangle in fact); Barnby and Anne Stepney and Dicky Umfraville (a triangle in embryo).

Umfraville triggers the events and associations evolving from the encounters at Foppa's restaurant. As the aging, somewhat dissolute playboy camouflaging a grain of rootlessness and defeat under a patina of insouciance, he creates a dark parallel with Charles Stringham,

> the similarity between [them being] of a moral rather than physical sort. The same dissatisfaction with life and basic melancholy gave a resemblance, though Umfraville's features and expression were more formalized and, in some manner, coarser—perhaps they could even be called more brutal—than Stringham's. (*AW*, 152-53)

This observation is but the first element in a schematic of related connections. Umfraville's eliciting from Milly Andriadis permission to "come round" for a nightcap makes it virtually impossible "to disregard the pattern of life which caused [him] not only to resemble Stringham, but also, by this vicarious invitation, to reenact Stringham's past behaviour," while Nick's place in it all makes it equally impractical to ignore the duplication of his own behavior. What he doesn't at first perceive is the general arrangement and placement of characters which validate the older pattern.

Take, for example, the faces in the crowd at Milly Andriadis' second party. Deacon, the painter, has been replaced by Barnby, another painter; Gypsy Jones by Lady Anne Stepney—a bit of upper-class fluff who, in breaking from her family, camping with artists, and

eventually marrying Umfraville, proves as radically ori-
ented and rebellious. Nick, of course, is the same, yet
not the same. While his present assault hardly differs
from his previous one with Stringham, his outlook
differs immeasurably:

> I was curious to see how [Milly's] circumstances would
> strike me on re-examination. Her party had seemed, at
> the time, to reveal a new and fascinating form of life,
> which one might never experience again. Such a world
> now was not only far less remarkable than formerly, but
> also its special characteristics appeared scarcely necessary
> to seek in an active manner. Its elements had, indeed,
> grown up all around one like strange tropical vegetation:
> more luxuriant, it was true, in some directions rather
> than others: attractive here, repellent there, but along
> every track that could be followed almost equally dense
> and imprisoning. (AW, 160)

Despite his balanced appraisal, Nick himself cannot
escape enslavement, and when he falls in love with Jean
his position is, ironically, somewhat fixed in the series of
relationships undergoing attrition. For Jean's confession
of her affair with Jimmy Stripling foreshadows her later
estrangement from Nick and her return to Duport (re-
ported in At Lady Molly's). The entire scene at Milly's
second party implies a faithful conclusion drawn from
the premises of promiscuity.

The triangles that are patterned on "love" (Jean,
Stripling, Duport; Nick, Jean, Duport; Milly, Stringham, Umfraville; Anne Stepney, Barnby, Umfraville)
and those patterned on "power" (Quiggin, Members, St.
John Clarke; Widmerpool, Stringham, Le Bas; Myra
Erdleigh, Giles, Stripling) are, like the personalities that
form them, protean and complex. Still, they do not fully
exhaust the novel's lines of interplay. Love, in the last
analysis, must be taken jointly with power; as intense
forces, each activates the other. Midway—like a bit of

metal between the poles of a magnet, now attracted this
way, now repelled that—wavers Nick in his affair with
Jean:

> I thought of love, which, from the very beginning per-
> petually changes its shape: sometimes in the ascendant,
> sometimes in decline. At present we sailed in compara-
> tively calm seas . . . yet sometimes . . . I was aware of an
> odd sense of antagonism . . . of being out of key with
> her. . . . Then, all at once, tension would be relaxed;
> always, so it seemed to me, some mysterious force
> emanating from her: intangible, invisible, yet at the
> same time part of a whole principle of behaviour: a
> deliberate act of the will by which she exercised power.
> (*AW,* 136-37)

This very Proustian observation—one recalls that the
fifth volume of *Remembrance of Things Past* is entitled
The Captive—is at the heart of Nick's philosophy.
Power-in-love and love-in-power are reconcilable antin-
omies, for in the real sense (that is, beyond the abstract
paradox) love becomes power, power, love. Yet the problem is not one of analysis but control. Forces so strong,
so charged may be positive or negative. How does one
contain them or prevent them from cancelling out each
other? Nick finds that one usually doesn't. In other words,
he accepts the condition. The clash of sensuality and the
will is the rule in *The Music of Time.* For this reason
Nick and Jean's illicit liaison is—because balanced and
relatively sane—unique; but it is also short-lived. Structurally, it serves as an important foil for the central love-
power triangle in the novel—that formed by Templer,
Quiggin, and Mona—and the first close-up of marriage.

Whatever the metaphorical meaning of "acceptance"
might be so far as other things are concerned, it is
hardly applicable to marriage; in this case "rejection"
becomes an ironic transposition of the title. With few
exceptions, and of these Nick is one, the younger gen-

eration marries and repents in haste, and marries in haste again. Marriage is unsatisfactory, if not catastrophic.

Jean, after all, is separated from her husband; Stringham is divorced from his wife; and Mona and Templer are on the rocks. Though it is true that "different couples approach with varied technique the matrimonial vehicle's infinitely complicated machinery," the mechanism (as Powell suggests) runs down quite of its own accord. Each partner (geared to his own track) guards his rights; and the couple remains "two entirely separate individuals, giving no indication of a life in common." Each stands in delicate balance on either side of the marital line, sensing the vibrations of breakup, helplessly watching the rift widen.

By these standards the Templers seem typical, though Quiggin's acquisition of Mona perhaps less so. Like Nick, one may be justifiably surprised that the gauche Quiggin could woo so cunning a woman from the wealth, style, and charm of Templer. But then, of course, the novel's comedy relies just on the very sort of reversal that directs "Mona, as Anna Karenin . . . towards Karenin as a lover, rather than Vronsky as a husband." Savage, feline, sexual, she seems an odd complement to the truculent, sober Quiggin, though in effect both are animalistic and willful, passionate in their desire for individuality. Why Quiggin gets Mona remains moot; that he does is of greater import. Striving for recognition, he acquires a prize beauty and domination over St. John Clarke, simultaneously. The exercise of love and power are fused; Quiggin coheres in a moment (if for only a moment), more completely than any one in the novel.

Nick's cohesiveness, though tardy, is projected as more permanent. In his adulterous affair with Jean he is not very different from Quiggin in his with Mona. Both men have women of expensive tastes and both are relatively insolvent, but where Quiggin exercises power over Mona, Jean wields it over Jenkins. Suffering the pangs and tortures of all good lovers, Nick accepts this, placing great faith in anything that establishes unity. And when friends' marriages topple, love gains a higher premium still. Not found in marriage, love must be sought apart from it—elsewhere, anywhere—a consideration that demands increasing shifts of perspective.

The change in Nick's outlook on love (and its ultimate acceptance) is the synthesizing motif of *The Acceptance World*. First seen in Giles's rooms after those romantic contretemps depicted in earlier novels, Nick displays eagerness for an affair but still maintains in this (as in most everything) his severely high standards. Myra Erdleigh's telling of his fortune (" 'I expect he wants to hear about *love*' ") naturally piques his interest. Her prediction that Nick will soon meet someone is commonplace enough, though he is less encouraged by her performance than amused (remaining more impressed with the teller than the tale) and forgets the entire incident until chance throws him and Jean together.

Belief or disbelief in fate is, of course, not the point here. Nick's dismissal of the prophecy as hokum reflects a smug, but justifiable, skepticism about fortune-telling as well as love, while the later realization that Mrs. Erdleigh has forecast truly underscores his vulnerability to both. Powell even compounds the irony. For, though the meeting is predictable, love itself, as Nick learns, is most emphatically not. Chance, too, all but arranges Nick and Jean's first embrace as they are motoring with the Templers to the latter's home outside London. And chance again takes a hand at the Templers', where amidst that strange assortment of forces and personalities—he, Jean, Mona, Peter, Quiggin, Mrs. Erdleigh, Jimmy Stripling—Nick is frustrated by having Jean ideally, but not physically. The whole weekend is a kind of dream: she, the surroundings, his new-found love, all unreal. The session of planchette—in which the sophisticated ouija spells out jumbled Marxian dicta and sentences of crises, signing off with a sole, indecent monosyllable—is the *reductio ad absurdum* of relationships dependent upon so sterile a method of sustaining interest and communication. Love, at least, gives little opportunity for boredom.

But for all its bitter comedy the weekend is the last time all goes smoothly. From then on revelations multiply, and the veneer of idealism is stripped away layer by layer. Conversely, Nick gradually undergoes a hardening. Love may be an "escape from the world" but it is real, too, and even a bit sordid. His faith in the ideal withers almost completely upon Jean's disclosure of her previous intrigue with Stripling, in Nick's opinion "an object of perpetual derision." Unfortunately, the joke is on Nick, who, himself a surrogate, can scarcely bring recriminations against his mistress.

A "separateness" (different from that in marriage but a "separateness" all the same) is at last the lot of a lover whose vision penetrates beyond foggy idealism. Yet, upon this discovery, the bond between Nick and Jean does not, like some fairy nimbus, dissolve. Knowing at last that while a relationship may be artificial, love itself never can be, Nick is prepared to "accept" the fraud as an historical phenomenon; it has survived the ages, as have few other things.

Toward the end of *The Acceptance World,* Nick strolls in the direction of Jean's flat, cynically musing on a picture postcard "showing a man and a woman seated literally one on top of the other in an arm chair . . .

[exchanging] ardent glances," which informs him of the hour he should arrive:

> One could not help thinking how extraordinarily un-like the real thing was this particular representation of a pair of lovers; indeed, how indifferently, at almost every level except the highest, the ecstasies and bitterness of love are at once conveyed in art. . . .
>
> Even allowing a fairly limited concession to its charac-ter as a kind of folk perception—an eternal girl sitting on an eternal young man's knee—the fact remained that an infinity of relevant material had been deliberately omitted from this vignette of love in action. These two supposedly good-looking persons were, in effect, going through the motions of love in such a manner as to convince others, perhaps less well equipped for the strug-gle than themselves, that they, too, the spectators, could be easily identified with some comparable tableau. They, too, could sit embracing on crimson chairs. Although hard to define with precision the exact point at which a breach of honesty had occurred, there could be no doubt that this performance included an element of the confi-dence-trick. . . . Perhaps, in spite of everything, the couple of the postcard could not be dismissed so easily. It was in their world that I seemed now to find myself. (*AW*, 213-14)

While Nick doubts the sincerity of his *own* affair, he gradually eschews any quixotic idealism and accepts the relationship with Jean as a substitute for "the real thing"—not because he is at all superficial or callous, but because he needs to feel that even the "confidence-trick" gives him something on which to fasten. From the kiss spontaneously given on the Great West Road, to Jean's surrender at the Templers', discreet meetings around town, troubled or abandoned scenes of love-making, discoveries of harsh truths, Nick has totally experienced the relief of a lover's fulfillment and the agony of his disappointment. But, more importantly, he has grown. Myopic optimism in matters of love has been replaced by a maturer realism. Even when love, the anticipated ace-in-the-hole, turns out to be the joker, he sees it as an animated symbol and fact connecting individuals in a way that none of the impersonal forces of a disintegrating society can. In "accepting" Jean with all her faults, even with the imposture, Nick accepts the design for happiness, however temporary. Placed side by side, the postcard from his uncle and that from his mistress form the long-sought pattern that is the synthesis of love.

10

At Lady Molly's

Opening the second "trilogy" of *The Music of Time, At Lady Molly's* spans the brief period between Nick's connection with Jean Templer and his engagement to Isobel Tolland, showing his exchanging an ambience of love without responsibilities for a world of marital preparation. The novel reflects noticeable shifts in tone and technique, provocative without being distracting, innovative without being obtrusive. First, the tone of the novel has grown brighter. The comedy is more brittle and mannered than previously; the graying horizon at the end of *The Acceptance World* has momentarily lightened, awaiting the onrush of the darker clouds of marital discord and death in *Casanova's Chinese Restaurant*. Second, the narrative has undergone revision. Less introspective and inverted, more swiftly paced and flexible, it links, rather than subordinates, character to theme. Dialogue embraces a wider range of subtlety, vignettes sparkle, characterization is deft, and action has not been interrupted for observation. Powell's energy and comedy are in evidence everywhere. *At Lady Molly's* is his happiest book.

In retrospect one realizes that by the closing pages of *The Acceptance World* a density of character had begun to obscure the extensive comic world of *The Music of Time*. Powell's inventiveness and sense of timing dissipates this atmosphere in *At Lady Molly's*. Rather than seeking surprises among the same old gang—even the best of whom have grown a trifle wan through yeoman service—Powell has filled the novel with originals who doubly succeed by being fresh and lively in their own right and new to the sequence. The regulars—Quiggin, Members, Widmerpool, Templer—still make their presence felt, but they receive stiff competition.

Equally animating is Nick's attitude. He recedes more than slightly into the shadows, and this apparent uninvolvement counterpoints the anxieties of others, especially the men of will who are experiencing their bitterest disappointments so far. His status among the new cast is different as well. No one menaces him, no one is set out as his rival, no one seeks his sanction, no one—except possibly, and in the most limited way, Widmerpool—reflects his particular problems, and no one has a better way of solving them. He is, if it can be summed up in a single word, relaxed. Now accepted and accepting, he has matured in refining impression and fact; and though still passing through a period of apprenticeship to art and life, he exercises the strictest control over his role as observer and performer, wedding actuality and memory, focusing more on the present than the past.

The past, however, is always viable. An important motif in *At Lady Molly's*—"settling down" after "acceptance"—is self based upon the conclusions of the preceding work, while one of Nick's epigrams—"all human beings, driven as they are at different speeds by the same Furies, are at close range equally extraordinary"—hitherto tentative, lays the groundwork for a survey of memorable eccentrics.

The very form of the novel, in fact, links the leading motif of "settling down" with Powell's gallery of eccentrics. There are, to begin with, the two parties thrown by Molly Jeavons in an atmosphere thoroughly respectable, but agitated, frenetic, and a bit chaotic. At one party Nick runs across Widmerpool, eminently successful and affianced to the notorious Mildred Haycock; at the other he finds Widmerpool's engagement off and his own on. Next, there are his two conversations with the voluble old extrovert, General Aylmer Conyers: the first an abbreviated appraisal by Nick of Widmerpool's virtues; the second an assessment by the octogenarian of Widmerpool's sexual insufficiencies. Finally, there is a frugal dinner given by Lord Warminster (known more popularly as Erridge), at which Nick meets his future wife, Erridge's younger sister.

The matter of "settling down," then, crops up at odd times, and in odd circumstances and surroundings. Indeed, the orthodox meaning of the term grows progressively obsolete throughout the course of the novel. No one ever suggests that "settling down" means becoming settled. Those who have lived free and immune do not sanction quiescence, no matter how respectable, and even those who are married are not insensitive to pleasures beyond marriage. Despite Nick's representation of the world of normality, one comes away from the novel feeling that the laissez-faire attitude of the upper classes and the spectrum of eccentricities within it preclude ever getting settled at all.

In writing of the idiosyncratic, Powell follows a tradition of English literature as old as *The Canterbury Tales,* but he is also developing a theme integral to the entire *Music of Time.* Up to the fourth volume of the series much of his attention has been given to the egocentric man of will—his advent, onslaught, achievement—the circles of society in which he moves, and the man of imagination he so often bests. The dominant note sounding throughout is a weary and depressing one: excess of either power or sensuality leads to the annihilation of the social entity. Combining cunning and pride with megalomania, the power seekers relinquish their basic humanity. The sensualists, on the other hand, abandoning themselves to dreams, debilitating stimulants, and introversion, surrender theirs. Such undesirable alternatives—made even more distasteful by being hopelessly entangled with family, friends, class— have at points impeded Nick's search for a proper balance, or corrective, but they have given it some impetus as well. While correctives never prove totally satisfactory, they sustain temporarily.

As buffers against the oppressive excesses of power and sensuality, eccentrics have their attractive side. Nick is attracted to them because of their humanity and ingenuousness, for they are not quacks, frauds, or loonies. The eccentric characters in *At Lady Molly's* are strong willed and energetic, with muscular intelligence, balanced perceptions, and an eye for fine discriminations. They are models of their kind: neither egocentric, ego-restrictive, nor ego-destructive. Most importantly, they keep Nick from falling into the pococurantism of *nil admirare* and preserve his outlook of *nil desperandum.*

The extroverted General Conyers, "in" with all "the right people," is one eccentric extreme; Erridge, introverted, *déclassé,* is the other. Bound with Nick's past, emerging out of the "family myth [that established him] not only as a soldier with interests beyond his profession, but even as a man of the world always 'abreast of the times,' " the General perseveres as a figure of independent mind. He has got on through "influence" but has maintained his dignity, cultivating certain avocations that have prevented his becoming either severely chastened or mechanized by his military profession.

Though nearly eighty, Conyers is no superannuated man; age has vitiated none of the life force and he defies obsolescence by immersing himself totally in the present. Without being tediously oracular, the General has achieved a ripeness that respects and weighs all knowledge and experience that is old and, without being senile, still preserves the childish wonder for all things new. What accounts Conyers "odd" is his enthusiasm. In much younger men, enthusiasm, as well as energy and ambition, is expected; after eighty it may not unreasonably be labeled eccentric. For example, the General's devotion to the cello approaches religious adoration. The melancholy instrument wails throughout the house day after day, emitting "notes . . . mysterious, even a shade unearthly, as if somewhere in the vicinity gnomes were thumbing strange instruments in a cave." Preoccupied with attaining a belated—and by now impossible—technical facility, searching for the subtle shading of a shop-worn Romantic piece, caught up in the phrasing of a Baroque one, Conyers pursues his absurd but salutary hobby.

His entrance finds him musing on the botch he has made (and habitually makes) of *"Nunc et in hora mortis nostrae,"* a line from Gounod's famous *Ave.* Here is an example of that Powellian crystallization of character, rendered expertly, but vastly underplayed. So involved is the General with his subjective, healthy excesses, that he fails to discern the potential irony of his own obsession. There is, however, no smell of mortality about him. Colorful, candid, strong willed, discerning, expansive, his very guffaws ringing "like the inextinguishable laughter of the Homeric gods on high Olympus," he seems invested with a mythic resistance to all the forces that deaden virility.

If Conyers (partisan of his class, but nevertheless susceptible to frequent, healthy retreats into fancies) makes a virtuosity of eccentricity, Lord Warminster (Erridge), a rebel lord of Marxist persuasions goaded by idealism, makes an eccentricity of his virtue. Even as an antihero of sorts, Erridge is an awkward one, more awkward perhaps than the principles to which he is dedicated. Set beside Conyers, whose polish, taste, elegance, aggressiveness, and "natural distinction" give his character breadth and scope, Erridge cuts an almost pathetic figure. Nick's earliest recollection of him at the Huntercombes' memorable dance—"angular, sallow and spotty . . . usually frowning angrily to himself, weighed down with anxiety, as if all the troubles of the world rested on his shoulders" —is confirmed by later impressions.

But Erridge is no object of ridicule. Powell uses "eccentricity" as a focus for pinpointing the weaknesses in class, not as a weakness in itself. Characters of deviation are necessary in the range of any long novel, as they are in life, for illuminating an experience in itself, or another by comparison. To be sure, Powell views the aristocracy as bordering on (if not already partially undergoing) a private *Götterdämmerung,* but he sustains sympathy for those sinking, like their myths, into twilight.

Conyers (the eccentric pragmatist) and Erridge (the eccentric idealist) are attractive because they resist the stultifying forces of classification by ordering their own worlds; but they also appear refractory when they posit

philosophies—scientific, social, otherwise—to account for
the flesh-and-blood predicament. Powell realizes how
close eccentrics can come to riding a liberating fancy to
the ground and pinning the human beneath the abstract. Naturally, Conyers' passion for amateur psycho-
analysis is less extravagant at eighty than Erridge's
obsession with professional causes at thirty. With
Erridge, alienation from all *but* "causes" paradoxically
marks him as one "spending much of his time in boredom and loneliness, yet in some way inhibited from
taking in anything relevant about other people." Carried aloft on the utopianism of the period, he dreams of
crusades abroad, ironically immune to the friction of his
own domestic situation. Cozened and cheated by his
dipsomaniac butler, plagued and teased by innumerable
sisters, badgered and solicited by Quiggin, cajoled and
vamped by Mona—he closes down his estate and bolts
for China and another cause. Erridge's "escape" into
action is of the same quality as the General's, if at
different intensity.

Although Conyers and Erridge emerge as memorable
representatives in the flourishing tradition of English
eccentrics, they are interwoven in the sequence's overall
pattern. Operating outside the norm they are barriers to
the narrow disciplines of broad conventions; being men
of will as well, they are foils for men like Quiggin and
Widmerpool who seek mastery over everything, including the imagination. Circumspect of absolute successes,
antipathetic toward restraint, at times even incredulous
of their own controlling influence, such eccentrics
inadvertently acknowledge a fallibility in themselves
while uncovering that in their symbolic counterparts.
Erridge's compulsive flight abroad with Mona reflects a
loosening of Quiggin's hold. And Conyers' indelicate
discovery of Widmerpool's impotence brings to light

Widmerpool's most crushing reversal since he paid for Gypsy's abortion. Such is the energy of eccentricity that can counter, however briefly, the forces of power.

Quiggin's reversal is dramatic but predictable. His relationship with Mona has appreciably deteriorated during the brief time they have been together. The charming isolation of their cottage outside London only heightens its occupants' forced retreat. Their nerves are frayed and their sensibilities ragged. Living with a radical journalist has lost much of its novelty for Mona. The kind of woman who thrives on variety, she has gone to seed without it, looks sloppy, flaccid, and even a trifle sluttish.

Quiggin, however, whether swayed by Mona's sexuality or, more mysteriously, the "hidden force" of her firm, ruthless personality, still senses her domination. Being flattered that she should prefer him to Peter Templer does not, however, make him any more adept at handling her. Mona craves whimsy, and Quiggin is not a whimsical man. Perhaps, as Nick perceives, naïveté and sophistication combined prompt Quiggin's encouragement of Mona's sudden desire for a career in films. The idea, at least, sustains her and relieves the boredom, however temporarily. Of course, Quiggin—the man driven by will—seldom experiences boredom and is therefore the natural antithesis of his mistress. Wrapped up in his writing, the pure professional engaged in his trade or pulling strings to further it, he is always stimulated, though not stimulating.

Nor is he sufficiently wealthy for Mona, who has been spoiled by Templer and still demands occasional "treats." Absorption in dozens of literary ventures has not swelled his pocketbook by much. Quiggin is not above cutting corners by living rent-free on Erridge's estate, nor above exploiting his bank account. Alternately urging and relaxing his principles, Quiggin, always alert, considers scruples as something flexible. He is, after all, a seeker after power. That he is hoisted with his own petard furthers the irony. Who is exploited by whom—Erridge by Quiggin, Quiggin by Erridge, both by Mona—is hardly comic if taken as a struggle between revolutionary and aristocrat, but the situation is violently so when seen as a kind of reel danced by the man of will, the eccentric, and the sensualist.

Quiggin in love is amusing, but the comedy is Erridge's; Widmerpool in love is ludicrous and the comedy is all his. As the saint, when he embraces temptation, falls body and soul, the man of will yields as completely to the emotion he has supposedly overcome. Love (as he construes it) is Widmerpool's undoing (at least for a while). One expects him to be impotent—the impotency of the man of will is so thoroughly Nietzschean—yet Powell makes no heavy work as he moves toward the crucial revelation; it is comedy all the way.

Widmerpool makes his first appearance in the novel netted by love. Looking like "a fish made of rubber or some artificial substance," he sails with his fascinating fiancée, Mildred Haycock, the sister-in-law of General Conyers, into the Jeavonses' drawing room while one of Molly's parties is in high gear. He strikes one as being obviously ill at ease at the thought of having relaxed his will, especially for a woman. Nick recalls those memorable fiascos involving Barbara Goring and Gypsy Jones, Widmerpool's monkish avowal that "he would never again have anything to do with a woman who 'took his mind off his work,' " and dubiously considers the "tall, elegant, brassy," fast, terribly competent, and highly experienced Mildred.

Widmerpool is never more comic than when he takes himself seriously, which he does at his tête-à-tête with Nick. The backdrop at Widmerpool's exclusive club provides the setting for a dialogue reflecting his poverty of imagination and lack of appetite for matters of love. Dining on "cold tongue and a glass of water," he eases Nick into the role of confidant and gradually forces him into that of counselor regarding the advisability of pre-marital relations. Hemming, hawing, and hedging, Widmerpool finally gets down to cases:

> "I should not wish to appear backward in display of affection . . . merely because certain legal and religious formalities take time to arrange. In short, Nicholas, you will, I am sure, agree . . . that it would be permissible on my part to suppose—once the day of the wedding has been fixed—that we might—occasionally enjoy each other's company—say, over a weekend——"
> He came to a sudden stop, looking at me rather wildly.
> "I don't see why not. . . ."
> "In fact my fiancée—Mildred, that is—might even expect such a suggestion?"
> "Well, yes, from what you say."
> "Might even regard it as *usage du monde?*"
> "Quite possible." (*LM*, 60)

Widmerpool, despite Nick's advice, never has the chance of attacking the problem. Shortly after this interview he is seized with an acute, almost symbolic, hepatitis: a malaise caused as much by fear as frustration, and perhaps contributing the physical factor to an impotence that evolves pretty much psychologically.

So, it seems, General Conyers feels. Widmerpool has his opportunity with Mildred and botches it miserably, although the comedy is played offstage with classic composure. The events filter through the detached eye of Conyers, whose undue interest in things sexual heightens the comedy. Embalmed in the fantasy of his own psychological research, he invites Nick into clinical confidences:

> "It seems to me . . . that [Widmerpool] is a typical intuitive extrovert—classical case almost. Cold-blooded. Keen on a thing for a moment, but never satisfied. Wants to get on to something else. . . . That's the category in which I'd place him. . . . No use denying subjective emotions. Just as well to face the fact. All of us got a lot of egoism and infantilism to work off." (*LM*, 230-33)

The General's psychological diagnosis occurs at Nick's engagement party and is so placed for maximum comic effect. A young man contemplating marriage hardly wishes to explore a friend's impotency, even though he has no particular fears on the subject. Apart from being comic, the scene is thematically crucial. Being engaged, Nick is neither fish nor fowl. He dangles between the impressionableness and irresponsibility of his colleague Chips Lovell (Nick as he was in *The Acceptance World*), and the disappointments of Widmerpool and Quiggin, who may have failed in settling down. Fears about marriage may seem justified where few marriages have succeeded. Eccentricity has saved the General's marriage, but then it is not possible for everyone to cultivate eccentricity. Conyers' pronouncement that marriage, like war, is "not an exact science but a terrible and passionate drama" is less homiletic than his ex cathedra analysis of Widmerpool, and strikes Nick as more significant:

> Marriage was a subject upon which it was hard to obtain accurate information. Its secrets, naturally, are those most jealously guarded; never more deeply concealed than when apparently most profusely exhibited in public. However true that might be, one could still be sure that even those marriages which seem outwardly dull enough are, at one time or another, full of the characteristics of which he spoke. (*LM*, 234)

Conversely, those that outwardly sparkle may be sham, drained of all passion. The refinement of these extremes, and the exploration of the range between them, is reserved for fuller treatment in *Casanova's Chinese Restaurant*. Here, the theme is adumbrated in the settling and unsettling aspects of Jeavons and Lady Molly's marriage.

It is difficult to dissociate Jeavons from Molly, and almost impossible to dissociate Molly from her parties. A Molly Jeavons gathering is one at which anything might happen, but upon closer inspection little happens at all. The social swirl into which one settles is busy without being productive and must be left behind for the world outside where things get done. The parties are points of beginning rather than of termination. People return to them changed, while Molly and Jeavons change very little. Engaged by their common activities, they are disengaged (as so many of Powell's couples are) by that "moral separateness"; yet they are vital. Something of a phenomenon in *The Music of Time,* they have reached an understanding—i.e., the acceptable deviation within the bounds of convention—of their marital roles. Despite many shortcomings, they become symbolic guides for Nick.

Molly's life is centered in her gatherings. A gaudy social butterfly, she flits from party to party, guest to guest, pollinating one idea, then another, alluring those by her brilliant array, ensnaring herself sometimes through excessive temerity. Molly finds relief from class stagnation by combining a raffish respectability with a temperate unconventionality:

> She had occupied a position many women must have envied, jogging along there for a dozen years without apparent dissatisfaction or a breath of scandal; then contentedly taking on an existence of such a very different

kind, hardly noticing the change. While married to [Lord
Sleaford] Molly remained a big, charming, noisy young
woman, who had never entirely ceased to be a schoolgirl.
When [that] frame was removed, [i.e., when she married
Jeavons] like the loosening of a corset of steel, the unconventional, the eccentric, even the sluttish side of her
nature became suddenly revealed to the world. (*LM,* 158-
59)

Ted Jeavons, too, has burst from the social chrysalis,
though to Molly's queenly butterfly he plays the squire
moth. (The analogy is explicit, in fact. Nick's first impression of Jeavons amidst the melee through which
Molly moves so easily is that of a man standing remote,
exhibiting "a vacant expression," looking like "some
rare insect enclosed in amber.") But Jeavons' servility is
superficial and his subservience an accommodating
sham.

In a way, he is no less competent than his wife, no less
exceptional, no less in control. Periodic pub-crawling,
for him, like partying for Molly, has become the outlet
for purging "too much domesticity." Actually, the
Jeavonses' actions are of a piece. Both as literal expressions of differing personalities, and as structural aspects
of the novel, they are well gauged, since each time of
release precedes one of Nick's revelations. Thematically,
Jeavons' monologue in Umfraville's club may be the
most significant. Less showy than the General's, less
comic than Widmerpool's, it is a more substantial treatment of the difficult normalities of marriage rather than
its anomalies; it is a balanced composite of the other
speeches:

"We've lost all our bloody illusions. Put 'em all in the
League of Nations, or somewhere like that. Illusions, my
God. I had a few of 'em when I started. You wouldn't
believe it. Of course, I've been lucky. Lucky isn't the
word, as a matter of fact. Still people always talk as if

marriage was one long roll in the hay. You can take it from me, my boy, it isn't. You'll be surprised when you get tied up to a woman yourself. Suppose I shouldn't say such things. Molly and I are very fond of each other in our own way. Between you and me, she's not a great one for bed. A chap I knew in the Ordnance, who'd carried on quite a bit with the girls, told me those noisy ones seldom are. Don't do much in that line myself nowadays, to tell the truth. Feel too cooked most of the time. Never sure the army vets got quite all those separate pieces of a toffee-apple out of my ribs. Tickles a bit sometimes. Still, you have to step out once in a way. Go melancholy mad, otherwise. Life's a rum business, however you look at it . . ." (*LM*, 178-79)

Nostalgia here verges on pathos; but all is comically righted when Jeavons discloses his brief affair with Mildred Haycock during a hospital leave in World War I. One commends him for having gotten Milly, fleers at Widmerpool for not; but perhaps approbation is really leveled at the art of chance as opposed to the artifice of calculation. Weak, mild, likable, ingenuous, Teddy Jeavons hasn't much left of his conquests save pieces of "toffee-apple" and the disillusionment of the depressingly sane; while Widmerpool, even in his defeat, brazens it out to the last:

"Curious how our situations have been reversed. You are getting married, while Mildred and I decided in the end it would be better not. We talked things over quietly, and came to the same conclusion. I think it was all for the best. She has returned to France. She prefers to live there. That was one of the bones of contention. Then, of course, there was also the disparity in age. Between you and me, I was not anxious to take on those two sons of hers. They sound an unsatisfactory couple. . . . You know, Nicholas, it is wise to take good advice about such a thing as marriage. I hope you have done so yourself. I have thought about the subject a good deal, and you are always welcome to my views." (*LM*, 238, 239)

So much of the truth has gone into the novel that one's sensibilities might be offended at having it end with so bald a lie, so blatant a bluff. But Widmerpool's rationalizations strike the correct, hollow note. His last-ditch attempt at raising the false front fails; and in the futility is the comedy, for Nick knows all. He knows, too, how thoroughly unsettling the business of settling down can be, knows what to expect of himself as well as of others. As always, he is left holding the "mixed-bag" of paradoxes and ironies; but he has now firmer mastery over the strings that open and close it. In *At Lady Molly's* the masks of relationships and marriages have been eased off; it is for *Casanova's Chinese Restaurant* to trace more deeply and darkly the faces that lie beneath them.

11

Casanova's
Chinese
Restaurant

Casanova's Chinese Restaurant is at once Powell's most restrained book and his most tragic. Its subject, simply stated, is marriage, but the theme is transformed into gloomy variations on infidelity, frustration, and failure, or played against a darker passacaglia of disintegration and death. Not since Poussin's painting has Powell formulated so complete an image that establishes a mood sustained to the very end.

> Crossing the road by the bombed-out public house on the corner and pondering the mystery which dominates vistas framed by a ruined door, I felt for some reason glad the place had not yet been rebuilt. A direct hit had excised even the ground floor, so that the basement was revealed as a sunken garden, or site of archaeological excavation long abandoned, where great sprays of willow herb and ragwort flowered through cracked paving stones; only a few broken milk bottles and a laceless boot recalling contemporary life. In the midst of this sombre grotto five

or six fractured steps had withstood the explosion and formed a projecting island of masonry on the summit of which rose the door. Walls on both sides were shrunk away, but along its lintel, in niggling copybook handwriting, could still be distinguished the word *Ladies*. Beyond, on the far side of the twin pillars and crossbar, nothing whatever remained of that promised retreat, the threshold falling steeply to an abyss of rubble; a triumphal arch erected laboriously by dwarfs, or the gateway to some unknown, forbidden domain, the lair of sorcerers. (*CCR*, 1)

Marriage and death comprise the objective world of *Casanova's Chinese Restaurant,* but ghosts haunt its ethos. The flesh-and-blood realm of *At Lady Molly's*—its party lights, brilliant eccentrics, comic relief—dissolve into the darkness of abandonment, the barrenness of the "abyss."

The novel is set in 1936-37, when the historic shadows of destruction are already lengthening. Events of the Spanish Revolution link the marshaling of furies in *The Kindly Ones,* the war itself in *The Valley of Bones*; Franco and the rape of Spain, Hitler and the fall of Czechoslovakia ordain the rubble and ruin of the blitzed restaurant that revives memories of a previous decade. But, as in all of Powell's work, global circumstance provides only the backdrop for personal tragedy. Ghosts of chaos and anarchy become incidentally important to the private, orderly ghosts summoned by Nicholas Jenkins.

Two such motifs underscore the major themes in *Casanova's Chinese Restaurant.* Powell's investigation of marriages evolves from conversational evenings in a grubby restaurant endowed with the name of the immortal libertine; and preoccupation with death and infidelity (figuratively the death of marriage) is suggested by associations with an amusement park operation called the Ghost Railway on which Nick and the composer Hugh Moreland rode in days of freedom and irresponsibility.

As an image, the railway is by far the more direct and self-contained. Its ghosts are specters of paradox. Crazily jerking through the erratic motions of a piece of vital, intricate machinery, the roller coaster is made analogous to the indeterminate, capricious, but somehow controlled functions of Nick's society,

> slowly climbing sheer gradients, sweeping with frenzied speed into inky depths, turning blind corners from which black, gibbering bogeys leapt to attack, rushing headlong towards iron-studded doors, threatened by imminent collision, fingered by spectral hands, moving at last with dreadful, ever increasing momentum towards a shape that lay across the line. (*CCR*, 229)

At the fun fair, the shape (grim as it may seem) is an illusion, a mechanism, whisked away at the last moment, forgotten. In life, as Moreland tells Nick, it can hardly be considered a phantasm of any sort:

> "Do you remember when we used to talk about the Ghost Railway and say how like everyday life it was—or at least one's own everyday life?"
> "You mean rushing downhill in total darkness and crashing through closed doors?"
> "Yes—and the body lying across the line. The Maclintick affair has reminded me of the disagreeable possibilities of the world one inhabits; the fact that the fewer persons one involves in it the better." (*CCR*, 219)

For Nick and Moreland, the Ghost Railway precipitously plunging toward some vague shape symbolizes their lives, the lives of their friends, and their generation.

Keyed slightly lower, but with a provocative range of possibilities, are the connotations supplied by the London restaurant, whose "Italian name, Chinese cuisine,

French décor, English waitresses and interracial clientele"[1] are admittedly curious, though far less curious in Soho than elsewhere. To take it as "a symbol of Powell's theme of cultural confusion," however, is too broadly critical, since the novel scarcely concerns "cultural confusion" at all, or only in the way that any piece of a fifty-year history might. Actually, Casanova is considerably more important than the restaurant, though evenings in the restaurant give rise to discussions of him. He is linked to Nick and Moreland's central dialogues on marriage: the first anticipating joy—their respective weddings; the second presaging sorrow—Maclintick's suicide. But implications go beyond this.

Marriage, as the theme of the novel, is bared, then dissected. Seen in all its anatomical unpleasantness, it is viewed as an omnipresent malady, basically confining, potentially tragic. From this the ironies begin unfolding. *Casanova's Chinese Restaurant*—centering on several bleak years of the thirties—becomes a disturbing treatise on modern marriage; the eponymous hero's memoirs comprise an entertaining portrait of a confident, optimistic age. Casanova's rogueries and amours, licentious but proper, calculating but naïve, launched blissfully on tides of irresponsible love, are implicitly juxtaposed with scuttled marriages. Bobbing about in uneasy seas, trying to stay afloat despite the tensions and banalities that can choke marriages, Nick's acquaintances are sorry, unheroic figures. Compared to Casanova they appear (when not ludicrous) pathetic; and their marriages, set against his conquests, seem (when not farcical) tragic.

---

1. *Time,* September 26, 1960, p. 108. Powell's title is disturbing, one must agree. It gets at what he wants, but it is misleading in tone. *Casanova's Chinese Restaurant* is an amusing title, but the book is not very funny at all.

For the sequence as a whole, Casanova thematically ties in with Powell's bolder design of illustrating the continuing conflict between men of will and men of imagination. Casanova belongs with the latter, quite obviously. Poised, easy, gracious, charming, he is the acme of libertinism, activated by simple passions and desires, perhaps even superior to his counterpart, Don Juan, who, neurotically compulsive, is actually bored by sex and looks upon it as a mere outlet for domination and control. Moreland, in discussing marriage and sex with Nick, differentiates the two by placing them over their lowest common denominator—love:

> "But Don Juan was not at all the same as Casanova. . . . The opera makes that quite clear. . . . Don Juan merely liked power. . . . He obviously did not know what sensuality was. If he knew it at all, he hated it. Casanova, on the other hand, undoubtedly had his sensual moments, even though they may not have occurred very often. . . . No doubt he ended as a complete Narcissus, when love naturally became intolerable to him, since love involved him with another party emotionally." (*CCR*, 34-35)

Moreland's observations are just, but incomplete. Casanova represents the sensual, potentially narcissistic man in a novel crowded with narcissistic, potentially sensual men. Again, having risen to the top of his profession—the art of seduction—he becomes the image of success, holding up a mirror to failure. *Casanova's Chinese Restaurant* keynotes failures; few escape serious reversals, professionally or personally. Disappointment and nonfulfillment troubling the reflection make Casanova's successes an ironic running commentary on the novel's themes. He fits in, but not for what he was—rather for what he wasn't.

These two motifs of the Ghost Railway and "the lascivious Venetian" are stated in the first chapter, a fresh recapitulation of the years 1929-36, the time covered by *The Acceptance World* and *At Lady Molly's*. The cast of characters has again changed, as well as the milieu. At Casanova's one is introduced to a cross section of the musical population: Maclintick, the musicologist, Gossage, the critic, the intransigent Carolo (a violinist who began his career as boy-genius and never quite evolved into man-genius), and Hugh Moreland, a young composer of promise. Nick, a friend of Moreland, finds himself on the periphery, professionally alien, until marriage draws him toward the center and uncomfortably involves him with the recurrent marital problems of his acquaintances.

Fittingly, music leads Nick and the reader into the novel. Even as memories, stirred by visions of the bombed-out pub, begin shaping in Nick's mind, more complex associations are generated by the coincidental, almost magical song,

> strong and marvellously sweet, of the blonde woman on crutches, that itinerant prima donna of the highways whose voice I had not heard since the day, years before, when Moreland and I had listened in Garrard Street the afternoon he had talked of getting married. (*CCR*, 1)

These sudden strains are at once an evocation of the past and a resolution. The crippled singer becomes an apt correlative for a novel treating the crippled lives of musicians; her song—a languorous, sentimental tale of lotus-eating narcosis, recounting escape, warmth, quiescence, beauty, exoticism—an ironic contrast to the circumscribed, cold, prosaic world of marriage.

In itself, however, there is nothing ironic about the opening section of *Casanova's Chinese Restaurant*. Marriage is not yet considered the bugaboo it is to become. And freedom, youth, art—everything apart from marriage—*are* exotic. Casanova and the street singer's song are now the realities; the spectral puppets of the future have not been set in motion. But outlooks change after marriage has become an accomplished fact. The thematic textures and tonal patterns of Powell's manual become increasingly complex as harmonious relationships are transformed—perhaps as a further extension of the musical motif—into atonal and dissonant ones. With direct insights into Nick's life and the lives of others, Powell shifts from the bold major opening of Chapter 1 into a relative minor key.

While not a striking example, Nick's own marital status is a case in point. (Actually, in the course of the novel little space is devoted to Nick's wife, Isobel Tolland. She weds offstage on one page and is convalescing from a miscarriage several pages later.) Powell's refining the Jenkinses out of the picture is less awkward than it might seem, and, for his method, an actual necessity. As a neutral agent who narrates character and impressions rather than actions, Nick must seem knowledgeable, yet uninvolved. Still a bit uncomfortable in his double role as husband and member of the Tolland family, always seeking the pattern that lends meaning to new experiences, he carefully assesses the Sunday gatherings at his mother-in-law's: for what they offer in themselves, and for what they display as "a kind of parade of different approaches to marriage."

Lady Warminster's "at homes" are rather different from Lady Molly's parties: certainly more sobering, if not more instructive. The "lack of exhilaration" about the house at Hyde Park, the "quiet, almost despondent . . . note" are forcibly contrasted with the atmosphere at the Jeavonses' and in keeping with the subdued tone of the novel. Oddly enough, the focus of conversation is surprisingly similar. Erridge, owing to his eccentricity and improprieties, still provokes speculation, though his return from China and subsequent scheme for going to Spain excite less interest than his dropping of Mona: quite reasonably, Erridge's death would prove far less provocative than a bad marriage.

Then there is the matter of George Tolland. A man who has lived by the creed "I can never see the objection to being a snob" would seem a predictable barometer of actions. One remembers George as the constant butt of his Aunt Molly, whose icy wit solidifies his snobbery:

> "What a correct young man—*what a correct young man!* I don't think I ever met a young man who was so correct. I can't see how we are ever going to get him married, he is so correct—and even if we found a correct wife for him, I am sure they would both be much too correct to have any children. And even if they did, what frightfully correct children they would have to be." (*LM*, 35)

George thwarts all expectations and wriggles free from so strict and devastating a definition by marrying a divorcée, a warm, earthy creature, and nestling comfortably under her thumb.

By contrast, Roddy Cutts, M. P., and his wife, Susan Tolland—a couple superficially alluring—turn out smug, pallid, objectionable. Their marriage, a predictable affair so far as class is concerned, has ostensible deficiencies compensated for by the ambitious drives of both parties. Nick finds his brother-in-law formidable, as a home, king, and country man, and finds his sister-in-law beautiful; and class and beauty work hand in glove for the advancement of each other.

The marriages of Cutts and Tolland seem, in the long run, tranquil, composed, solid, even happy. Nick is partially convinced (after these Sunday get-togethers) that however disappointing wedlock is in particulars, it is salutary in general. Without embracing the doctrine

that any marriage is better than none at all, Jenkins
nearly takes the position that no marriage lacks redeeming features, but he pulls himself up short before
committing the blunder. Surfaces are fine, but is one by
now not rightly suspicious of surfaces? If so exacting a
type as Roddy, so simple a soul as George—members of
an intimate family circle—have proved how wrong hasty
conclusions can be, how difficult to resolve complex relationships!

> A future marriage, or a past one, may be investigated and
> explained in terms of writing by one of its parties, but it
> is doubtful whether an existing marriage can ever be
> described directly in the first person and convey a sense
> of reality. . . . To think at all objectively about one's
> own marriage is impossible, while a balanced view of
> other people's marriage is almost equally hard to achieve
> with so much information available, so little to be be-
> lieved. Objectivity is not, of course, everything in writing;
> but even casting objectivity aside, the difficulties of pre-
> senting marriage are inordinate. Its forms are at once so
> varied, yet so constant, providing a kaleidoscope, the
> colours of which are always changing, always the same.
> The moods of a love affair, the contradictions of friend-
> ship, the jealousy of business partners, the fellow feeling
> of opposed commanders in total war, these are all in
> their way to be charted. Marriage, partaking of such—and
> a thousand more—dual antagonisms and participations,
> finally defies definition. (*CCR*, 97)

Despite such protests, the second half of the novel is
given over to a scrupulous attempt at definition; and, as
Nick soon discovers, exposure outside Hyde Park proves
illuminating and painful. Picking up again with Moreland and Maclintick after a year's lapse provides repeated occasions for scrutiny. Burdened somewhat by
conventional responsibilities, the composer has grown
noticeably disenchanted with wedlock and increasingly
depressed by reversals; the critic has found the normal

run of rows transformed into agonies. Both marriages are soon careening toward the rocks. Personal and artistic success redeem Moreland's, as he navigates to safety; Maclintick's failures wreck his, though the relationship founders long before. Anatomizing marriage, Powell also analyzes the men, building their character, their respective ruin and reconstruction, upon the favorite cornerstones of heredity and environment. Separately, in juxtaposition, Moreland and Maclintick (as man and as husband) are Powell's fullest studies of the creative and assimilative personality.

Moreland's innate genius was fostered by upbringing. He had heard from a musical uncle "famous men discussed on familiar terms; not merely prodigies read of in books, but also persons having to knock about the world like everyone else." As a consequence, his temperament developed into something both practical and ethereal, the cause of emotional dissonance. When Nick first meets him, he is having difficulties with women.

> Women found him amusing, were intrigued by his unusual appearance and untidy clothes, heard that he was brilliant, so naturally he had his "successes"; but these, on the whole, were ladies with too desperate an enthusiasm for music. Moreland did not care for that. . . . he remained a hopeless addict of what he used to call, in the phrase of the day, a "*princesse lointaine* complex." This approach naturally involved him in falling in love with women connected in one way or another with the theatre. (*CCR*, 8)

The pursuit of Matilda Wilson—an actress, and former mistress of Magnus Donners—strikes no one as sensible, Nick least of all. Shaggy, masculine, Moreland cuts an awkward figure as a wistful, whistling, stage-door-johnny, prowling among theatrical girlies and primping homosexuals. Matilda, too, seems an unlikely complement to the composer. Gay, fast, clever, thoroughly "theatrical," she and her crowd clash violently with Moreland. One is steeled against another Mona Templer. But appearances deceive. At bottom, Matilda is alert, sober, capable, domineering in the pleasantest of ways. She takes over Moreland while letting him remain master; she is his equal in most ways, superior in her sense of social amenities, her poise, her overall balance and control—the very things with which his excessive romanticism is at odds. Withal, Nick comes round to the conclusion that the enterprising Matilda possesses "ideal, even miraculous, qualifications for becoming [Moreland's] wife."

Moreland's qualifications prove less satisfactory. His sensible theorizing about marriage ("I am going to marry. . . . Otherwise I shall become just another of those depressed and depressing intellectual figures who wander from party to party, finding increasing difficulty in getting on with anyone.") is upset by its *Realpolitik*. It is the "business" of marriage that especially depresses Moreland, makes him feel he is sometimes "going off" his head. The death of his infant daughter, his wife's severe illness, a bout with a recurring lung disorder, the lack of commissions do not assuage the feeling. "Everything went wrong," Nick says. The business and responsibility of marriage far outweigh its past novelty. Despite protestations that he is not some pre-Raphaelite Bohemian but "the sane Englishman with his pipe," Moreland demands novelty, and before quite realizing it he becomes involved with Nick's sister-in-law, Priscilla Tolland.

Symbolically, however, Moreland's greatest entanglement is with the times. His crisis develops throughout 1936 and parallels the events leading to the Abdication. While the Duke of Windsor's case is not precisely Moreland's own, it has compelling affinities: the loosing—one dislikes calling it the "evading"—of wider responsibilities for personal fulfillment, the break with tradition, the sacrifice of duty to love. Expressing the fear that news of the Abdication might overshadow the première of his symphony, Moreland ironically records more than general discontent:

> "Isn't this just my luck?" he said. "Now nobody is going to listen to music, look at a picture, or read a book, for months on end. We can all settle down happily to discussions every evening about Love and Duty."
> "Fascinating subjects."
> "They are in one's own life. Less so, where others are concerned."
> "You speak with feeling."
> "Do I? Just my naturally vehement way of expressing myself." (*CCR,* 137)

Soon after, his symphony is performed and he is embrangled with Priscilla. Conflicts over "love" and "duty" are removed from theory and made part of the messy clichés of marriage.

Most profoundly affected by Moreland's philandering is Matilda, who, in a levelheaded way that is quite maddening, pinpoints the besetting disillusion of most marriages. Some ugly differences between the Maclinticks—publicly aired at the party celebrating the première—provoke her sensitive dialogue with Nick:

> "They should lay off for an hour or two on occasions like this," [Nick said]. "A short rest would renew their energies for starting again when they return home."
> "That is just married life."
> "To be married to either of the Maclinticks cannot be much fun."
> "Is it fun to be married to anyone?"
> "That is rather a big question. If you admit that fun exists at all—perhaps you don't—you cannot lay it down

categorically that no married people get any fun from the state of being married."

"But I mean *married* to someone," said Matilda, speaking quite passionately. "Not to sleep with them, or talk to them, or go about with them. To be *married* to them." (*CCR*, 157)

That she is qualified as an authority Nick surmises; how qualified surprises him. Knowledge of Matilda's checkered career and her being kept by Donners complements the revelation of a previous marriage to the shadowy, dour Carolo. Her divorce picks up the thread of the Abdication motif. Previously seen as a factor of disintegration, divorce now seems acceptable on certain terms. As a bilateral agreement between parties, it may offer particular salvation at the risk of undermining institutions. But, Powell asks, which is more important, the individual or the marriage? Matilda "saves" Moreland; Audrey, in a grimmer way, Carolo. Mona, Peter Templer, Charles Stringham go to seed after their divorces; Maclintick commits suicide contemplating his. Standards are ambiguous, values suspect, results paradoxical. The independent dramas enacted in *Casanova's Chinese Restaurant* and the Abdication are of a piece with *Tosca, Turandot, Tamburlaine, The Duchess of Malfi*—works casually but significantly alluded to throughout the novel. All are studies in the universal conflict of love and duty, and its unsatisfactory, generally tragic unilateral solution.

Tragedy, diverted in Moreland's case, becomes imminent in Maclintick's. Heredity has played the critic false, endowing him with neither talent nor looks; environment forces him to brood about it. "Bad-tempered" without a redeeming charm, "grumpy" without a compensatory sagacity, "disapproving" without a vindicating productivity, he moves toward a dead end. Maclintick's unimaginativeness and "a congenital lack of amiability" make his ungrudging, unalloyed veneration of Moreland seem more painful and practically masochistic. He is drawn to Moreland, whose character, genius, probable fame are searing reminders of the critic's own deficiencies, for Maclintick is a dejected, disappointed, defeated person: plagued by a melancholic temperament, frustrated by a sterile occupation, destroyed first by an execrable marriage, then his own hand.

Not until the day before his suicide does Maclintick detail the circumstances involved with the most ruinous step of his life. By then, Nick is prepared to accept the grim truth that from passion, understanding, sympathy, and love something as destructive as marriage can be born.

But Jenkins has sensed much of this on his first visit to the Maclinticks. Though primed by Moreland to expect a strained atmosphere in a strange household, Nick can't shrug off a profounder feeling of uneasiness. Forebodings become manifest even as he and Moreland pass through the critic's forbidding section of London:

> We . . . passed on foot into a vast, desolate region of stucco streets and squares upon which a doom seemed to have fallen. The gloom was cosmic. We traversed these pavements for some distance, proceeding from haunts of seedy, grudging gentility into an area of indeterminate, but on the whole increasingly unsavoury, complexion. (*CCR*, 106)

The landscape is of course symbolic of Nick's state of mind on the one hand, and of the Maclintick's situation on the other. As the opening description of the blitzed restaurant occasions a flashback, the setting here previews destruction. In the scenes dealing with the Maclinticks, Powell's writing often reaches its finest and fiercest pitch. His probings into the tortured personalities of the couple comprise the most thorough analysis of marriage in *The Music of Time,* and perhaps in contemporary literature.

Opposed physically and temperamentally, Maclintick and his wife cannot be expected to come up with a satisfactory solution to differences that are assignable to no one thing. Certainly Powell sees cause and effect as indivisible agents of marital upheavals. Audrey is simple, restless, passionate, ignored; Maclintick is cold, discontented, troubled in other ways. Drinking and whoring satisfy his masochistic tendencies, but only indulge the other weaknesses that legitimately account for failure. Forever at work on a tome of musical criticism that seems as much a mechanism of escape as a labor of dedicated scholarship, he suffers a paralysis and a predictable obscurity. For Maclintick, one is contingent upon the other, and both develop from his morbid pursuit of isolation. Neither unsalutary nor damning in general, isolation becomes devastating when it involves others. Married, Maclintick hastens toward a destruction which, if single, he might have avoided. That "quite separate entity" known as marriage rises impervious between him and his wife, cutting them off from each other, making their isolation more complete and more terrible.

To realize that marriage is based on a paradox—that forces of unification are also forces of separation—is the first step toward its preservation. Chipping away at the weaknesses in that barrier becomes the sole way that marriage can be made durable and not unbearable. Moreland and Matilda seek the loose stone in the wall, Maclintick and Audrey the chink in one another's armor. Audrey's baiting her husband at the party for Moreland ("Do take your hands out of your pockets. . . . You always stand about everywhere as if you were in a public bar.''); her denigrating him ("I told him he was standing about as if he was in the Nag's Head. That is a pub near us where all the tarts go."); and ultimately her twisting his evaluation of Moreland's symphony ("What did you think of [it]? . . . Not much of a success Maclintick thinks."), all drive Maclintick to an uncontrollable, public declamation:

> "I didn't say anything of the sort, you bloody bitch," Maclintick said, "so keep your foul mouth shut and don't go round repeating that I did, unless you want to get hurt. It is just like your spite to misrepresent me in that manner. You are always trying to make trouble between Moreland and myself, aren't you? What I said was that the music was 'not Moreland's most adventurous'—that the critics had got used to him as an *enfant terrible* and therefore might underestimate the symphony's true value. That was all. That was what I said. You know yourself that was all. You know yourself that was what I said."
> Maclintick was hoarse with fury. His hands were shaking. His anger made him quite alarming. (*CCR*, 150-52)

Maclintick's loss of such chances for catharsis marks his decline. When Audrey at last flees with Carolo—her flirtation at the party with Stringham perhaps a foreshadowing of this ultimate decision—all the fight is taken out of him. Once sustained by hatred for his wife, Maclintick goes quietly, insidiously to pieces without it. Lying in his sordid, smelly rooms, having rambled on about his present freedom, reviewed (now nostalgically, now philosophically) his past relationship with Audrey, grown progressively drunker and more confessional, Maclintick plays with Nick and Moreland a scene that moves toward a final, terrible, nihilistic statement:

> "We'll have to go," [said Moreland.]
> "You don't expect me to see you out, do you? Kind of you to come."
> "You had better go to bed, Maclintick," said Moreland.

"You don't want to spend the night on the sofa."

"Why not?"

"Too cold. The fire will be out soon."

"I'll be all right."

"Do move, Maclintick," said Moreland.

He stood looking down with hesitation at Maclintick. . . . I remembered the scene when Widmerpool and I had put Stringham to bed after the Old Boy Dinner, and wondered whether an even odder version of that operation was to be re-enacted here. However, Maclintick rolled himself over into a sitting position, removed his spectacles, and began to rub his eyes . . .

"Perhaps you are right, Moreland," Maclintick said.

"Certainly I am right."

"I will move if you insist."

"I do insist."

Then Maclintick made that harrowing remark that established throughout all eternity his relationship with Moreland.

"I obey you, Moreland," he said, "with the proper respect of the poor interpretative hack for the true creative artist."

Moreland and I both laughed a lot, but it was a horrible moment. Maclintick had spoken with that strange, unearthly dignity that a drunk man can suddenly assume. (*CCR,* 214-15)

Memory, compulsively and logically, links Maclintick with Stringham, whose appearance at his mother's party only several months before had filled Nick with a "pang of horror." On the dole from his mother and Buster Foxe, discussed by them "as if he had been put away from view like a person suffering from a horrible, unmentionable disease, or become some terrifying legendary figure," Stringham, a dipsomaniac, having totally capitulated to his weakness, lives a self-imposed imprisonment under Tuffy Weedon. Miss Weedon's love for Stringham—for "love" it is, even so perversely disguised—binds her to him in a kind of pseudo-

wedlock, overpowers him. Slipping gradually into helplessness and impotency, Stringham, like Maclintick,
becomes the victim of his own isolation and masochism,
seems, in effect, to be slowly dying. Maclintick's suicide
is only the dramatic extension of the Stringham case.
Given his values, the temperament of Audrey, and the
potentially destructive powers of marriage, it is totally
explicable. Certain movements, as Nick comes to realize,
are unalterable, certain chances for survival unrealistic.
Thus, though faith is shaken, it is not annihilated; faith
based on reason, even on tragic recognition, is the most
secure trust. Here, death provides faith's logic.

And, less paradoxically or abstractly, death provides
positive conclusions. Often, it may correct life's un-
avoidable faults better than life ever could. Ironically,
the dead Maclintick, having made such a botch of his
own career and marriage, saves those of his friend:

> Maclintick, in doing away with himself, had drawn atten-
> tion, indeed heavily underlined, the conditions of life to
> which Moreland was inexorably committed. . . . I think
> Moreland's realization was in the fact of Maclintick's
> desperate condition; Maclintick's inability to regulate his
> own emotional life; Maclintick's lack of success as a mu-
> sician; in short the mess of things Maclintick had made,
> or perhaps had had visited upon him. Moreland was
> probably the only human being Maclintick had whole-
> heartedly liked. In return, Moreland had liked Maclin-
> tick; liked his intelligence; liked talking and drinking
> with him. By taking his own life, Maclintick had brought
> about a crisis in Moreland's life too. He had ended the
> triangular relationship between Moreland, Priscilla, and
> Matilda. Precisely in what that relationship consisted re-
> mained unrevealed. What Matilda thought, what Priscilla
> thought, remained a mystery. All sides of such a situation
> are seldom shown at once, even if they are shown at all.
> Only one thing was certain. Love had received one of
> those shattering jolts to which it is peculiarly vulnerable
> from extraneous circumstances. (*CCR,* 220-21)

To find any particular moral implied in Nick's last statement would detract from its universality. Everything, everyone, is vulnerable to "extraneous circumstances." Precisely because fate directs the actors, the human comedy revives unstaled. Life "jolts" along: capricious, chancy, yet somehow suitably patterned. Significantly, *Casanova's Chinese Restaurant* ends with the surprise announcement of Chips Lovell's engagement to Priscilla Tolland. Auguring marriage, perhaps even happiness, the novel has come full circle. Though the hoarse, hollow, ironic laugh of Casanova seems to reverberate as the Ghost Railway hurtles into the dark future, fate may yet fulfill illusion, and, like the magical mechanism in the amusement park, resurrect at the right moment the "shape [lying] across the line."

12

The
Kindly
Ones

Three-quarters through *The Kindly
Ones,* Nick travels to the small, bleak seaside resort
where Giles has died in order to complete arrangements
for his cremation. It is the summer of 1939: oppressively
hot, fearful, tense. Looming large, war hovers over Europe like the blade of a guillotine. But neither the
finality of death nor the incipience of war long preoc-
cupy Nick on his mission. The major force is the past,
which, permutable, evasive, protean, refuses to be
shaped and continually surprises. At a chance encounter
with Bob Duport in the resort town, Nick is button-
holed into listening to intimate details of Jean's past
excesses, in particular her affair with Jimmy Stripling.
Justifiably uncomfortable in posing as bright-eyed confidant to his ex-mistress's ex-husband, Nick stifles any
awkward reaction and ruminates on the dead past with
interested disinterest:

I well remembered the frightful moment when Jean herself had first informed me, quite gratuitously, of having
undergone the experience to which Duport referred. I
could recall even now how painful that information had
been at the time, as one might remember a physical
accident long passed. The matter no longer worried me,
primarily because I no longer loved Jean, also because
the whole Stripling question had, so to speak, been resolved between Jean and myself at the time. All the
same, the incident had been a disagreeable one. . . .
However, present recital could in no way affect the past.
That was history. (*KO*, 175-76)

This cocksureness is undermined immediately. As
Duport begins turning up a variety of lovers, Nick
imagines he himself will be presently discovered. The
irony that he is not is a fine jest on Duport, who hasn't
the least notion of his former wife's most flagrant esca-
pade. But the greater irony has been reserved for Nick.
Far from being a collection of settled, dead, and buried
"facts," history becomes a parody on facts, a shocking
reality, for Jenkins learns that while he was Jean's lover,
she was secretly seeing Jimmy Brent, and perhaps others. That Nick now finds himself merely one link in the
chain is a blow to his pride; history, created anew, generates hubris:

I thought of the grave, gothic beauty that once I had
loved so much, which found fulfilment in such men. . . .
If her lovers were horrifying, I too had been of their
order. That had to be admitted. . . . For the moment,
angry, yet at the same time half-inclined to laugh, I could
not make up my mind what I thought. This was yet another example of the tricks that Time can play within
its own folds, tricks that emphasise the insecurity of those
who trust themselves over much to that treacherous concept. I suddenly found what I had regarded as immutable
—the not entirely unsublime past—roughly reshaped by
the rude hands of Duport. That was justice, I thought, if
you like. (*KO*, 180-81)

Here, and throughout the novel, Nick is caught between the ordering forces of justice and time: justice,
not predicated on the moral premises of retribution, but
attuned to the classical principles of harmony, broadly
social, fundamentally poetic; time, the substance and
essence of historical order, allied to the shifting lines of
history which are cyclical and finite, parallel and infi-
nite. These two ideas gradually fuse as Nick is transplanted from childhood during the First World War to
manhood and maturity in the early weeks of the Second.

The theme of *The Kindly Ones*—the regaining of an
historic perspective which enables one to revaluate the
fluctuating social order and function within it—plays
back and forth between these two periods, separated by
twenty-five years but linked by their corresponding values. Conscious of this interplay, realizing that the end of
one war and the beginning of another have marked
crucial stages in his development, Nick would impart a
justness to the contingencies and consequences of history, or seek an historic justice in things that have tran-
spired. Carrying Jenkins forward once again, the novel
may immediately reflect little more than variations on
the hero's continuing search for patterns in life and society. But as the last volume in the second trilogy of
The Music of Time, capping several decades, it tran-
scends Nick's plight and becomes most closely connected
with the theme of history itself.

Powell gains historic continuity between the first long
chapter of the novel (focusing on 1914), and the latter
three chapters (covering 1938-39) through a linking
motif of the Furies: crones of destruction who terrorized
under the name Erinye ("the angry ones") and were
propitiated by being euphemistically called Eumenides
("the kindly ones"). The contemporary mythic importance of the Furies is self-evident. O'Neill and Eliot

evised the old myths, made them new, and, like Aeschylus, kept them morally relevant. Yet the symbolic relevance of the Furies for the fifth century differs from that for the twentieth, quite as naturally as Orestes differs from Orin Mannon and Harry Monchensey. If the three playwrights have anything at all in common it is their insistence on the literal interpretation of the symbol, and the fact that in each of the plays the problems belong more to the maddened hero than to the dramatist.

This mythic view of history enables the artist somehow to slip free if he chooses; the *historic* view of history does not. Powell subscribes to the latter: analytic rather than intuitive, realistic rather than impressionistic, and of course comic rather than tragic, he sends *his* Orestes to ferret out the Furies and the problems of society—not the abstractions behind them. Looking backward on one war, forward to another, Jenkins gains several perspectives at once, sees the Furies in a light which accords them power but denies them reverence. Double vision makes the metaphor of the novel ironic as well as symbolic. If history must repeat itself, the Eumenides really *are* kindly. One may convert the shadows of the past into the substance of future action.

The shadows, long in the extreme, touch at more points than either fate or history might have predicted. At his home, Stonehurst, in 1914, Nick first learns of the Furies via a lesson in classical mythology. As avenging deities, "bringing in their train war, pestilence, dissension on earth," they are to be presently translated into storm petrels of World War I, though the young Nick and his schoolmates, his family, peripheral relations, friends, and servants only mildly anticipate so thorough a disaster. Days at Stonehurst are halcyon, happy, irresponsible, when goddesses menace in textbooks only,

when personal irritation and confusion are reflected in
the inconvenient arrival of Giles wishing to discuss the
Trust; in Albert the cook's leaving to marry; in the
advent of Billson, the maid, naked in the drawing
room; in the awkward proximity of an eccentric theoso-
phist's colony.

Such are the few ripples on the generally tranquil
surface. But Nick senses that below the calm move continual undercurrents, subtler in a way, and fiercer: the
very private furies of the individual mind. Long before
they are "precursors of fire and destruction," the
Eumenides symbolize an almost indefinable apprehen-
siveness mingling with the well-being and Georgian
optimism prevalent at Stonehurst. Albert's nightly closing of the shutters against local suffragettes, or "Virgin
Marys" as he calls them (a name reflecting his own
limited misogyny, his distrust of marriage and female
domination), the soldier-servant Bracey's "funny days"
(periods of melancholia and agitation related to his
unrequited love for Billson), her obsession with Stonehurst's "ghosts" (a sexual frustration of the most obvious order), "Dr. Trelawney's place," the center of his
fashionable occultism (like Yeats's, an attempt to
impose mythical order upon chaos and to save the intellectual élite)—all are reflections of uneasy states of
mind, all euphemisms to propitiate the Furies of conscience.

But the times work against propitiation. At the peak
of tense optimism, Europe now begins its descent into
holocaust, exploding all hopes of imaginative solutions
to problems of power. Indeed, *The Kindly Ones,* which
deals with the beginnings of the two "great" wars, expands Powell's favorite theme globally, suggesting perhaps that power ultimately destroys not only the body,
but the body politic. Something of this is recalled by

Nick in recounting a curious impression at Stonehurst:

> Once, we saw Dr. Trelawney and his flock roaming through the scrub at the same moment as the Military Policeman on his patrol was riding back from the opposite direction. The sun was setting. This meeting and merging of two elements—two ways of life—made a striking contrast in physical appearance, moral ideas, and visual tone-values. (*KO*, 29)

"Two ways of life"—the way of the will, the way of the imagination—are irreconcilable. Pawns in a game more disastrous and terrible than the mere pricking of conscience, the Furies cannot be propitiated. War ensues, the imaginative way out crushed by the willful way in and by the finality of it all. "Childhood," Nick says, "was brought suddenly, even rather brutally, to a close. Albert's shutters may have kept out the suffragettes: they did not effectively exclude the Furies."

In the rapid shift from Nick's past at Stonehurst to his present in London the symbolic momentarily becomes literal. The private consciences and methods of appeasement of 1914 are now the collective conscience and method of 1938. Chamberlain, the embodiment of the Choephori, moves out to propitiate the powers that be; Godesberg becomes a latter-day Argos. And, like Agamemnon, Czechoslovakia is betrayed. The Furies, demobilized and quiescent for over two decades, are activated by world guilt. The lesson that appeasement teaches is simple: it doesn't work. But this is being wise after the fact, and Powell never cheapens his ironies by capitalizing on hindsight. In 1938 Nick and his contemporaries wrestle with the question "Will there be war or won't there?"

Importantly Nick is now older. The thought of war goes beyond anticipation or speculation. He must consider action, must consider casting off the cloak of imagination and donning the uniform of power: a quick change that imaginative men are so often ill prepared to make, though the general war climate and the range of Nick's own sensibilities make gearing up to the change more credible:

> Like one of the Stonehurst "ghosts," war towered by the bed when you awoke in the morning; unlike those more transient, more accomodating spectres, its tall form, so far from dissolving immediately, remained, on the contrary, a looming, menacing shape of even greater height, ever thickening density. (*KO,* 86)

Though situations constantly force evaluation of his feelings of inadequacy, Nick nevertheless remains dependent on the fateful agencies controlling call-up lists. He, like England, can do little but wait, and sink further and further into depression.

The nadir is reached at Stourwater. Peter Templer chauffeuring, the Morelands and the Jenkinses are driven to Sir Magnus Donners' estate for cocktails, dinner, and revelations. The evening, beginning somewhat awkwardly, devolves into *dolce vita* abandon when the guests, humoring Sir Magnus in his avocation of photographer, pose tableaux of the Seven Deadly Sins. The interlude is comic and banal, but not without its serious overtones. In assigning the various vices, Donners hands Nick the role of Sloth, without, he says, "personal implications." The irony is of course Powell's, not Donners'. Nick has already lived with the role too long, although with increasing discomfort. For him, at least, the diversion doesn't quite fulfill its object of offering "temporary relief from the personal problems, from the European scene." And Nick's feelings of impotence are heightened when, in the midst of the charade, Widmerpool, bulky, uniformed, sober, "a sinister figure, calling the world to arms," suddenly materializes. As always,

Widmerpool is several steps ahead of Nick. Not only has he a commission but he soon makes connections for getting appointed to the general staff. Never have the "personal implications" seemed greater!

If the voice of Widmerpool is the forbidding mechanism that clicks off Nick's revery and returns him to reality, Giles's death (coming one year after the German-Soviet pact) urges him to shake off lethargy and reexamine values. Widmerpool calls to the present from the present; Giles calls to it from the past, almost as a mythic figure. Ineffectual in life, he is grander in death, inadvertently leaving Nick a sizable legacy. But it is his role as ex-captain that endows him with almost disproportionate significance. In no way else, at no time else, might Giles's death have proved so inspirational. Nick, once plagued by the fear of ending up like his uncle in seedy hotels, now wonders if he can, when the time comes, match him in the things that really count. A commission from Queen Victoria, found among Giles's effects, sets Nick pondering further:

> While I thus considered, rather frivolously, Uncle Giles's actual career in contrast with the ideal one envisaged by the terms of his Commission, I could not help thinking at the same time that facile irony at my uncle's expense could go too far. No doubt irony, facile or otherwise, can often go too far. In this particular instance, for example it was fitting to wonder what sort of a figure I should myself cut as a soldier. The question was no longer purely hypothetical, a grotesque fantasy, a romantic daydream, the career one had supposed to lie ahead as a child at Stonehurst. There was every reason to think that before long now the tenor of many persons' lives, my own among them, would indeed be regulated by those draconic, ineluctable laws, so mildly, so all embracingly, defined in the Commission as "the Rules and Discipline of War." How was it going to feel to be subject to them? My name was on the Emergency Reserve, although no one at that time knew how

much, or how little, that might mean when it came to
joining the army. At the back of one's mind sounded a
haunting resonance, a faint disturbing buzz, that was
not far from fear. (*KO,* 159)

In apprehending those obligations his uncle has already fulfilled, Nick (despite momentary, intellectual
fear) critically advances his personal sense of responsibility—his need to act, if not his desire to; while in
juxtaposing the very idea of two wars, Powell implies
the overall responsibility of one era toward another. As
Powell made clear in *Casanova's Chinese Restaurant,*
one can learn from ghosts; and in *The Kindly Ones,* the
present is instructed through the specters of the past.

Giles's death occasions a series of such revelations as
the past is quickened at the resort town. The disquisi-
tion on army life and the meeting with Duport are the
more sobering circumstances; the encounter with Dr.
Trelawney, the Blavatskyite of Stonehurst days, the
most fantastic one. Now disciple-less and hypochondriac,
transformed by the years, Trelawney has retreated to
the Bellevue.

Nick still feels uneasy in his presence, and the uneasiness stems from that earlier juxtaposition at Stonehurst
of the military policeman out on his rounds and the
Trelawney flock out for a ramble. At that time, both the
doctor and the soldier seemed disturbing, but fleeting
intrusions. Now a new note is struck. At close hand,
Trelawney's eccentricity turns the grotesque into the
fearful, the bizarre into the truthful; his way of life no
longer conflicts with the military's but merges with it:
"There was something decidedly unpleasant about him,
sinister, at the same time absurd, that combination of
the ludicrous and alarming soon to be widely experienced by contact with those set in authority in wartime." It is here that Trelawney becomes associated

with the mystique of the novel. (One recalls that Widmer-pool, too, was a sinister figure "calling the world to arms"). Nick feels instinctively menaced and places himself "on guard," not for fear of falling under the doctor's spell but as "a tribute to his will." Except for his desire to act, his knowledge that action is contention, the imaginative man by nature dreads power. Again, in every way, Trelawney's theosophy, turgidity, egoism are (as willful inflations of the self) monstrous and outlandish.

But the doctor has more in common with Nick than the younger man imagines. Both are harassed by the Furies of the past; both rely on patterns of the past to aid in its unwinding and reweaving. Nick works through reflection, evaluation, interpretation; Trelawney through premises formulated on mystical apothegms ("The Essence of the All is the Godhead of the True. . . . The Vision of Visions heals the Blindness of Sight."). Each man, in short, has his own historic method.

If Trelawney's theosophy seems an ironic abstraction, the doctor himself is no mere bloodless one. He is singular, at times humorous, at times lucid and almost prophetic—even when sinister, even when pontifical:

> "What do you think, Dr. Trelawney?" [asked Duport. "Will there be a war?"]
> "What will be, must be."
> "Which means war, in my opinion." said Duport. . . .
> "Could this situation have been avoided?" I asked.
> "The god, Mars, approaches the earth to lay waste. Moreover, the future is ever the consequence of the past."
> "And we ought to have knocked Hitler out when he first started making trouble?" . . .
> "The Four Horsemen are at the gate. The Kaiser went to war for shame of his withered arm. Hitler will go to war because at official receptions the tails of his evening coat sweep the floor like a clown's." (*KO*, 192)

What Trelawney is suggesting is the theme of Greek tragedy; the coming from humiliation into triumph, an egocentric, but scarcely invalid view of history! In fact, his cornucopia overflows with aphorisms on power:

> "The education of the will is the end of human life. . . . One who is afraid of fire will never command salamanders. . . . You must emancipate the will from servitude, instruct it in the art of domination. . . . Power does not surrender itself. Like a woman it must be seized." (*KO*, 192-93)

Trelawney, having failed to turn theory into practice, is something of a Widmerpool *manqué*—older, deteriorated, addicted less to the powers of life and death than to the powers of drugs. He exists, it seems, in fatal combination with Mrs. Erdleigh, who feeds his fancy, his secret whims, his nervous system. That Trelawney, anticipating a hypodermic heaven, envisions himself as one of the "votaries of the Furies" strongly suggests the drugged will's desire to propitiate (not face) the past, to relax (not entirely lose) its grip. As Trelawney might have said, and for once not have been cut down by irony: Ignorance of the Will means enslavement to History.

Or vice versa. Certainly the past wears a mask, or more often a face marred by mythic features, which Nick fights to penetrate. He is given repeated opportunity. The weird triangle at the Bellevue formed by Giles, Mrs. Erdleigh, and Dr. Trelawney bears an unsettling resemblance to that at Stonehurst among Bracey, Billson, and Albert Creech. History does repeat, can be instructive, both below and above stairs. Albert, now owner of the Bellevue, is as perdurable as if he had walked out of the mythical past, though he has truly come from the historic one. Nick christens him a Sisyphus or Charon, thereby elevating an otherwise enforced stoicism to the higher plane of action. And unlike many who have faded in time, Albert has endured:

> For a man who thoroughly disliked danger, Albert faced the prospect of total war pretty well. At best its circumstances would shatter the props of his daily life at a time when he was no longer young. All the same, the Germans, the Russians, the suffragettes were all one when it came to putting up the shutters. He might be afraid when a policeman walked up the Stonehurst drive; that trepidation was scarcely at all increased by the prospect of bombardment from the air. Indeed, his fear was really a sort of courage, fear and courage being close to each other, like love and hate. (*KO*, 201)

Albert's pluck is inspiring. Without intellectualizing his lot he goes about it. To rationalize past performance is, for Nick, to see present paralysis. With control lacking, "the falcon cannot hear the falconer . . . the center cannot hold." Betty Templer's breakdown during the charade at Stourwater, while a relatively minor incident, is part of this major problem. Trembling, protesting mildly at the thought of acting out a "sin," she collapses completely when her turn comes, made hysterical by her thespiphobia and by her husband's previous enactment of "Lust" with Donners' mistress. The past and present are paralleled as Nick juxtaposes the immediate scene with one that occurred at Stonehurst:

> For some reason my mind was carried back at that moment to Stonehurst and the Billson incident. This was all the same kind of thing. Betty wanted Templer's love, just as Billson wanted Albert's; Albert's marriage had precipitated a breakdown in just the same way as Templer's extravagances with Anne Umfraville. Here, unfortunately, was no General Conyers to take charge of the situation, to quieten Betty Templer. Certainly her husband showed no immediate sign of wanting to accept that job. However, before an extreme moral discomfort could further immerse all of us, a diversion took place.

> The door of the dining-room, so recently slammed, opened again. A man stood on the threshold. He was in uniform. He appeared to be standing at attention, a sinister, threatening figure, calling the world to arms. It was Widmerpool. (*KO*, 133)

In Stonehurst's drawing room (like Stourwater's, "a place for action") there was "a display of the will." Then, Conyers bundled the naked Billson in a spare shawl and gallantly escorted her from the room. Now, no one moves. Widmerpool's entrance aborts one grim scene; but in recalling the players from illusion he offers them the realities of a grimmer one. The disparity between "acting" and "action" is manifest. Ironically, Mrs. Jenkins' reflections as Billson stood stark and terrified—"I thought it was the end of the world"—echo with renewed force as Nick is shamed into realizing the lack of action and control: "There can be no doubt whatever that the scene was disturbing, terrifying, saddening, a moment that summarised, in the unclothed figure of Billson, human lack of coordination and abandonment of self-control in the face of emotional misery." The moment passes; and, as Nick points out, life becomes normal again once the spell is broken.

Such incidents mark the end of one stage of life and the beginning of another. But it is the casual, rather than violent, revelations that create the transitions in *The Kindly Ones*. Chance encounters of persons, a word slipped in between sips of tea, an unannounced visit are the understated circumstances that decide fate. Giles, both trial and joke to his family, breezes into Stonehurst with his eternal umbrella and Gladstone bag, and between windy importunities sandwiches in some world-shattering news:

> "I wanted to have a talk about business matters. . . . There has been rather a crisis in my own affairs. I'd like

to ask your opinion. I value it. By the way, did I mention I heard a serious piece of news in Aldershot? . . . Some royalty in a motor-car have been involved in a nasty affair today. . . . They've just assassinated an Austrian archduke down in Bosnia. Did it today. Only happened a few hours ago."

Uncle Giles muttered, almost whispered these facts, speaking as if he were talking to himself, not at all in the voice of a man announcing to the world in general the close of an epoch; the outbreak of Armageddon; the birth of a new, uneasy age. He did not look in the least like the harbinger of the Furies. (*KO*, 67, 69-70)

Nor does Widmerpool at Stourwater; but they both are. Even dead Giles sustains the resemblance; for it is a Gladstone bag ("perhaps the very one with which [he] had arrived at Stonehurst on the day of the Archduke's assassination") that Nick symbolically turns up at the Bellevue. Obviously, Furies cannot be so easily packed away. Several days later, over morning coffee, Nick reads of Germany's and Russia's nonaggression pact, hears of Duport's ruinous involvement in the chromite venture, and ostensibly decides to push for his commission. Stonehurst, Stourwater, Bellevue, and at last London, form for Nick the critical bridge across a gulf separating the past from the present, action from inaction.

Action is both theme and method of the final section. London, gradually making the shift into wartime, becomes the proving ground for Nick's success. As the earlier three chapters depicted locales insulated from spheres of accomplishment, depicted differing worlds of illusion (Stonehurst: childhood; Stourwater: "playacting"; the Bellevue: speculation) the chapter on London discards mere revery over action and thrusts Nick into the real world of happenings.

Aylmer Conyers—the paramount symbol of action from Stonehurst days—is the first whom Nick solicits for help in getting his commission. Though now widowed, the General is unbent by grief. Still dedicated to the cello, displaying that same paradoxical air of vigor and remoteness, eccentric grace, strength, and sensitivity, Conyers inspires simply by existing. He communicates at once life-force and action; indeed, frozen momentarily in an attitude, he becomes reminiscent of an "unbearded Jehovah inspiring life into Adam through an extended finger." Unable to help Nick, Conyers is not unable to astound him. Trotting out "Tuffy" Weedon (nicely coy and girlish) as his future bride would be a ludicrous gesture were it not such a grand one:

> There could be no doubt that General Conyers had taken on a formidable woman; equally no doubt that he was a formidable man. If he could handle Billson naked, he could probably handle Miss Weedon clothed—or naked, too, if it came to that. I felt admiration for his energy, his determination to cling to life. There was nothing defeatist about him. (*KO*, 217)

Miss Weedon's news of Stringham's sober comeback and attempts at enlistment, and the General's extraordinary situation balance Nick's feelings of defeatism and give him heart for the interview with Widmerpool—the unwelcome, but sane, voice of action that resounded through the halls at Stourwater. Security grafted on pomposity, Captain Widmerpool embodies the organization man now swollen with military power. Naturally he can do nothing for Nick, and gets himself straightway off the hook before begging a reciprocal favor:

> "The fact is," said Widmerpool . . . "you ought to have joined the Territorials before war broke out."
> "I know."
> "No good just entering your name on the Reserve."
> "There were difficulties about age."
> "Only after you'd left it too late."
> "It was only a matter of months."

"Never mind. Think how long I've been a Territorial officer. You should have looked ahead."

"You said there wasn't going to be a war after 'Munich'."

"You thought there was, so you were even more foolish. . . ."

"You think there is nothing for me to do at present?"

"You could enlist in the ranks."

"But the object of joining the Reserve—being accepted for it—was to be dealt with immediately as a potential officer."

"Then I can't help you." (*KO*, 220)

Nick accommodates Widmerpool however by taking him round to Lady Molly's, where Ted Jeavons' brother, Stanley, is to arrange with Mrs. Widmerpool about lodgings in her cottage for London evacuees. Pausing at an antiwar rally only long enough to discover that the vehement, indelicate, gat-toothed orator is Gypsy Jones, Nick senses the discord he has fortunately escaped, while, for an agonizing instant, Widmerpool confronts the Erinyes incarnate:

> I felt my arm caught tightly. It was Widmerpool. I turned towards him. He had gone quite pale. His thick lips were trembling a little. The sight of Gypsy Jones, rousing vague memories in myself, had caused him to react far more violently. To Widmerpool, she was not the mere handmaid of memory, she was a spectre of horror, the ghastly reminder of failure, misery, degradation. He dragged at my arm. (*KO*, 228)

As in the past, Widmerpool's dependence (however slight) on Nick, seems a triumph (however slight) for the man of imagination. Face to face with the Furies, whose existence he has probably never considered, Widmerpool weakens.

That Nick does not may suggest a symbolic surge of strength. He seems very much in control at Lady Molly's, where the same wild eccentricities prevail, but as a healthy complement to the anarchy of the street, or the grotesque, demoralizing, decaying environment at the Bellevue. At the Jeavonses', morale is high; things are bustling; life is action: "War," Nick points out, seemed to have accelerated, exaggerated, rather than changed the Jeavons way of life." Molly is irrepressible as ever, but Jeavons has "livened up." (Perhaps he is what Uncle Giles might have been when younger. Both men, in fact, made any career they had because of the war, and both thrived on it—not because they enjoyed bloodshed, but because they saw it as a way to action, not stagnation.)

But even Molly and Ted are dominated here by Stanley Jeavons. Brisk, efficient, practical, staid but quite cheerful, Stanley is the quiet, normative figure of authority, the counter to the boisterous and excessive figure Widmerpool cuts. Too, he is the active hand of fate, as Nick discovers in questioning him about his military occupation; Stanley processes reserve lists and promises to speed up Nick's application.

The Kindly Ones closes during a London blackout, on a challenging, yet optimistic, and almost elated note. War must be destructive universally, personally; but it can be reconstructive. The small shocks of life, the reversals, the decisions, the ultimate moves, the conclusions, work between two poles. In the novel Nick seeks and finds action. Hopefully Stringham may do the same. Less hopeful are those whom the war sets back. Duport is one; and Hugh Moreland, who, now in a somewhat desperate condition because his wife has bolted and because his bad lung keeps him away from the "show," is another. And yet personal disappointment is rapidly countered in the tragicomic world of Powell. Matilda Moreland leaves her husband for Donners and a possible title; Anne Umfraville picks up with Quiggin and

Members; Nick gets his promise of a regiment; Duport is left out on a limb; and Ted Jeavons is caught up in the fever of crisis, reveling in so simple a role as air-raid warden.

As Jeavons pins up the curtain to keep in the light, he repeats Albert's actions of fastening the shutters to keep out the suffragettes. But the Furies, once come, must be engaged, not propitiated. Walking through the darkened London streets, "exhilarated, at the same time rather afraid," Nick contemplates the realms of action to which he is now committed, "the region beyond the white-currant bushes, where the wild country begins, where armies forever campaign, where the Rules and Discipline of War prevail." An Orestes who no longer flees the Furies but goes in search of them, Nick has ruled his own conscience, reconciled the justice of history and his heritage.

13

The Valley of Bones

Nick's reflections at the conclusion of
The Kindly Ones anticipate ambivalences treated at
length in *The Valley of Bones,* the seventh volume in
The Music of Time and the first of a forthcoming "war
trilogy." The novel's ironic impact is not felt until well
into the last chapter, although certain paradoxes indicate commitment to the complex theme and practically
dictate the action. Both paradox and irony proceed
from the title, one of the most evocative to date. Explicitly the title suggests one thing; implicitly the novel
enforces another. And the irony, powerful, controlling,
is sustained through tension rather than ambiguity.

While imagistically macabre, Ezekiel's famous vision of
"the valley of bones" (Ezek. 37:1-10) is a straight-from-
the-shoulder admonition to the Hebrews, dishonored,
down-trodden, and dispersed under the Babylonian

captivity, to rally themselves and become a nation once again.

"The hand of the Lord was upon me, and carried me out in the spirit of the Lord, and set me down in the midst of the valley which was full of bones, and caused me to pass them round about: and, behold, there were very many in the open valley: and, lo, they were very dry. And he said unto me, Son of man, can these bones live? And I answered, O Lord God thou knowest. Again he said unto me, Prophesy upon these bones, and say unto them, O ye dry bones, hear the word of the Lord. Thus saith the Lord God unto these bones; Behold, I will cause breath to enter into you, and ye shall live. And I will lay sinews upon you, and cover you with skin, and put breath into you, and ye shall live; and ye shall know that I am the Lord. So I prophesied as I was commanded; and as I prophesied there was a noise, and behold a shaking, and the bones came together, bone to bone. And when I beheld, lo, the sinews and the flesh came upon them, and the skin covered them above; and there was no breath in them. Then he said unto me, Prophesy unto the wind, prophesy son of man, and say to the wind, Thus saith the Lord God; Come from the four winds, O breath, and breathe upon these slain that they may live. So I prophesied as he commanded me, and the breath came unto them and they lived, and stood up upon their feet, an exceeding great army."

The wild note of mystical heroics in Ezekiel's prophecy contains less the idea of warfare than the notion of legalistic expediency, and may seem somewhat far from the drill fields of Wales and Northern Ireland. But, basically, war martials elements from all class levels. The disparate entities that come together in *The Valley of Bones* for "the supreme effort" are disjointed, unrelated—a mass of professions and personalities that must be molded into an effective fighting unit; they must be, like the parched, bleached, scattered bones, articulated and fleshed out.

And eventually they may be; but *The Valley of Bones* is not a novel of articulation. The stirring force of the Lord now blows randomly through the chain of command, inspiring General Liddament's passionate expatiation on the virtues of porridge, rattling Rowland Gwatkin's sense of order, chafing relationships, stirring doubt and confusion. The hand and spirit of God are absent; instead, there are men—never very strong, often ineffective, seldom secure, always troubled. Ezekiel's allegory depicts the resurrection of a nation; Powell's narrative pictures the partial breakdown of an infantry company: the personal ossification of some men, the cracking of the mold in others, the failure (and even death) of still others. At distance from the pure vision is grubby practicality; far from the inspiriting romance of prophecy, the dispiriting coldness of daily reality.

Nick soon learns that war, like peace, doesn't alter basic human nature. Resolved at the end of *The Kindly Ones* to live by war's "Rules and Discipline," he becomes "geared" to its machine only to discover that the cogs turn little differently from those in the world he has left. War is, after all, like any closed society, only the sum total of those who comprise it. And so Rules and Discipline are only as perfect as the men who formulate or execute them, in other words, imperfect— subject to change and chance. These, then, become the modern visions and main themes of *The Valley of Bones:* the almost complete breakdown of rules and discipline accompanied by a glaring disenchantment, the gradual revelation that the romantic aura of war is dissipated finally in its near classic tediousness.

Powell comes at his theme directly through personality; and in this respect *The Valley of Bones* is hardly a conventional war novel at all. Fighting is far offstage, and perhaps for this very reason the book becomes a highly civilized discussion of the natural, but uncivilizing, phenomena of war and its peculiar code. Something in most men rebels against living by the book, against living an enforced, impossible excellence. Rules, discipline, order—in short, the bold and fine print in manuals—are military sacraments, but being sacred scarcely assures their durability. Even during war it is, in the last analysis, the human that must interpret the abstract, and any machine geared to reliance on human perfection must become slave to human fallibility.

The Valley of Bones throbs with this humanizing impulse, worked compellingly into the main themes. Because the majority of men are basically too human and vulnerable ever to become inhuman and precise, the system, and not really war, becomes their private Waterloo. In the brief, pathetic career of Nick's company commander, Captain Rowland Gwatkin, are concentrated theme and moral. Beginning ostensibly as one of the system's strongest links, Gwatkin ends as one of its weakest, his brittle ideals shattered by experience, his sense of order undermined by a disenchantment as debilitating as it is powerful. Gwatkin's decline marks the most significant movement in the novel. The world of "officers and gentlemen," he comes to learn, only outwardly glistens with the spit-and-polish of military *noblesse oblige*. Beneath the patina of comradery and Kiplingesque romance are the scarred surfaces of a grubby, routine existence, where success is not easy and where failure is severe.

Gwatkin conveys this ambivalence from the first moment Nick meets him in the barracks.

> He appeared on that occasion almost to perfection in the part for which he had cast himself: in command, something of a martinet, a trifle unapproachable to his subordinates, at the same time not without his human side,

above all a man dedicated to duty. It was a clear-cut, hard-edged picture, into which Gwatkin himself, for some reason, never quite managed to fit. . . . There was about him something melancholy, perhaps even tragic, that was hard to define. His excessively "regimental" manner was certainly over and above anything as yet encountered among other officers of the Battalion. . . . He gave the impression of being something more than a civilian keen on his new military role, anxious to make a success of an unaccustomed job. There was an air of resolve about him, the consciousness of playing a part to which a high destiny had summoned him. I suspected he saw himself in much the same terms as those heroes of Stendhal . . . an aspiring, restless spirit, who, released at last by war from the cramping bonds of life in a provincial town, was about to cut a dashing military figure against a backcloth of Meissonier-like imagery of plume and breastplate: dragoons walking their horses through the wheat, grenadiers at ease in a tavern with girls bearing flagons of wine. (*VB*, 12-13)

Idealizing his role, Gwatkin borders dangerously on becoming thoroughly incompetent in it. And over the weeks the more authority he assumes, the more his effectiveness diminishes. Every petty assignment becomes a crisis, engaged with futile intensity, and a direct challenge to the Stendhalian ideal. Gwatkin, terribly naïve, romantic, lacks the basic knowledge that is innate to even the "dirty, disobliging, quarrelsome" private, Sayce: the army works through collective, not personal, honor; criticism must never be taken to heart; one should avoid responsibility rather than court it. Nick describes the problem:

The fact was Gwatkin lacked in his own nature that grasp of "system" for which he possessed such admiration. This deficiency was perhaps connected in some way with a kind of poetry within him, a poetry which had somehow become a handicap in its efforts to find an outlet. Romantic ideas about the way life is lived are often to be found in persons themselves fairly coarse-grained. This was to some extent true of Gwatkin. (*VB,* 48-49)

It becomes increasingly obvious that Rowland Gwatkin's weaknesses are not simply symptomatic of situations in *The Valley of Bones,* but part of a syndrome relevant to *The Music of Time.* Despite his flirtation with power, the captain is basically a man of imagination, ill fitted for the role of limited greatness thrust upon him. His attempted reformation of Sayce is the first uncomfortable indication of how his imagination becomes self-defeating, for Sayce, despite Gwatkin's cajoling and consideration, turns out to be a perfect bounder, and Gwatkin an imperfect disciplinarian.

Still, standards raised high, he moves on untroubled, lost in the idealization of "the old days," which might be a shade shinier than the new, and in his "personal myth." Gwatkin's model hero is the Roman Centurion from *Puck of Pook's Hill.* It is not surprising that Gwatkin even resembles some anachronistic apparition as he forms up his company for the battalion's first coordinated field exercise:

He had draped a rubber groundsheet round him like a cloak, which, with his flattish-brimmed steel helmet, transformed him into a figure from the later Middle Ages, a captain-of-arms of the Hundred Years War, or the guerrilla campaigning of Owen Glendower. I suddenly saw that was where Gwatkin belonged, rather than to the soldiery of modern times, the period which captured his own fancy. (*VB,* 76)

Gwatkin's disastrous handling of the maneuvers is tinged with the same mixture of tragicomedy that portrays his life: desiring to excel, he fails, and one failure leads to a nexus of failures. Shortly after the exercises, Sgt. Pendry's suicide further blurs Gwatkin's visions of success and symbolically, if not overtly, implicates him.

Like Pendry, he begins with an excess of zeal, making a great show, being "keen"; like him, he achieves minor successes with the men, even with his superiors; but like him, too, Gwatkin broods on disappointment, converts it into disaster, and at the end witnesses his dreams fade and die.

The eloquence of Gwatkin's plight is finally voiced by David Pennistone, the officer Nick meets while en route to temporary duty at a special training center. Pennistone calls forth the shades of Alfred de Vigny, the French poet who served a fourteen-year military apprenticeship. In a way de Vigny is the *raisonneur* of *The Valley of Bones*. His view of the soldier as a "dedicated person, a sort of monk of war" renouncing "thought and action" for "passive obedience" challenges both Gwatkin's "keenness" and Sayce's "recalcitrance":

> ["De Vigny sees," Pennistone tells Nick,] "the role of authority as essentially artificial, the army a way of life in which there is as little room for uncontrolled fervour as for sullen indifference. The impetuous volunteer has as much to learn as the unwilling conscript." (*VB,* 108)

Equally ill tailored to the "Rules and Discipline of War," the enthusiast, as well as the malingerer, falls to ridicule, though men like Gwatkin, men of fine feelings and allegiances, fall harder.

Victimized as much by "half-baked romanticism" as by the "system," Rowland Gwatkin only gradually struggles free of captor fancies. At Castlemallock, in the spring and summer of 1940, the tedium of training starts to tell. In an atmosphere of tenseness, dislocation, "resignation," despair, with the war growing closer and the need for level-headed command greater, Gwatkin founders. Falling for the local barmaid is one folly; not making her is the second and worse one. A slave to procedural correctness, he is an acknowledged master of poor timing. His two great passions, love and war, run parallel disastrous courses downhill until, as he piles blunder upon blunder, they bump bottom. Failure to convey a critical codeword and the hasty arrest of Lieutenant Bithel put him in straits with the commanding general, failure to assert himself more vigorously with the barmaid raises the emotional impasse to what appears a dead end professionally. He loses his company to the cheerless Idwal Kedward, his girl to the beefy company buffoon (a corporal, to aggravate the rub), and in losing them both he loses the dream of "a glorious career . . . [or] an equally glorious romance."

Experience, however, does not wash over Gwatkin. Withal he gains a compensating, if not wholly satisfying, insight that Nick translates in another way:

> "A French writer who'd been a regular officer said the whole point of soldiering was its bloody boring side. The glamour, such as it was, was just a bit of exceptional luck if it came your way."
>
> "Did he?" said Gwatkin. . . . He smiled in an odd sort of way, as if he dimly perceived it was no good battling against Fate, which, seen in right perspective, almost always provides a certain beauty of design, sometimes even an occasional good laugh. (*VB,* 234-35)

This comic perspective elevates Gwatkin; he rises above most in *The Valley of Bones.* Like many other men of imagination who have come through experience to knowledge the hard way, he is an object of nostalgia as well as pathos. One cannot deny Gwatkin's incompetence or innocence; he has an ample measure of both. But his failures depend on a qualitative rather than a quantitative appraisal of shortcomings. *Where* he has gone wrong is simple enough to determine; *why* is more difficult, though Nick moves toward a tentative answer:

> All Gwatkin said [about his working hard] was true. He had worked hard. In many respects he was a good officer,

so far as he went. He was even conscious of such moral aspects of military life as the fact that the army is a world of will, accordingly, if the will is weak, the army is weak. I could see, however, that one of the fallacies that made him so vulnerable was the supposition that manners, good or bad, had anything to do with the will as such. (*VB*, 228)

Gwatkin, however, does not rise or fall by a syllogism. Few others in *The Valley of Bones* are as vulnerable, to be sure; but then few are as imaginative. The man of imagination, here and throughout *The Music of Time,* suffers the romantic fallacy, but he may equally possess a comic outlook which, however latent, finally permits him to laugh at himself. Few others in the novel are able to laugh in the same way. Bithel—soft, sluggish, bibulous, slightly fraudulent—is ludicrous; Kedward— hard, priggish, dull, mechanical—is dreary. As person- alities, as symbols, both men seem poles apart from each other and from Gwatkin, succeeding by virtue of their innocent (but depressing) mediocrity, while he fails.

But Powell seldom simplifies contrasts. True, Bithel is a direct foil to Gwatkin's religion of order, a parody, sometimes compassionate, sometimes grotesque, of "Rules and Discipline." Laxity and rootlessness have marked his career (if it can be called one) in civilian life:

"I was trained for professional life too—intended for an auctioneer, like my pa. Never cared for the work some- how. Didn't even finish my training, as a matter of fact. Always been more or less interested in the theatre. Had walk-on parts once or twice but I'm no actor. I'm quite aware of that. I like doing odd jobs in any case. Can't bear being tied down. Worked for a time in our local cinema, for instance. Didn't have to do much except turn up in the evening wearing a dinner jacket." (*VB*, 33)

Never having lived by method, he either sees no need for it or does not comprehend it; accustomed to varying order, he perhaps sees no need for romanticizing it. Again, if Gwatkin steps from the pages of knightly legend, Bithel walks out of the topsy-turvy world of Lewis Carroll, looking like "a sprite in pantomime; perhaps rather—taking into consideration his age, bulk, mustache—some comic puppet half-way between the Walrus and the Carpenter."

This contrast is just in conception, but, like many, ironic in implication. Bithel stands for everything Gwatkin would not want to, could not be—but quite nearly is; Kedward for the very things he needs to be—but isn't. Kedward, a Widmerpool in miniature, is made for the machine: tedious in himself and therefore effective at engineering tedium, robot-like and therefore adept at converting the mechanistic theory of order into practice. However depressing it is that Bithel should win out over Gwatkin—his heading up the Division's Mobile Laundry Unit constitutes a promotion of sorts— it is far more depressing (and consequently frightening) that Kedward, devoid of *all* imagination (and perhaps feeling), is so eminently successful. Bithel, because ineffective, is harmless; his victory is a fluke. Not so that of the Kedwards, who, by nature antipathetic to the Gwatkins, inevitably triumph over them.

Throughout, Kedward's sobriety is taken as a corrective to Gwatkin's excesses, but upon becoming captain Kedward proves to be the worst kind of martinet, rigorously adhering to the book, unresponsive to the human predicament. Power, which has whipped Gwatkin, seems potentially capable of warping Kedward. And the easy slide into the new commission is accompanied by a show of force, less significant for its range than its pettiness:

> "The Company needs a thorough overhaul," said Kedward. "There are one or two points I shall want altered in your own Platoon, Nick. It's far from satisfactory. I've

noticed there's no snap about them when they march in from training. That's always a good test of the men. They are the worst of the three platoons at musketry, too. You'll have to give special attention to the range. And another thing, Nick, about your own personal turn-out. Do get that anti-gas cape of yours properly folded. The way you have it done is not according to regulations." (*VB,* 219-20)

Recalled to Division, Nick is temporarily spared from further decline into the abyss of nit-picking regulations, from repeating, in effect, the identical pattern so recently completed with Gwatkin. Ironically, what Nick does not know, what he discovers in *The Soldier's Art,* is that Widmerpool is more a stickler for the religion of "bumph"—red tape—than Kedward.

Primarily a portrait of the preparations for war, *The Valley of Bones,* too, paints those peripheral lives that continue uninterrupted, but not unchanged, as the machinery of war grinds on. Powell captures the modified, but basically ordinary civilian routine that complements barracks activity. The interlude at the home of Nick's sister-in-law, Frederica Budd, while breaking the tediousness of training camps and field maneuvers, still suggests a corresponding sense of order: "The place had that same air of intense respectability Frederica's own personality conveyed. In spite of war conditions, there was no sign of untidiness about the garden, only an immediate sense of having entered a precinct where one must be on one's best behaviour."

Yet within these "precincts" adherence to the superficial sense of order is far less interesting than changes in the ideas of order. " 'The war seems to have altered some people out of recognition and made others more than ever like themselves,' " says Isobel Jenkins. Values and attitudes have shifted, and in some cases actually broken down. Perhaps Frederica herself best reflects the transformation. That "dreadful correctness" which had so thoroughly stamped her as of the upper class—a correctness notable less as an idiosyncracy than an "approach to life"—has been partially "dislodged" by events. Temporarily, at least, while war is "in," *snobisme* is "out."

New, odd forces are making themselves felt. That Odo Stevens, the inoffensively egoistic but slightly crude costume jewelry manufacturer, should find himself on equal footing with the Tollands, and, as an officer, superior in rank to Robert Tolland (a lance-corporal) reflects the continued capriciousness of change. War, not death, becomes the great leveler—linking, fusing, cross-pollinating. Dicky Umfraville, notorious for his vagaries in love, his four precipitous and short-lived marriages, turns up reformed and respectable, the unlikely fiancé of Frederica Budd (" 'My God, I never dreamed I'd marry one of Hugo Warminster's daughters, and I don't expect he did either.' "); while Robert, quiet, sensitive, warm, no great hand with women, has, with equal unlikelihood, taken up with Stringham's sister, twice divorced and Umfraville's former mistress.

The pressures of war not only alter people but, as Nick observes, force action. Action is common both to peace and war, though the latter punctuates the vitalistic theory that order and progress exist because of change, not despite it. Accompanying change is chance, which in this case either annihilates personal order or creates the suitable pattern into which it can be incorporated. At Frederica's, as elsewhere in the novel and in *The Music of Time,* Powell raises again the question of whether character is fate or vice versa, later to be spelled out more fully with the death of Robert Tolland, so literally complete, so symbolically unresolved:

> Some die in an apparently suitable manner, others like Robert on the field of battle with a certain incongruity. Yet Fate had ordained this end for him. Or had Robert decided for himself? Had he set aside the chance of a commission to fulfil a destiny that required him to fall in France. . . . The potential biographies of those who die young possess the mystic dignity of a headless statue, the poetry of enigmatic passages in an unfinished or mutilated manuscript, unburdened with contrived or banal ending. *(VB,* 196-97)

Unquestionably, Nick romanticizes Tolland's death, but only to find meaning and purpose in it, to liberate it from the tedium and triviality that is the rest of war. Here, however, the elegiac note is not to be construed as part of a tragic vision. Rather than emphasizing the inevitable interactions of fate and character, Powell treats the incongruous clashes between them; hence his vision is comic.

The final action of the novel tends to confirm this by pointing up the comedy of Nick's plight, even after the sudden death of his brother-in-law. Assigned to Division, Nick finds himself in the "power" of Widmerpool, who has extended his cold, finny feelers of control. Widmerpool surfaces, dominating all about him, and Jenkins as well. Life's incongruities have placed Nick in a situation that the sequence has been approaching from the beginning. Having traced and analyzed the force called Widmerpool, he now falls under it. To keep his comic perspective after that requires schooling to a new art.

14

The Soldier's Art

*T*he Soldier's Art is as fast, polished, and accurate as a Bren gun. It is one of the best examples—*Casanova's Chinese Restaurant* is another—of Powell's talent to compose, with surface simplicity, complex variations on a single theme. The theme here, variously orchestrated and shifting in intensity from comedy to irony, is the application of the term "art" to phases of the soldier's life and to his personality. "Art" implies as well an articulation that goes beyond the muddle and "balls up" of *The Valley of Bones,* and the ordering is managed by shifting the focus of the sequence back to its norm, Nicholas Jenkins.

Having accepted the "Rules and Discipline of War," Jenkins now takes up the trickier job of practicing its arts, without, of course, fully understanding them. On the tight little island where war has become at last a fact, all manner of breakup and disintegration give him the chance to test himself against its realities and abstractions. And though he is not given the opportunity to actually display heroism, it soon becomes apparent that he is made of heroic stuff. It is England's and Nick's finest hour.

To arrive at this assessment of Jenkins is first to note that Powell's method for exploring "the soldier's art" in terms of the novelist's is here rather special. Technique is controlled by a shifting dramatic perspective that can alternately view war as a mere backdrop for the dance, the "ineluctable shadow under which characters and events have their being,"[1] or as the actual subject that heightens and intensifies the relationships of all the dancers. Powell has taken great care with his theatrical effects, as one might call them, to make certain that everyone fits his role well for the "big show."

Nick is outfitted for his role in an opening scene that sets the theatrical motif while capitalizing fully on its inherent irony. "When, at the start of the whole business," he begins, and goes on to describe his purchase of an army overcoat at a shop that deals both in theatrical costumes and officers' supplies, and, it appears, double entendres. Mistaken for an actor, Nick finds himself "prompted" into the following exchange:

> "What's this one for?" [the assistant asked.]
> "Which one?"
> "The overcoat—if I might make bold to enquire?"
> "Just the war."
> "Ah," he said attentively. *"The War* . . . I'll bear the show in mind."
> "Do, please."
> "And the address?"
> "I'll take it with me. . . ."

1. Walter Allen, *The Modern Novel in Britain and the United States* (New York, 1965), p. 262.

"Tried to make a neat job of it," he said, "though I expect the theatre's only round the corner from here."

"The theatre of war?"

He looked puzzled for a second, then, recognising a mummer's obscure quip, nodded several times in appreciation.

"And I'll wish you a good run," he said, clasping together his old lean hands, as if in applause.

"Thanks."

"Good day, sir, and thank *you*." (*SA*, 2-3)

This sequence is of course very funny, but its appropriateness both to *The Soldier's Art* and *The Music of Time* goes beyond the rhetoric of comic misunderstanding. It anticipates subsequent, more serious ambiguities arising from the interplay of characters in the dance (of which acting is an extension), and projects an ironic view (not only about "life" but about life at this particular time) that is saving and salutary—which is what one would expect an ironic view, post facto, to be! If these images of "the play" soften the explicit tragedy of the human condition, they intensify its implicit ironies. Powell, as a comedian, is interested in showing tragedy as underlying comedy, not vice versa. Thus the theater may become a grand euphemism for war since both promote the grand illusion that character spontaneously controls fate, while in reality it is driven by larger forces toward an anticipated conclusion.

Here is the "big picture"; but the success of the metaphor depends really on the moment-to-moment ironies of the novel, those that enforce the many ways in which war—the war of *The Soldier's Art*, at any rate—becomes "dramatic." There is, first of all, attention to the setting. The nearest thing to action in *The Soldier's Art* is Nick's low-keyed description of a distant air raid, early in the novel. The explosion of bombs, the reports of the antiaircraft guns are muffled, like those offstage sounds one finds in many war plays, while the lighting of the stage itself is emphasized. The searchlights, playing back and forth across the sky trying to pinpoint enemy planes, and the shifting cloud formations create a kalei-doscope of "pastelled compositions of black and lilac, grey and saffron, pink and gold." Then the planes re-lease flares:

> Clustered together in twos and threes, they drifted at first aimlessly in the breeze, after a time scarcely losing height, only swaying a little this way and that, metamorphosed into all but stationary lamps, apparently suspended by immensely elongated wires attached to an invisible ceil-ing. Suddenly, as if at a prearranged signal for the climax of the spectacle—a set-piece at midnight—high swirling clouds of inky smoke rose from below to meet these flickering airborne torches. . . . All the world was dipped in a livid, unearthly refulgence, theatrical yet sinister. . . . (*SA*, 11)

The intensification of this scenic design, at once re-flective and poetic, contrasts purposefully with the very un-theatrical and un-sinister discussion that Nick is en-gaged in while all this is going on: a discussion with Bithel over a check that has bounced. "How everything turns away/Quite leisurely from the disaster," writes Auden in "Musée des Beaux Arts," which is perhaps the best commentary on the *idea* that Powell's irony intends to convey. Powell, like Auden, is quite aware that whimsies about bad checks operate concomitantly with matters of life-and-death, that as well as an urgency about disaster there is also a leisureliness. In war especially there seems all the time in the world to get on with things, perhaps because what one gets on with, oftener than not, is death.

Bithel's preoccupation with finances during the bom-bardment parallels similar interludes at higher levels. The rivalry of the Captains Biggs and Soper in Jenkins' mess, and the polite hostility of the Colonels Pedlar and Hogbourne-Johnson in the General's are of a piece with all the other mundanities that transpire as the universal tragedy mounts. This, for example, is the "dramatic" setting of General Liddament's mess: "A single oil lamp threw a circle of dim light round the dining table of the farm parlour where we ate, leaving the rest of the room in heavy shadow, dramatising by its glow the central figures of the company present." Powell's momentous analogy comparing the company with conspirators in the Gunpowder Plot crumbles into bathos minutes later as Eric Pedlar plays Alphonse to Derrick Hogbourne-Johnson's Gaston. Their dialogue grows replete with the innocuous brilliance and embarrassment of any vaudeville routine.

> "Fellow in my regiment was telling me just before the war that his grandfather laid down a pipe of port for him to inherit on his twenty-first birthday," [Colonel Pedlar] remarked. . . .
>
> "Twelve dozen bottles. . . . Pretty good cellar for a lad when he comes of age. . . ."
>
> "Twelve dozen, Eric?"
>
> "That's it, isn't it, Derrick? . . ."
>
> "You're wide of the mark, Eric. Completely out of the picture."
>
> "I am, Derrick?"
>
> "You certainly are, Eric."
>
> "What is a pipe then, Derrick? I'm not in the wine trade."
>
> "Don't have to be in the wine trade to know what a pipe of port is, old boy. Everyone ought to know that. Nothing to do with being a shopman. *More than fifty dozen.* . . ."
>
> "Is that a pipe, by Jove?"
>
> "That's a pipe, Eric."
>
> "I got it wrong, Derrick."
>
> "You certainly did, Eric. You certainly got it wrong. You did, by Jove."

> "You've shaken me, Derrick. I'll have to do better next
> time."
> "You will, Eric, you will—or we won't know what to
> think of you." (*SA*, 40-41)

The dialogue, which has other ironic implications to
be discussed below, immediately suggests affinities with
absurdist techniques, and indeed there is a sprinkling of
absurdity throughout this first long chapter of *The Soldier's Art,* especially in Nick's literary discussion with
General Liddament and in his fumbling attempts at
rapprochement with Private Stringham. But the deepen-
ing sense of the drama really comes with the second act,
the Spring of 1941:

> Sullen reverberations of one kind or another—blitz in
> England, withdrawal in Greece—had been providing the
> most recent noises-off in rehearsals that never seemed to
> end, breeding a wish that the billed performance would
> at last ring up its curtain, whatever form that took. How-
> ever, the date of the opening night rested in hands other
> than our own; meanwhile nobody could doubt that more
> rehearsing, plenty more rehearsing, was going to be
> needed for a long time to come. (*SA,* 88)

As it turns out, Nick broods upon an invasion of
England much less than upon an invasion of privacy.
His London leave—the civilian section of *The Soldier's
Art*—takes up in part a meeting with Moreland (now
the lover of Audrey Maclintick) and its several inter-
ruptions: the first by Chips, the second by Priscilla
Lovell. It is not hard to see that the episode, in construction at least, is intended to provide a double view
of breakup and re-formation, as they occur in life no less
than in war time: Chips and Priscilla are thrown apart,
Moreland and Audrey together. But Powell's finesse
with *mise-en-scène* only partially accounts for the climax
that the dramatic metaphor dictates and the war demands.

With Chips, for one, it is as much character as fate that balances the account. A volatile and engaging fellow, he is nevertheless an earnest one. To take another shot at reconciliation with Priscilla he plans to surprise her at the hotel where they had celebrated their engagement, a gesture that complements his "dramatic manner": "Everything had to be staged [Nick ruminates]. Perhaps he was right, and everything does have to be staged. That is a system that can at least be argued as the best." Chips, killed an hour or so afterward in a bombing of the hotel, doesn't benefit much from the validity of the argument. Yet in a neat, artistic way the dramatic metaphor is itself well validated. That a theatrical performance was taking place at the hotel solders the novel's metaphor to its structure by capitalizing on the earlier phrase casually interjected in Nick's misunderstanding at the costumer's: "theatre of war." Chips's is another case of tragedy underscored by comedy, with the added irony that he, a script writer, acts out the ultimate in scripts.

But Powell enlarges the dimensions still further. Priscilla, who never turns up at the hotel, is killed along with Molly Jeavons at Molly's house. A certain sadness attaches to these deaths that is lacking in Lovell's, a sadness heightened by the knowledge that while the bombing was going on, Nick, Moreland, Audrey, and Odo Stevens (Priscilla's current lover) were sitting around listening to Stevens' elegy on war and love. Too, there is the melancholy recognition that with Molly's death entire episodes of *The Music of Time* have been absorbed into the fluidity of the continuing dance, that with her death "a whole gay, eccentric world"—to paraphrase Waugh's Tony Last—"had come to grief."

Nostalgia, but nostalgia free of grief, has remained a

significant part of *The Music of Time* ever since death became a part of the series. But death has never rendered inelastic the tautness of life that expands from second to second. The sense of drama is never very far from the varied approaches to lives that go on in the face of the most shocking reversals and the most violent of deaths. "I wonder when the next [bomber] will arrive," says the nightclub entertainer Max Pilgrim after Chips Lovell has been killed. "Worse than waiting for the curtain to go up." And Stringham, upon learning that Widmerpool has wangled a still better duty, says with typically cynical lucidity, "How very dramatic." Powell knows that no matter how interesting the ironies and ambiguities attending death may be, those attending life are more interesting by far.

This point is at the center of *The Music of Time* and it is done over with special attention in *The Soldier's Art*. What then (to return to the central idea of the novel) is the "art" so conceived that illuminates for Nick new insights, and turns him, in his private, small, gentlemanly war, into heroic stuff. The title of the novel comes from a Browning poem which in turn was inspired by a line from Shakespeare. And if there is a good deal of confusion as to what Edgar means by the line in *King Lear* (III.iv.187), there is even greater confusion as to what Browning means by it in "Childe Roland to the Dark Tower Came." The particular ring of the final line in Browning is indeed heroic—much more heroic than when incorporated by Edgar in one of his errant juxtapositions—but the clean, sharp ironies of Shakespeare seem at cross-purposes with the profuse, tangled symbolism of Browning.

To oversimplify, "Childe Roland" is an allegory of quest and initiation, but whether it ends in hope or despair, triumph or defeat still remains sport for commentators. It is at least fair to say that Powell, whose penchant for Browning should be apparent after *What's Become of Waring,* has taken the *entire* poem as an analogy for the confusions, tensions, fears, and disasters of his own society during the war and has taken the fifteenth stanza to particularize the immediate problems confronting Nick in *The Soldier's Art:*

> I shut my eyes and turned them on my heart.
>> As a man calls for wine before he fights,
>> I asked one draught of earlier, happier sights,
> Ere fitly I could hope to play my part.
> Think first, fight afterwards—the soldier's art:
>> One taste of the old time sets all to rights.

"The good bit is about thinking first and fighting after," says Stringham, who has quoted the lines to Nick, and Nick goes on to comment archly that he hopes "the High Command have taken the words to heart." There is more to it than this. If to Childe Roland thought means emotional reflection and to Jenkins it suggests intellectual deliberation, both are, as far as Powell is concerned, right. The novel dramatizes the soldier's art of "thought": thought as imagination on the one hand, as will on the other, though there are various shadings in the shifts from the emotional to the intellectual plane. Too, the novel is concerned more specifically with how Nick adjusts to the thoughts of others: how, like Childe Roland, he must face the ambiguity of an ordeal and the ambiguity of its results.

Particularly with his minor characters—minor when fitted into the total scheme of *The Music of Time—* Powell pencils in the typical (and almost archetypical) behavior that constitutes a primitively imaginative or primitively intellectual application to "the soldier's art," at least as the characters themselves understand it.

Bithel, the genial dipsomaniac, has a dramatic flare for evading duty and discipline, a kind of symbolic function in a novel filled with evasion and red tape. Cocksidge, on the other hand, is eager to the point of "servility" and "subservience," his mind, Nick wittily projects, "perpetually afire with fresh projects for self-abasement before the powerful." Nick displays contempt for neither (though his sniping at Cocksidge comes close to it at times) for in truth he may almost admire how both have worked out plans for survival.

The dual relationships of Soper and Biggs, Pedlar and Hogbourne-Johnson offer greater variety and complexity. The worldly Soper, the easygoing, somewhat dull-witted Pedlar are in every way perfect foils for their disagreeable antagonists. Biggs and Hogbourne-Johnson, different sides of the same coin, look to the army as an outlet for their aggressive, bullying natures, which on the surface seem to thrive. Yet the irony of Hogbourne-Johnson's easy victory over Pedlar in the "port" dialogue becomes manifest later in the novel when a warrant officer, whom "H-J" has defended tooth-and-nail against Widmerpool's politick imputations of dishonesty, deserts. Betrayed by an underling, proved wrong by his nemesis Widmerpool, Hogbourne-Johnson loses face.

In the same way, Biggs's suicide is prompted by another "betrayal," that of his wife. The act is overshadowed by Germany's invasion of Russia, but not so overshadowed that the imperturbable Soper cannot reflect:

> "A fine kettle of fish. . . . Never thought Biggy would have done that. In the cricket pav of all places, and him so fond of the game. . . . Quite a change it will be, not having him grousing about the food every day." (*SA*, 228)

The comedy here is more than byplay; it is a totally central commentary, given Biggs as one who fights *first* and thinks *afterwards*. Biggs and Hogbourne-Johnson extend themselves too far and fare less well than either the goldbricking Bithel or the bootlicking Cocksidge.

Concern for the right and wrong ways of thinking is not new to *The Music of Time*. What is new, however, is that the mere utilitarian considerations of thinking rightly and making a "good" or "safe" choice, thinking wrongly and making a poor one, or simply not thinking at all have been seriously challenged by moral and ethical considerations. Schoolboy, professional, romantic rivalries—these are no longer the question; life itself may be. Thus Widmerpool, still master of the will and ever as strict an exponent of the utilitarian approach to "the soldier's art," forges ahead by hewing to the lines of discipline. No one blames Widmerpool for that; it is basic to his egoism, and his egoism has often been the inspiration for great fun. But when he arranges a disadvantageous, perhaps fatal, transfer for Stringham and leaves Jenkins stranded in an inferior post, fun gets a good stiff bash on the head. Stripped of probity and decency Widmerpool is less entertaining than downright dangerous. In this case, one looks to men of imagination to provide the ethical and moral balance.

Stringham partially supplies it. He has undergone a change for the better: a change indebted somewhat to the cliché of the army making one a man but owing as much to Stringham's new-found imaginative intelligence. He is proud of having overcome a good education and upbringing and prouder still of his own brand of autodidacticism. Of course, he cannot live down his education and upbringing at all. He is still witty, cultured, quick, and cynical. ("Awfully chic to be killed," he tells Nick.) But cynicism minus drink has sharpened his edges rather than blunted them. He has become a cynic of the old school, seeking practical virtue through a self-imposed morality that involves freedom from, not avoidance of, "class" responsibilities. Stringham has not "opted out"; his soul-searching is quite serious. His firm but gentle refusal to start up socially again with Nick is the preamble to expounding his own formula for "the soldier's art":

> "I know perfectly well, in practice, we could dine to-gether. . . . It isn't that. I just don't feel like it. Dining with you would spoil the rhythm so far as I'm concerned. I wouldn't go so far as to say I'm actively enjoying what I'm doing at the moment. . . . At the same time, what I'm doing is what I've chosen to do. Even what I want to do, if it comes to that. Up to a point . . . being in the ranks suits me. No strain in that particular respect. . . . You know I've been thinking a lot about myself lately, when scrubbing the floors and that sort of thing . . . and I've come to the conclusion I'm narcissistic, mad about myself. . . . My great amusement now is trying to get things straight in my own mind. That takes me all my time, as you can imagine. Funny, isn't it?" (*SA*, 78-82)

"Trying to get things straight in [one's] own mind" can't really be as odd as Stringham first imagines it. As Nick discovers later on in *The Soldier's Art*, acquaintances like David Pennistone and intimates like Hugh Moreland are engaged in a similar sorting-out process. Pennistone, who promises to play a major role in the concluding books of the series, has gone beyond Stringham, living neither for "money, power, women, the arts, domesticity" but for the mere love of "thinking about things, arranging his mind." And Moreland, too, always more of a "perfectionist" than Stringham, finds even in his civilian post that the "war clears the mind in a few respects."

It does for Nick. Possessing neither Widmerpool's callous industry nor Stringham's creative cynicism, he would seem a noble, albeit poor, candidate for either sorting things out or getting things done. But the total of what Nick appears *not* to do in the novel must be played against the little bit he does well. In the last analysis the novel really belongs less to those who seem to have mastered "the soldier's art" than to Nick, who feels himself "without any particular qualifications for practicing [it]."

Nick's career as an officer has looked unpromising from the outset. He just makes it into the army (*The Kindly Ones*), and he barely gets a decent post in which he can almost think for himself (*The Valley of Bones*) when he is snatched up by Widmerpool and assigned to work harder and think less. Under the thumb and aegis of Widmerpool, Nick feels the force of Biggs's cheerless saw: "There's nothing lower in the whole bloody army than a second-lieutenant." The empirical fact, however, is only stepson to the moral one. Nick's ethical worth ranks higher than his pips might indicate, and Powell makes the contrast between Widmerpool and Jenkins effective merely by throwing them together. Nick is hopeful, fearful, concerned about the war, but still concerned about people; Widmerpool is not. Where Nick is frank, Widmerpool is false, forever promising to "put [Nick] in the picture" while scrupulously excluding him. And as Widmerpool is nearly ready to snafu the entire division in order to place his own man in a choice post (and scarcely raise a finger to help Stringham), Nick does all his rank will allow to improve Stringham's lot.

This shot at mediator is a tricky role for Nick, and a new one. Why he bothers is the important question. He is not, as he sees it, driven any longer by friendship for Stringham, for "the all-obliterating march of events" has pretty much disposed of opportunities for it. But that he would almost risk a showdown with Widmerpool reflects, even in so narrow a sphere as a Division HQ, something of the heroic. Of course, this humanistic impulse is as germane to Jenkins' nature as it is foreign to Widmerpool's, which is why Nick is surprised to discover (upon returning from leave) that Stringham has been transferred to the mobile laundry unit. Nick imputes this change of heart to a "good nature" which, because of certain exigencies of Widmerpool's rank, was hiding behind a "bleak façade."

"Façade" (Nick soon discovers) is the crucial word and one more side of "the soldier's art." Widmerpool's "act of pure kindness" (as Stringham calls it in all sincerity before he finds out what is really up) turns out to be a fiction. Stringham has obviously proved an embarrassment to Widmerpool and has become expendable:

> "You've known for some time they were going to move
> . . . when you transferred Stringham?" [Nick asks Widmerpool.]
> "That was precisely why I posted him to the Laundry."
> "So he'll go to the Far East?"
> "If that's where the Laundry's bound. . . ."
> "Will he want to go?"
> "I have no idea. . . . Why should it be your job—still less mine—to keep Stringham wrapped in cotton wool?
> . . . Nicholas, have you never heard of the word discipline? . . . I applaud my own forethought in making the arrangement about him I did. . . . Let me add that all this is entirely a matter of principle. Stringham's presence would no longer affect me personally."
> "Why not?"
> "Because I am leaving this formation." (*SA*, 189-90)

The Stringham affair, more than any composite of incidents in the novel, galvanizes Nick into assessing the basic element of "the soldier's art"—survival:

I was annoyed, even disgusted, by Widmerpool's attitude towards Stringham, this utter disregard for what might happen to him, posted away God knows where. However, worse now threatened. . . . Now, at Widmerpool's words about leaving, I was unwelcomely conscious of self-interested anxieties, throbbing hurriedly into operation. What was Widmerpool's present intention towards myself, if he were to go elsewhere? Would my fate be as little of interest to him as Stringham's? That was my instant thought. (*SA,* 190-91)

Naturally the answer is "yes." But admitted that Widmerpool is an opportunist who has had inordinate luck in wedding foresight and initiative, it is not as if Nick, on behalf of self-interest, has not tried his hand at improving his "military condition." The point is that through it all Nick does not degrade his character. He preserves an ethical superiority over Widmerpool because—and his reflections on self-interest come as a truth rather than a rationalization—the wish for survival and advancement has not been concealed "within some more or less hypocritical integument."

Powell's aim in *The Soldier's Art* is not solely to assert the moral ascendancy of Jenkins. That would not be hard to do. Widmerpool, starting off in *The Music of Time* as a bit of a pig, becomes, with no great labor, something of a swine. Rather, Powell is out to show that Jenkins can survive with dignity and honesty intact, on his own terms yet at the expense of no one else. By avoiding throughout the novel the entanglements of red tape that threaten to strangle and stultify any decent actions, Nick emerges as the perfect foil to Widmerpool and a stable yardstick for measuring Powell's ironies. In the last analysis Widmerpool is revealed as nakedly specious, still invulnerable to be sure, but generally ineffectual. Few of his plans pan out: his man is *not* placed; Stringham looks upon transfer to the Far East as a challenging and almost fulfilling experience; Sunny Farebrother makes colonel while he remains a major; and Nick, plucked at the sleeve again by Fate, is called to the War Offices as the novel ends.

Nick remains the darling of Fate, but his character is continually strengthened by opportunity as, conversely, Widmerpool's is weakened by opportunism. Absorbing experience, his character has enlarged itself until Nick now dwarfs everyone in *The Music of Time,* even so comic, original, and vital a creation as Kenneth Widmerpool. The present volume, while transitional in the sequence, goes the furthest in affirming Nick's stature. As Jenkins ultimately realizes it, "the soldier's art" means more than remaining human in the face of the dehumanizing processes of the war machine—a view partially exposed in *The Valley of Bones.* It means, almost conclusively, remaining human in the face of the more dangerous and impersonal dehumanizing processes of men themselves, who, miles from the front, dramatically engage in reduced, but nevertheless imperative, social and ethical struggles. *The Soldier's Art* proves a rich expression of the limited heroism of Nick Jenkins and the unfettered intelligence and art of Anthony Powell.

Conclusion

Any critical conclusion on a work-in-progress is rash. The critic's vision may match the novelist's, but rarely can it anticipate it. This is so true as to be commonplace, and the case with Anthony Powell is no exception. One has only to read (or re-read) the body of reviews that has appeared over the past decade or so to discover the high mortality rates among "conclusive" judgments on *The Music of Time*; to discover, too, how viewpoints have veered, tastes shifted, analogies been disproved. In all fairness to earlier critics, it must be pointed out that in 1951, the year *A Question of Upbringing* was first published, no one could possibly have known what Powell had in mind. Even when *The Music of Time* began taking shape—after, that is, the first trilogy—a certain amount of circumspection still retarded full support for Powell's work. While critics were beginning to make out his design, they had not quite measured his range.

Inevitably things came into focus. Reactions to individual novels remained (and still remain) warm or cool, but with the series now two-thirds complete its total impact and scope have achieved for Powell the status of a major contemporary novelist. For *The Music of Time,* in revealing an energy, force, and sustaining power that outstrips many postwar novels one-third its length, deals not simply with the "big" problems of the English upper class—the biggest being its decay and the likelihood of its extinction—but with major problems of our century.

Yet to measure Powell's stature is only partially fulfilling. There is a natural (in a way hazardous) curiosity among readers of the series to anticipate its direction as well as its conclusion. Considering that Powell has primarily focused on character throughout, and has even acknowledged his discomfort at laying out plot,[1] it is always surprising to recall how much has really gone on in *The Music of Time* since Widmerpool first donned his sweatsuit and came puffing up the fog-enshrouded road. Thus, when a new swatch from the lives of Jenkins and his circle is added to the others, the reader feels a temporary sense of completion at seeing one more piece fitted into place. At the same time, there is a sense of impatience to know what shape the next piece will take, and (perhaps most importantly as the sequence draws toward a conclusion) what the final picture will be. But before being prophetic it might first be wiser to chart several of the more sweeping movements of *The Music of Time* to date.

1. Powell observed this in a broadcast I prepared on his life and work. The program, produced by Walter P. Sheppard, was first aired over WRVR in New York City on September 21, 1966.

First, the major change in a series dealing with change has been within Nicholas Jenkins himself. From his shadowy beginnings as narrator and his often obvious role as author-surrogate, he has emerged into a full-blown hero. *The Soldier's Art* has confirmed this. Critics of *The Music of Time* can no longer suggest that Powell has not told us enough about Nick, or given him enough to do. What he is and what he does are now clear. *The Soldier's Art,* even though a transitional volume within the war trilogy and the sequence as a whole, offers the surety that no matter what realignment of characters occurs in later volumes Nick will always remain the principal hero of *The Music of Time,* its central and most fully developed character, for he has at last learned how a student of history and society should confront the uses of the past and of men.

This leads to a second consideration, not only of character but of technique. While Nick's knowledge is cumulative—*The Music of Time* is in great part a novel of education—it is never cumulative in the sense of experiences piling up, or, worse, of weighing Nick down. Nick's views are at times erroneous (Powell's ironic method depends on his narrator's oversights) but a later perception does not produce a sudden or violent change. Nick can accept the alteration with a minimum of pain and with understanding. He has been growing all along, with the other characters, but also independently of them. Hence his vision is sound and complex but never tangled. One volume of the sequence may overlap its immediate predecessor (and consequently all the other volumes that have preceded it), but it never attempts to summarize its antecedents. This, as much as incident or character, gives rise to the comic movement of the series. Neither time nor history, even within a fictional framework, can be successfully summarized without offering, as Proust, Faulkner, and Durrell have shown, a basically tragic sense of life.

In other words, to get on to point three, Powell is never trying to tie the whole thing together. When the last volume is in, it will not be a *recueillement* of the series so much as a coda to it. Clearly, Powell is not recapturing the past—with all its tragic implications—and this accounts for his disinterest in knotting together all the threads. If the past has proved important in playing on the sensitivity and sensibilities of Nicholas Jenkins, it has inspired no cataclysmic revelations, but low-keyed, meaningful insights. This is the way it should be in a work that sets out to be both life and fiction, history and myth, that attempts to strike a balance between what has really happened in the past fifty years and how the novelist has viewed its happening.

The question as to whether or not the writer of a novel sequence makes a distinction between the art of the novel that historicizes and the art of history that fictionalizes is, in the last analysis, pretty much as Powell himself has suggested: "I suppose all novelists who write about their own period use an element of historical materials, whether they like it or not, for future historical research."[2] Both critics of literature and historians will undoubtedly uncover the suggestion (implicit in *The Music of Time*) that decay has attended the growth of our century. To the historian, however, such decay will emerge as a single, simple fact; as, for example, the fall of any empire is a "fact," though the totalities involved in accounting for it are never as factual or as simple as one might like them to be.

There is yet a further perspective to be gained, one which a novelist is aware of and one which a critic of

2. Another observation of Mr. Powell's from the same program.

the novel may more willingly accede to than the historian. Powell's "anatomy of decay" (as someone has
tagged the sequence),[3] does not set out, like Proust's, to
dissect the habits, practices, excesses, secrets, and perver-
sions of the upper class. Powell writes about decay, but
decay is only one part of change; growth is another; and
both are part of the historic process. The very looseness
of the sequence's plot structure suggests the author's
studied attention to avoid making any final "point,"
either moral, social, philosophical, or otherwise.

Thus, in a way, one is relieved of the burden of
prophecy, for what one can forecast about *The Music of
Time* is somewhat irrelevant. To return to the historical
analogy above, the plot of the novel parallels the "facts"
of history, and what the plot will be, while of considerable interest, seems least worthy of conjecture. Naturally,
it will be intriguing to see how far Widmerpool rises in
the Cabinet after the war, if Stringham gets through the
war and recoups his powers, if Nick turns out to be a
successful novelist and how he goes on to adjust to postwar conditions and (for Powell) the principal struggle
of the century: the struggle between the man of will
and the man of imagination.

More intriguing, however, will be to discover how
Powell will go about refurbishing his supply of characters. For *The Music of Time is* its characters, all radiating from a hub of conflict, all converging as well as
diverging, all moving between these crucial poles of will
and imagination. Whether the sequence will ultimately
confirm the triumph of one over the other is again for
Powell to say. One can glean from the novels to date
that power has always been balanced by a correspondent
sensuality, and that as the men of will become mechani-

3. W. D. Quesenbery, Jr., "Anthony Powell: The Anatomy of
Decay," *Critique,* VII (1964), 5-26.

cally perfect, the fallible men of imagination become more highly prized for their humanity. This has been the outline in the past, and the outline has been considerably filled in recently in *The Soldier's Art.*

Beyond the present even the most fervent prophet of *The Music of Time* must remain mute. One can take comfort in realizing that Powell has always worked from design. And in seeking some pattern, some answer, one should remember that Powell's synthesizing metaphor is still the dance—a measured motion in which themes and steps (even those beyond recall) may eventually be repeated, sometimes as one would wish them in life, but always as they are necessary to art.

Index of Titles